## Exploring Malicious Hacker Communities

Malicious hackers utilize the World Wide Web to share knowledge. Analyzing the online communication and behavior of these threat actors can help reduce the risk of attacks. This book shifts attention from the defender environment to the attacker environment, offering a new security paradigm of "proactive cyber-threat intelligence" that allows defenders of computer networks to gain a better understanding of their adversaries by analyzing assets, capabilities, and interests of malicious hackers. The authors propose models, techniques, and frameworks based on threat intelligence mined from the heart of the underground cyber world: the malicious hacker communities. They provide insights into the hackers themselves and the groups they form dynamically in the act of exchanging ideas and techniques, buying or selling malware, and exploits. The book covers both methodology – a hybridization of machine learning, artificial intelligence, and social network analysis methods – and the resulting conclusions, detailing how a deep understanding of malicious hacker communities can be the key to designing better attack prediction systems.

ERICSSON MARIN, California State Polytechnic University, Pomona

MOHAMMED ALMUKAYNIZI, King Saud University

SOUMAJYOTI SARKAR, Arizona State University

ERIC NUNES, Arizona State University

JANA SHAKARIAN, Cyber Reconnaissance, Inc.

PAULO SHAKARIAN, Arizona State University and Cyber Reconnaissance, Inc.

# Exploring Malicious Hacker Communities

## Toward Proactive Cyber-Defense

ERICSSON MARIN
*California State Polytechnic University, Pomona*

MOHAMMED ALMUKAYNIZI
*King Saud University*

SOUMAJYOTI SARKAR
*Arizona State University*

ERIC NUNES
*Arizona State University*

JANA SHAKARIAN
*Cyber Reconnaissance, Inc.*

PAULO SHAKARIAN
*Arizona State University and Cyber Reconnaissance, Inc.*

Foreword by

EDWARD G. AMOROSO
*TAG Cyber*

**CAMBRIDGE**
**UNIVERSITY PRESS**

University Printing House, Cambridge CB2 8BS, United Kingdom

One Liberty Plaza, 20th Floor, New York, NY 10006, USA

477 Williamstown Road, Port Melbourne, VIC 3207, Australia

314–321, 3rd Floor, Plot 3, Splendor Forum, Jasola District Centre, New Delhi – 110025, India

79 Anson Road, #06–04/06, Singapore 079906

Cambridge University Press is part of the University of Cambridge.

It furthers the University's mission by disseminating knowledge in the pursuit of education, learning, and research at the highest international levels of excellence.

www.cambridge.org
Information on this title: www.cambridge.org/9781108491594
DOI: 10.1017/9781108869003



First published 2021

Printed in the United Kingdom by TJ Books Limited, Padstow Cornwall

*A catalogue record for this publication is available from the British Library.*

*Library of Congress Cataloging-in-Publication Data*
Names: Marin, Ericsson, author. | Almukaynizi, Mohammed, 1987– author. | Sarkar, Soumajyoti, 1992– author. | Nunes, Eric, author. | Shakarian, Jana, author. | Shakarian, Paulo, author.
Title: Exploring malicious hacker communities : toward proactive cyber-defense / Ericsson Marin, Mohammed Almukaynizi, Soumajyoti Sarkar, Eric Nunes, Jana Shakarian, Paulo Shakarian.
Description: Cambridge ; New York, NY : Cambridge University Press, 2021. | Includes bibliographical references and index.
Identifiers: LCCN 2020051654 (print) | LCCN 2020051655 (ebook) | ISBN 9781108491594 (hardback) | ISBN 9781108869003 (epub)
Subjects: LCSH: Cyber intelligence (Computer security) | Hackers–Social networks. | Social sciences–Network analysis. | Data mining. | Hacking–Prevention. | Cyberterrorism–Prevention.
Classification: LCC HV6773 .M3718 2021 (print) | LCC HV6773 (ebook) | DDC 363.325–dc23
LC record available at https://lccn.loc.gov/2020051654
LC ebook record available at https://lccn.loc.gov/2020051655

ISBN 978-1-108-49159-4 Hardback

# Contents

# Foreword

Hackers talk. This has been well known since the earliest cyberpunks of the Eighties and Nineties shared their preferred tactics over primitive bulletin boards. Witness also, for example, that one of the most famous hackers of that era – Kevin Mitnick – could not resist blabbing his methods and his conscience to a tech reporter while on the run from the FBI. So, hackers talk. This is no secret – and interestingly, this has not changed much over the past four decades. Such propensity to blab raises the question of whether intelligence can be actively derived from such on-going chatter. We know, for example, that law enforcement has gotten its best tips in the past from young snitches who are disgruntled (or cornered), and who are often pushed by their parents to cooperate with the Feds to enable a normal life. Former uber-hacker Kevin Poulsen is a good example – he is now a contributing editor at The Daily Beast.

Perhaps the best option would use technology to automate the collection, aggregation, and interpretation of threat intelligence from the discussion forums that have evolved. Generally referred to as hacker communities, these trust zones, whether created ad hoc or planned carefully, contain useful nuggets of insight into the most likely methods being used by hackers to target valued assets. They shed light onto what mal-actors are thinking and doing.

This new volume, Exploring Malicious Hacker Communities, provides a comprehensive and fascinating foundational base on which cyber defenders, threat investigators, and the like, might begin to derive good intelligence from hacker talk. Written to introduce the creative and original research being done at three universities and two interesting start-ups, the book provides readers with a thorough introduction to this important topic in cybersecurity.

Now – readers should be forewarned: This is not a light read, nor is it designed for casual perusal by marketing experts looking for some sales edge for their intelligence product. Rather, it is a deeply researched and thoroughly traveled computer science volume, replete with the mathematic explanations and models required to explain the technology accurately. You will need to devote time and energy to absorb this book. It is not for the faint-hearted.

If you are an undergraduate or graduate student, or if you are a professional researcher, then pay particular attention to the earlier material in Chapters 1 and 2. Do not skip these pages and just jump to the graphs, algorithms, and models. You will need the up-front information to ensure that you maintain proper context for the research presented. This is applied research and development with a clear practical purpose. This is not pure mathematics. Regardless of your background or motivation for picking up this volume, I hope you enjoy and profit from the fine material in *Exploring Malicious Hacker Communities* as much as I have.

Dr. Edward G. Amoroso
Chief Executive Officer, TAG Cyber
Distinguished Research Professor, NYU

# Preface

Malicious hackers utilize the World Wide Web to share knowledge. Previous work has demonstrated that information mined from online hacker communities can be used as signals for predicting cyber-attacks. In today's world, where technology systems are wrecked by continued cyber-attacks and when security alert systems are still facing high false positive rates, analyzing the online communication and behavior of threat actors can help reduce the risk of attacks. This approach gives birth to a new security paradigm denominated "proactive cyber-threat intelligence," and the main idea here is that defenders of computer networks gain a better understanding of their adversaries by analyzing the current assets, capabilities, and interests of malicious hackers. By shifting the attention from the defender environment to the attacker environment, this book proposes models, techniques, and frameworks to enhance cyber-defense based on threat intelligence that underpin the underground cyber-world: the malicious hacker communities. Particularly, we scrutinize the hackers themselves and the groups they dynamically form while exchanging ideas and techniques and buying/selling malware and exploits, as well as the patterns of hacking activity that can signal impending cyber-offensive operations. In this book, we describe methodologies that build hybrid models utilizing machine-learning, artificial intelligence, and social network analysis and underline some of the resulting insights. We detail how a deep understanding of malicious hacker communities can be the key for designing better attack prediction systems.

The authors would like to acknowledge the generous support and collaboration from Cyber Reconnaissance, Inc. (CYR3CON). CYR3CON provided financial support, software support, and collaboration – directly contributing to both scientific results and the writing of this book. Additionally, some of the work was supported by the Army Research Office (grant W911NF1910066), the Office of Naval Research Neptune program, the Intelligence Advanced Research Projects Activity (IARPA), the King Saud University (Riyadh, Saudi Arabia), and the Brazilian National Council for Scientific and Technological Development (CNPq-Brazil). We also extend a special thanks to Lauren Cowles, our editor at Cambridge University Press, whose assistance throughout the creation of this book was much appreciated.

# 1
# Introduction

With the wide spread of cyber-attack incidents, such as those recently experienced by Facebook, Dow Jones, AMC Networks, T-Mobile, Disney+, and US Customs and Border Protection [82], cyber-security has become a serious concern for organizations. A security bulletin published by the Kaspersky Lab [86] reported that 2,672,579 cyber-attacks were repelled daily by the company in 2019 (30 per second on average), which reflects the average activity of criminals involved in the creation and distribution of cyber-threats. Worldwide, cyber-attacks cost organizations an estimated US600 billion in 2017 [68] (0.8% of global income), and US5.2 trillion in additional costs and lost revenue are expected until 2024 [2].

A credible explanation for this threatening scenario, which is corroborated by many cyber-security researchers [145], is that malicious hackers are increasingly using the World Wide Web (the Web) to share knowledge and achieve their goals. Many works detail how threat actors rely on online hacker communities to (1) identify software vulnerabilities, (2) create or purchase exploits, (3) choose a target and recruit collaborators, (4) obtain access to the infrastructure needed, and (5) plan and execute the attack [152], making what was once a hard-to-penetrate market accessible to a much wider population [126, 145]. Although this hacker behavior helps to produce a huge amount of malware, it also provides intelligence for defenders, as the information shared by hackers on online communities can be leveraged as precursors to various types of cyber-attacks [10, 11, 51, 83, 148]. Thus, a deep understanding of the adversaries present in those environments can help organizations deal with the risk of attacks, moving their perspective toward a more proactive, intelligence-driven security.

The state of the art for cyber-security primarily provides information on what is already deployed by cyber-attackers, setting a dominant viewpoint of cyber-defense that solely focuses on the defender's environment [144, 145].

For example, consider the current technologies used for quantifying, monitoring, and managing cyber-risk. On one hand, most of those tools only consider technical characteristics of the defender's networked assets and their vulnerabilities, such as the number of public-facing hosts, the number of vulnerable software products they run, and the ease of exploiting these software vulnerabilities. These tools use a wide range of data sources, such as security advisory databases, software vendor websites, penetration testing tools, and vulnerability databases. On the other hand, most of those security tools focus on detecting abnormalities already present in the defender's systems and networks, such as traditional firewalls, intrusion detection systems, spam filtering, and technologies that leverage anomaly detection or threat signatures using data shared among different organizations. This security perspective has a main shortcoming: the lack of a holistic consideration of the attacker's activity. Fortunately, in the recent few years, significant interest has grown towards tools, systems, and analyses for understanding and monitoring the hacker activity using cyber-threat intelligence gathered from online hacker communities. This trend arose as a response to the growing broad realization of the importance of the attacker's role, allowing organizations to effectively deploy security measures and allocate resources by exploring the ability to anticipate future cyber-attacks. The speed of those contemporary attacks, along with the high costs of remediation for recovering from the reputation, revenue, or data losses produced, overall incentives avoidance and impacts limitation over response. For instance, according to the National Cybersecurity Institute at Excelsior College (NCI), about 60% of small and mid-sized businesses that are seriously breached go out of business within six months [89], strengthening the security specialists' claim toward prevention.

In order to understand adversarial settings and achieve proactive cyber-threat intelligence, important information should be continuously mined from the ever-evolving malicious hacking communities, especially from the main platforms leveraged by malicious hackers to share knowledge: forums and marketplaces. By analyzing data about market dynamics within those communities, the rise and fall of particular personalities and venues, the nature of the conversations that take place in the forums, and the overall evolution of these communities, organizations can design more accurate attack prediction systems. Those attack predictions, in turn, can lead to a variety of strategic decisions to avoid infections, including prioritizing certain patches, discontinuing the use of a piece of software, purchasing or developing software, and segregating certain computers from the rest of the network. Thus, the explosive increase in popularity of exploit markets and hacker forums existing in and across all layers of the Web (the surface-web, the deepweb, and the so-called darkweb) also has a bright side for cyber-security. The cyber-defenders can now leverage the hackers' digital traces existing in those environments to get valuable insights into evolving cyber-threats and into a pending cyber-offensive well before malicious activity is detected on a target system [101, 102, 127, 155].

For instance, the WannaCry ransomware attack directed against hospitals in the United Kingdom and numerous other worldwide targets was discussed several weeks prior on a darkweb forum [176]. Hackers likely involved in this attack discussed the number of unpatched machines, the exploit to be used, the industry verticals, and the method of attack (ransomware) – which encrypts the hard drive data and demands a ransom payment to have it recovered (see the WannaCry's home screen in Figure 1.1). The discussions were made in several languages, and medical institutions were chosen as prime targets based on the history of paid ransom from similar institutions. WannaCry's example demonstrates how malicious hacker platforms provide valuable information regarding the capabilities and intent of threat actors. The attack did not come out of nowhere: it exploited a known flaw in Microsoft Windows that hackers knew was left unpatched on many machines. They just needed to share the

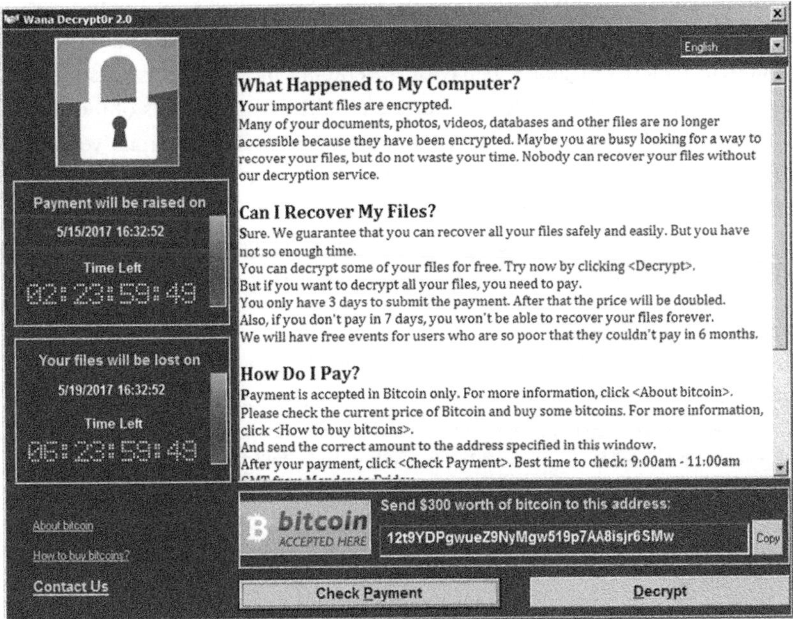


Figure 1.1 WannaCry's home screen with instructions for victims of the cyber-attack.

information and get online help to troubleshoot obstacles. Thus, by looking in the right place at the right time, defenders can mine the interest of malicious hackers, adopting a proactive behavior that can protect their assets before the attackers operate.

This book is intended to give an overarching view into how to explore malicious hacker communities to achieve proactive cyber-threat intelligence. After introducing those communities and giving general information on the cyber-security domain, we conduct a series of studies that demonstrate how artificial intelligence, machine learning, and social network analysis techniques can be used to make sense out of large quantities of hacker community data for security purposes. We divide those studies into two parts. In the first part, formed by Chapters 3, 4, and 5, we use those techniques to gain additional insight into the structure of online hacker communities as well as the behavior of their members. We focus there on scrutinizing the threat actors creating and distributing malicious code online and getting knowledge about dynamic reputation systems, user engagement, and highly specialized groups of hackers that can aid in the identification of credible threats. In the second part, formed by Chapters 6, 7, 8, and 9, we leverage those techniques to effectively predict future cyber-threats, either by identifying exploits-in-the-wild, predicting enterprise-targeted external cyber-attacks, or finding at-risk systems. We focus there on analyzing online hacker communication to find confident patterns of attack behavior, leveraging those patterns to anticipate future cyber-incidents. Table 1.1 summarizes the two main parts of this book.

Throughout the book, we use data collected from a commercial version of the system that we proposed in [126, 145]. This system, currently maintained and provided by Cyber Reconnaissance, Inc. (CYR3CON) [42] through API, is responsible for gathering cyber-threat intelligence from various social platforms of the Web. We query data originally hosted across multiple network

Table 1.1 *The two main parts of the book*

| | | |
|---|---|---|
| Understanding the Behavior of Malicious Hackers | Chapter 3 | Mining Key-hackers |
| | Chapter 4 | Reasoning about Hacker Engagement |
| | Chapter 5 | Uncovering Communities of Malware and Exploit Vendors |
| Predicting Imminent Cyber-threats | Chapter 6 | Identifying Exploits in the Wild Proactively |
| | Chapter 7 | Predicting Enterprise-Targeted External Cyber-attacks |
| | Chapter 8 | Bringing Social Network Analysis to Aid in Cyber-attack Prediction |
| | Chapter 9 | Finding At-Risk Systems without Software Vulnerability Identifiers (CVEs) |

protocols (the surface-web, the deepweb, and the "darkweb"), informing in each chapter what type of data is being used for the corresponding study. In addition to data obtained directly from the hacker discussions on forums and marketplaces, data from other resources, including social media platforms, Chan sites, paste sites,[1] exploit archives, vulnerability databases, and bug bounty programs,[2] are obtained through this system.

The remainder of the book is structured as follows. Chapter 3 leverages content, social network, and seniority analysis to mine key-hackers on hacking forums, identifying reputable individuals who are likely to succeed in their cyber-criminal goals. Next, as hackers often use Web platforms to advertise and recruit collaborators, Chapter 4 analyzes forum engagement by predicting where and when hackers will post a message in the near future given their recurrent interactions with other hackers. After that, Chapter 5 demonstrates how vendors of malware and malicious exploits organically form hidden organizations on online markets, analyzing the similarity of product offerings in different networks.

The next four chapters (Chapters 6, 7, 8, and 9) directly measure the risk of cyber-attacks, either by predicting exploits-in-the-wild, anticipating cyber-incidents at particular enterprises, or conducting assessment of threats to particular systems. Particularly, Chapter 6 predicts if exploits are going to be used in the wild by analyzing multiple sources of threat intelligence generated after vulnerability disclosures. Differently, Chapter 7 describes a temporal logical framework to learn rules that correlate malicious hacking activity with real-world cyber-incidents, leveraging these rules for predicting enterprise-targeted external cyber-attacks. With the same prediction goal, Chapter 8 measures network features and user/thread posting statistics to hypothesize that the interaction dynamics focused on a set of specialized users and the attention broadcast by them to others can be relevant to generating cyber-attack warnings. Finally, Chapter 9 looks at online hacker discussions to identify platforms, vendors, and products likely to be at risk, gathering indicators regarding the hacker capability of targeting systems to conduct the corresponding threat assessment.

Chapter 10 wraps up the book, presenting the overall contributions of all studies conducted, the challenges overcome, and future research directions to further empower cyber-security. The latter is done by addressing current limitations of the book as well as by discussing new models and methods that will contribute to enhancing proactive cyber-threat intelligence.

[1] Type of online content hosting service where users can store plain text, e.g., source code snippets.

[2] Deal offered by sites and organizations by which individuals can receive recognition and compensation for reporting bugs.

# 2
# Background

## 2.1 Introduction

Online communities built around content of pentesting,[1] hacking, and malware – malicious or otherwise – can be found on various networks. For it is not the method of exploiting vulnerabilities to traverse a network or breach a computer system that is per se malicious, but the motivation behind it and the intent of what to do after the access is gained. Visionary, capable hackers always pushed the boundaries of technology to innovate and stretch out the horizon of what is possible. Pentesters harden the security stance of organizations by using Red Team[2] tactics – informing the CISOs[3] beforehand and leaving them emboldened.

It is neither the method nor the tools that make a breach illegal, but the intent behind the compromise. In a time in which at least half of the work in the form of proof-of-concept[4] up to entire exploits are legally available on the *surface-web*[5] and all that is needed is customization toward the target's environment and (equally easily obtainable) payload(s), information hosted on the surface-web is extensive. Actually, this information mainly includes deepweb resources, which constitute a large part of the surface-web not indexed by search engines.[6] However, to escape the ever-increasing

[1] Process that simulates cyber-attacks on a computer system to evaluate its security. It is usually performed to identify software vulnerabilities.
[2] Offensive security professionals who are experts in attacking systems. In opposite, a Blue Team is formed by defensive security professionals who protect organizations against cyber-attacks. On a Purple Team, offense and defense work together to strengthen the cyber-security of an organization.
[3] A chief information security officer.
[4] Code developed to demonstrate security flaws in software or networks.
[5] Also called "clearnet," denotes the open portion of the World Wide Web (the Web) where sites are publicly accessible from any browser and largely indexed by search engines.
[6] Websites can implement non-indexing requests that search engines are bound to oblige.

surveillance and tracking of the open portions of the Web, a variety of network protocols offer additional functionalities, most notably increased (though not absolute) privacy.

*Darkweb* refers to a collection of websites that are hosted on networks requiring additional software, being not indexed by regular search engines and not accessible by traditional browsers.[7] It is a region that relies on protocols dedicated to protect the privacy of its users by obscuring traffic analysis as a form of network surveillance. Criminals who want to shield their online communications from government surveillance may require the cover of the darkweb. Some cyber-criminals and malicious hackers demand an infrastructure to safely and anonymously share and commercialize their illegal cyber-threats, keeping their activities hidden from law enforcement agencies.

Despite the clear advantages of the darkweb for malicious hackers, there is a downside. Networks requiring specific protocols or the sharing of bandwidth among users, such as The Onion Router (Tor),[8] I2P, ShadowWeb, Hyperboria, and Freenet, among others, often confront their users with at least a small number of acceptable compromises: duplicate content that is already available in more easily accessible sources, lagging content serving last come first, and unstable sites. The choice of network also depends on where the administrator hosts a website. Bandwidth restrictions and the absence of legal concerns obviate the need to host a site on Tor or another member of the so called darkweb network family. In some countries, the network protocol is not available for download and technical restrictions prevent the use of the technology. However, whenever the user values anonymity more than comfort and availability is not an issue, the darkweb composes a part of the underground networks to be explored, especially the hacking communities existing on forums and marketplaces.

## 2.2 Inside Online Hacking Communities

As in every meritocratic system, and developer communities in general, hacker communities value problem solving and autodidactic acquisition of knowledge. Clever hacks and innovation are rewarded with social recognition, which, in online forums, are represented through reputation scales. These sentiments also express themselves through a marked disdain for questions easily researched online, because the posting of these shows a lack of effort.

[7] Sometimes the term *deepweb* is mistakenly used to refer specifically to or include the darkweb.
[8] See the Tor project's official website with trend lines of usage metrics at www.torproject.org/.

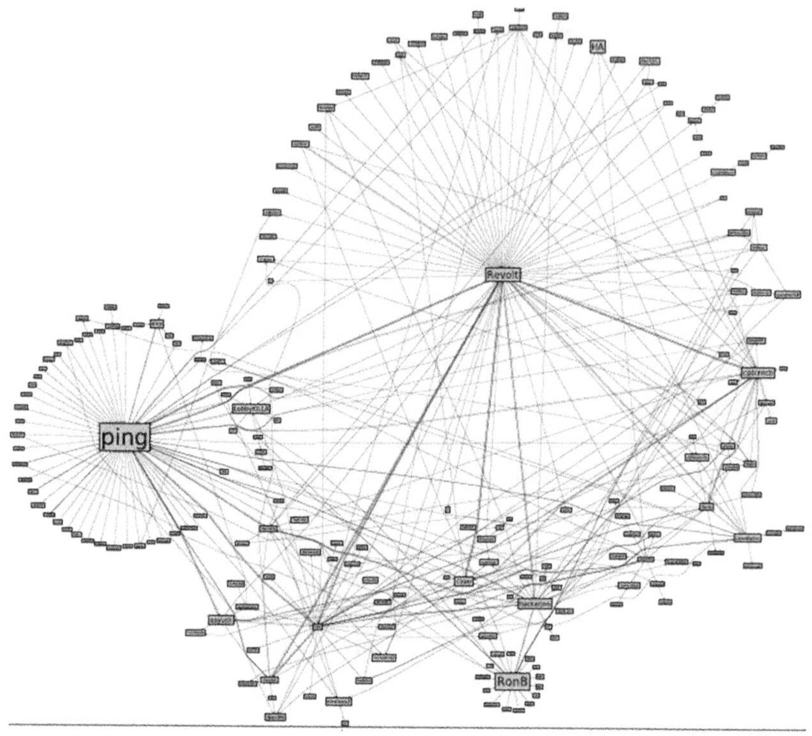


Figure 2.1 Social network of a now defunct Tor-hosted forum, generated in early 2016.

Because acquiring skills and recognition are main reasons to engage in online forums, trivial content is often decried and sometimes altogether removed in order to curate or maintain a reputable image for the forum.

Online forums might be structured in boards and child-boards by topic, or they may consist of a single rolling board – like in Chans.[9] Content placement and access in closed forums are controlled by administrators and moderators, who head up the social hierarchy. These functions tend to cause those individuals to represent central nodes in social network graphs, as shown in Figure 2.1. When it is available, each site maintains its own peer reputation

[9] A type of web forum, mostly image boards, that encourage visitors to anonymously post content. Chans are distinct from online forums in their lack of structure. Some Chan sites are found to be leveraged by activists, such as the well-known hacktivist group Anonymous, to advertise their campaigns. Sites 4chan and most undeservedly 8chan – now 8kun – rose to prominence due to the complete lack of content policing, which led to hate speech – induced actual violence more than once in the past.

system, which makes it difficult to compare users across platforms. Even highly active users are the spokes of subgroups and connect communities within forums (bridge nodes).

At the other end of the spectrum, low-activity forum members tend to interact with moderators only, not belonging to any particular community. Reputation tends to concentrate within the nodes rather than at the edges. When comparing members' reputations across sites in regard to competence, instead of basing the comparison on a normalized scale of the various reputation systems, more stable and ubiquitous factors may serve better. Aside from rating the value of content, other marks of reputation include the number of posts over lifetime (activity volume), seniority (lifetime), number of responses to posts (secondary posts volume), diversity in user interactions (i.e., variety in authors who respond to posts), number of initiating posts (primary posts volume), and quality of replies – which could be assessed through the threads' length (simple word count), its content validation (NLP, presence of important keywords), or the length and quality (sentiment) of the responding posts, as well as membership in like (reputable) forums (ego distribution).

Trust and trust building online differ greatly from face-to-face interactions [73] – let alone in spurious communities, as has been extensively laid out in related works. In meritocracies, trust and prestige are developed through sharing valuable content, such as successes, helpful advice, or the general display of relevant knowledge on a consistent basis. Because reputation is extraneous to build, we observe many forum members as well as vendors act against OpSec[10] principles by reusing their online handles across multiple online communities. The recognition value is tremendous: it offers access to closed forums and instant reputation and establishment in (new) marketplaces.

Online forums are virtual communication arenas almost as old as the Internet. Though addresses change more often than names do, the content has not changed much over the history of online forums. One of the most notorious, Dark0de, was founded around 2004 and shut down by a concerted effort of law enforcement agencies around the globe in 2015. Operation Shrouded Horizon, as the sting was called, resulted in 70 arrests spanning 20 countries, including in North America (United States, Canada), South America (Costa Rica, Brazil, Colombia), Africa (Nigeria), Europe (United Kingdom, Denmark, Sweden, Finland, Latvia, Germany, Romania, Cyprus, Bosnia and Herzegovina, Macedonia, Croatia, Serbia), and West Asia (Israel). Although access to this forum required a recommendation from a member, the FBI had infiltrated it and throughout months collected information on its approximately

[10] Operations Security.

Figure 2.2 Home screen of Hell forum.

300 members. Besides that any tool that could help break a system was likely to be found here, members were offering botnet[11] and malware for trade or purchase (including 0days[12]) as well as sensitive information such as credentials and dumps with personally identifiable information. Hosted on Tor in the past, in spring 2019 the forum reopened across the surface-web and started strong with more than 12,000 registered users and more than 55,000 postings in more than 6,000 threads. It appeared to have moved to Tor and drawn criticism from some due to its new layout.

One historically popular forum hosted on Tor and simply called "Hell" – illustrated in Figure 2.2 – was home to a relatively small population of malevolent and criminal hackers, who exchanged stories about their online endeavors, sought partnerships, and exchanged tips for OpSec. There are a few rumors on the causes of its first shutdown in the summer of 2015.

After a few months, the site came back up (as "Hell Reloaded"), but now required Javascript enabled, which aroused the suspicion of many members that the site was an "LE" (law enforcement) honeypot. Eventually, the site shut down completely, because it could not convince its members that it was safe.

11 Collection of infected computers that can be used in tandem for malicious purposes.

12 Exploits designed to leverage previously undiscovered vulnerabilities. A zero-day attack happens once a software or hardware vulnerability is exploited and before a developer has an opportunity to create a patch to fix it. Thus, those attacks occur on the same day a software weakness is discovered ("zero-day" or "0day").

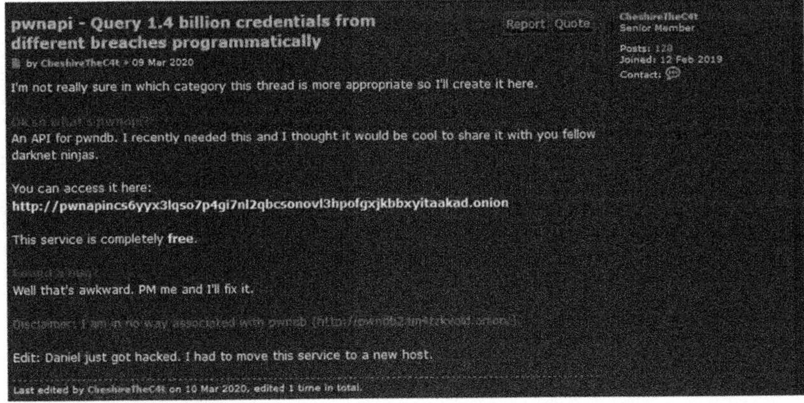


Figure 2.3 Example of forum content, in which a genuine tool is shared for a data feed.

For a while thereafter, staunch Hell members formed a group on a Tor social media site and later moved to set up a site that was strictly access controlled. To gain access to this site, users either had to have reputable names[13] or fill out an online questionnaire detailing their hacking skills and past exploits. The site offered training in the form of CTFs[14] and other game structures. It appears as though they were a bit too strict in censoring their access, as the site was not publicly available for very long.

Aside from the proliferation and exchange of experiences with various kinds of weapons and drugs as well as pornography unfortunately encompassing all ages, much of the so-called darkness is populated by privacy-conscious hosters. Regarding cyber-security content, the exchange of high-profile events (hacks, news, etc.), new techniques and tools (e.g., code at various degrees of maturity, that is, deployability – as illustrated in Figure 2.3), but also questions and help for assistance make up a large part of the content (see Figure 2.4).

With the more recent merging of forums and marketplaces observed in the past one or two years, vendors offer personally identifiable and other sensitive information, accounts to e-commerce and payment service platforms, bank

13 However notorious the admin of Hell, "ping," may have been, he did not gain access here. Though well known and greeted, the rumor started by some forum members that he may have been a "snitch" appeared to have stuck and shut doors for him.

14 A capture the flag (CTF) contest is a cyber-security competition where participants try to solve computer security problems and/or capture and defend computer systems.

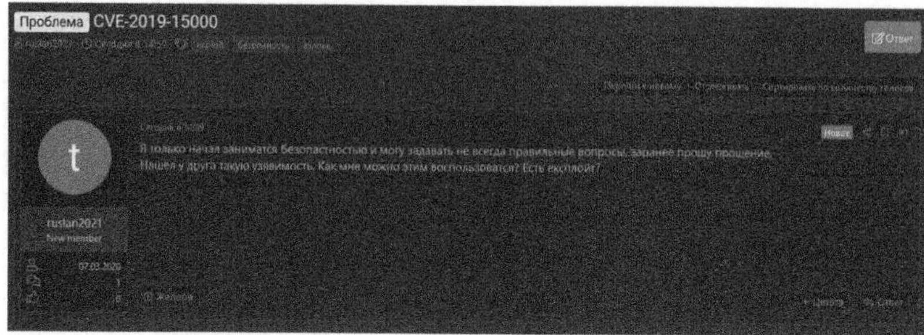


Figure 2.4 Example of forum content in which a question is posed whether a software vulnerability is exploited/exploitable.

account and credit card information, and data leaks across all sites. More static content advertises hacking-as-a-service skills and rents out DDoS attacks[15] at various time-intervals, effectively communizing skills and technologies once available to only a few. Pure marketplaces offer products like keyloggers,[16] skimmers,[17] and other tools for capturing credit card information on point-of-sale devices and ATMs, social media, e-commerce, and/or payment service accounts or tutorials on how to hijack them, tutorials on how to cash stolen credit cards, network and physical layer hacking, WiFi tools and information (wardriving, coopting, etc.) dumps, remote access Trojans (RATs), browser-affecting tools, remote desktop protocol (RDP) tools, exploit kits, mobile phone and Windows-affecting malware, password cracking, email hacking and phishing[18] tools, botnets, and invitations to hacking groups and lists of new forums and marketplaces. Vendors often sell on multiple marketplaces to optimize their profits by addressing a larger audience. Well-known and prestigious marketplaces may also serve well on the resume for a vendor who traded there, even though the marketplace is long defunct – provided the site did not close down due to an exit scam (in which the administrators cashed in the cryptocurrency[19] held in wallets on the site).

[15] A distributed denial-of-service (DDoS) attack is a malicious attempt to disrupt normal service of a website or other network resource, by overwhelming the target infrastructure with a flood of Internet traffic produced by multiple compromised computer systems (e.g., botnets).

[16] Software designed to secretly monitor and log all keystrokes.

[17] Hardware device or malicious software designed to steal information stored on payment cards.

[18] Internet fraud in which the cyber-criminal tricks individuals into providing their sensitive information, such as usernames, passwords, and credit card details, by disguising himself or herself as a trustworthy entity.

[19] Digital currency distributed across a large number of computers that implements cryptography to secure and verify transactions and control the creation of new units. Most darkweb transactions are made with the Bitcoin cryptocurrency, where users send/receive bitcoins without giving personally identifying information.

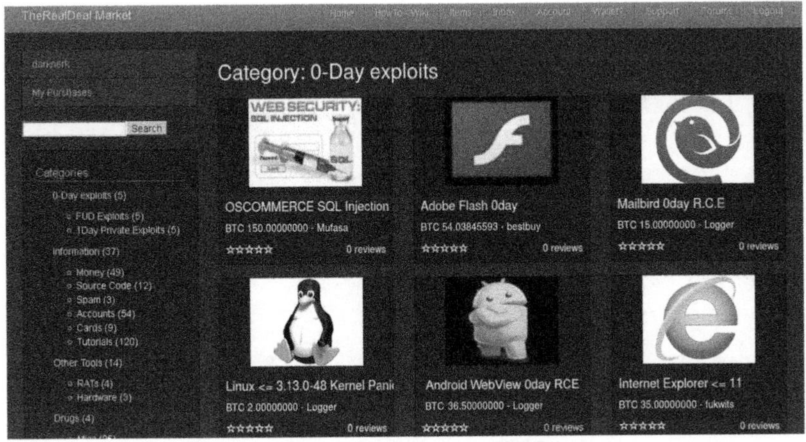


Figure 2.5 Examples of 0days exploits offered on TheRealDeal marketplace.

Popular reputable markets for cyber-criminals were TheRealDeal and, to some extent, AlphaBay. Both were hosted on Tor, though the latter was longer serving. TheRealDeal was purportedly arranged around a gifted Russian hacker and his accomplices who sold his products. Among those products were 0days (see Figure 2.5) and exploits of all kinds. They were joined slowly by other sellers. After DDoS attacks in September and a doxxing[20] event discussed on the now defunct DeepDotWeb[21] suggesting internal tensions, it shut down in November 2016. The AlphaBay marketplace was not focused on cyber-criminals, but sellers offered a wide range of products between 2014 through summer 2017, when an international law enforcement effort shut it down together with other like sites. It was recognized to be the largest darkweb marketplace in 2015, with more than 200,000 registered users (vendors and buyers).[22] Vendors offered everything from stolen digital content to e-commerce accounts, software licenses, tutorials of any kind, some malware, data leaks (dumps), and medicine. The site switched between at times 55 mirror URLs. Figure 2.6 presents some hacking-related products and guides offered on the AlphaBay marketplace.

20 Practice of publishing private information about an individual or organization on the Internet.
21 DeepDotWeb was a news site dedicated to events in and surrounding the darkweb.
22 At the time it was taken down, it had doubled the number of users reaching nearly 400,000 listings.

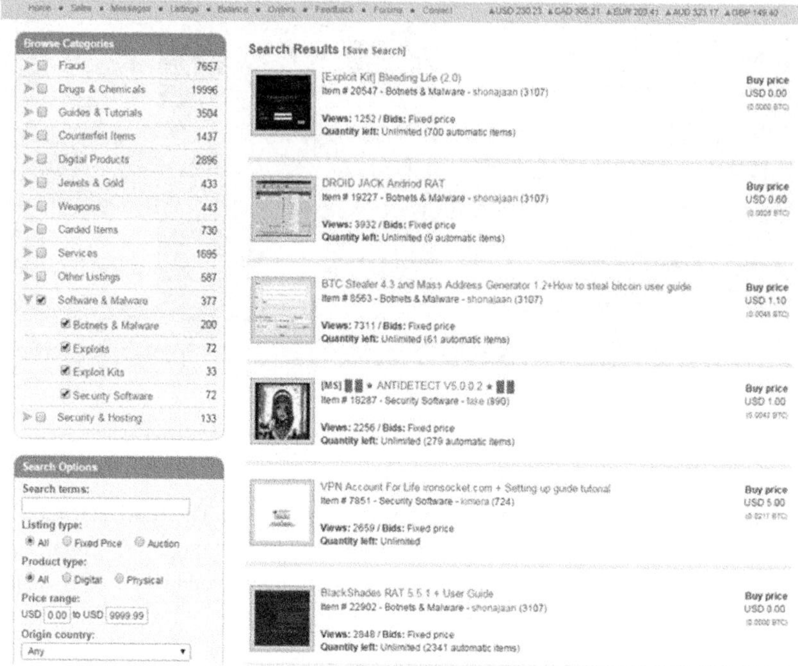


Figure 2.6 Example of hacking-related products and guides offered on the AlphaBay marketplace.

In the next chapters, we discuss the implementation of real cyber-threat intelligence gathering systems, built on top of the data mined those malicious hacker communities.

# PART I

# Understanding the Behavior of Malicious Hackers

# 3
# Mining Key-hackers

## 3.1 Introduction

Malicious hacker communities have participants with different levels of knowledge, and those who want to identify emerging cyber-threats need to scrutinize these individuals to find key cyber-criminals [98, 106, 200]. We denote those malicious cyber-actors as key-hackers, since they have higher hacking skills and influence when compared to the great majority of users present in online hacker communities. As this select group of hackers foment a promising vulnerability exploitation threat market [5], it forms a natural lens through which security alert systems can look to predict cyber-attacks.

To support our assumption, consider when beginners or standard-level hackers are planning to launch an attack. As those actors are utility maximizing, they opt for rewarding vulnerabilities for which there exist threats with demonstrated attack and concealment capabilities to increase their chances of success [5]. Overall, the skills to implement and spread those threats belong to key-hackers [9], as they are able to craft advanced hacking tools,[1] find zero-days vulnerabilities,[2] recruit and orchestrate teams in attack campaigns,[3] and maintain low profiles of activity [130, 175]. As key-hackers often succeed in their cyber-criminal goals [116], they provide profitable resources that are more attractive to other hackers [96].

The challenge here is that key-hackers form a small percentage of the community members, making their identification a complex problem. In the

[1] Examples of advanced hacking tools crafted by key-hackers: Retefe and Trickbot Go banking Trojans, Nitol and DoublePulsar backdoors, Gh0st RAT, EternalRocks and MicroBotMassiveNet computer worms, WannaCry, NotPetya, and UIWIX ransomwares.

[2] Examples of zero-day exploits crafted by key-hackers: Stuxnet computer worm, 666 RAT, Tobfy ransomware, and LadyBoyle action script.

[3] Examples of APT watering hole attack campaigns conducted by key-hackers: Web2Crew, Taidoor, th3bug, and Operation Ephemeral Hydra.

literature, two approaches have been empirically considered for this task: content analysis [1, 53, 200] and social network analysis [149, 199]. In both approaches, the idea is to generate features and rank the users based on their feature values, with the top-ranked ones being considered key-hackers [1]. However, there is an additional problem faced by those studies: the lack of ground truth (the key-hackers of the communities) to validate the results. As it is difficult to obtain this information, previous work basically neglected this validation task or has it done manually, that is, by leveraging security consulting companies [125]. Finally, it is unclear if these methods can generalize to multiple hacker communities, as training and testing are done using the same forum data.

In this chapter, we address the key-hacker identification problem and systematically validate the results using data collected from three highly ranked hacking forums. Particularly, we study how content, social network, and seniority analysis perform individually and combined. Information related to activity, expertise, knowledge transfer behavior, structural position, influence, and coverage is mined to develop a profile for each community member, aiming to understand which features characterize key cyber-criminals. To train and test our model, we use an optimization metaheuristic and compare its performance with machine learning algorithms. We leverage the users' reputation provided by the three analyzed forums to cross-validate the results among them; that is, models trained in one forum are generalized to make predictions in different ones. Our work is novel since it offers researchers a solid strategy to find key-hackers in forums that do not provide users' reputation or that provide a deficient user reputation system. We observe that this is the case for the vast majority of hacker forums, representing over 80% of the 36 forums scraped for this work. We summarize the main contributions of this chapter as follows:

1. We show that a hybridization of features derived from content, social network, and seniority analysis is able to identify key-hackers up to 17% more precisely than those derived from any of these strategies by itself.
2. We explain and evidence why the reputation of malicious actors present on online hacker forums can be used as a strong indicator of key-hackers.
3. We demonstrate how a model learned in a given hacker forum to identify its key-hackers can be generalized to a different forum that is not used to train the model, obtaining 52% of ranking consistency.
4. We compare the performance of different models when trying to identify key-hackers, showing how an optimization metaheuristic obtains 35% of predictive improvement over machine learning algorithms.

The remainder of this chapter is organized as follows. Section 3.2 details our forum dataset. Next, we show in Section 3.3 how we leverage users' reputations to obtain ground truth data. Section 3.4 informally defines our problem. Section 3.5 describes the features we derive to profile hackers. Section 3.6 presents our experiments and exhibits the corresponding results. Section 3.7 shows some related work. Finally, Section 3.8 concludes the chapter.

## 3.2 Dataset

For this chapter, we select three popular English-language hacker forums from our data repository detailed in Chapter 1. We anonymize these forums here, representing them as *Forum 1*, *Forum 2*, and *Forum 3*, and show their statistics in Table 3.1. All these forums comprise hacking-related discussions organized in a thread format, where a user initiates a topic with a post that is usually followed by many users' replies.

In order to prepare the data for feature extraction, we retrieve the users' interactions over time to generate a network of hackers. We denote a set of users $V$ and connections $E$, as the nodes and edges in a directed graph $G = (V, E)$, while $\Theta$, $\mathcal{M}$, and $T$ correspond to a set of topics, messages, and discrete time points. The symbols $v, \theta, m, t$ will represent a specific node, topic, message, and time point. We denote an activity log $\mathcal{A}$ containing all posts (topics and replies) as a set of tuples of the form $\langle v, \theta, m, t \rangle$, where $v \in V$, $\theta \in \Theta$, $m \in \mathcal{M}$, and $t \in T$. It describes that "$v$ posted in topic $\theta$ a message $m$ at time $t$." A directed edge $(v, v')$ is created when users $v$ and $v'$ post together in a given topic, so that the posting time of $v$ is greater than of $v'$. We formalize the set of direct edges $E$ in Equation 3.1:

$$E = \{(v, v') \mid \exists \langle v, \theta, m, t \rangle \in \mathcal{A}, \exists \langle v', \theta, m', t' \rangle \in \mathcal{A}, \ s.t.\ v \neq v', t > t'\}. \quad (3.1)$$

Table 3.1 *Statistics of the three analyzed hacker forums*

| | *Forum 1* | *Forum 2* | *Forum 3* |
|---|---|---|---|
| Time period | 2013-12-24 : 2016-03-16 | 2013-12-24 : 2016-08-16 | 2002-09-14 : 2016-03-15 |
| Number of users | 4,380 | 2,495 | 2,802 |
| Number of topics | 5,571 | 1,077 | 5,805 |
| Number of posts | 36,453 | 25,115 | 49,078 |
| Distinct values of users' reputations | 134 | 102 | 37 |

| Topic A | | Topic B | |
|---|---|---|---|
| User | Post Time | User | Post Time |
| 1 | 01-01-2015 10:23:15 | 2 | 01-02-2015 15:20:10 |
| 2 | 01-01-2015 10:25:10 | 1 | 01-02-2015 16:10:05 |
| 3 | 01-01-2015 10:30:20 | 3 | 01-02-2015 16:18:47 |
| 2 | 01-01-2015 10:31:46 | 2 | 01-02-2015 17:04:46 |
| 5 | 01-01-2015 10:40:14 | 4 | 01-02-2015 20:49:14 |

(a)

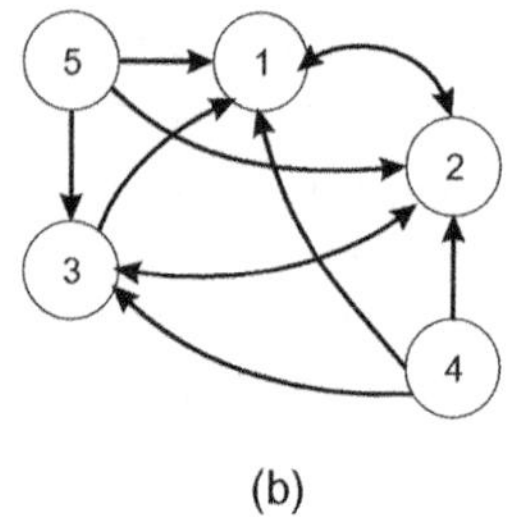


(b)

Figure 3.1 Directed graph generated using user posts

Table 3.2 *Network component analysis*

| | *Forum 1* | *Forum 2* | *Forum 3* |
|---|---|---|---|
| Giant component size | 4,313 | 2,417 | 2,737 |
| Component size = 11 | 0 | 1 | 0 |
| Component size = 3 | 1 | 0 | 0 |
| Component size = 2 | 19 | 6 | 7 |
| Component size = 1 | 26 | 55 | 51 |

The intuition here is to make visible to users who are posting in $\theta$ at time $t$ all other users who have already posted in $\theta$ prior to $t$, but not vice versa. We believe this strategy can better reproduce the interaction process on online forums (compared to the general strategy of creating a complete undirected graph, including all users who post together in a topic [149]), since users will only know about previous posts. Figure 3.1 illustrates this process by showing the original users' posts in panel (a), and the corresponding directed social network generated in panel (b).

After generating the social networks, we remove all users who do not belong to the giant component of their corresponding forum since they can produce misleading centrality values. The issue happens because some centralities are computed and normalized for each component, which tends to produce high values for users in small parts of the networks. Because of their few connections, these individuals would hardly be considered as key-hackers. Table 3.2 shows the size of all components of each forum, detailing that 67 users from *Forum 1*, 78 users from *Forum 2*, and 65 users from *Forum 3* were removed.

## 3.3 Leveraging Users' Reputation to Obtain Ground Truth Data

As hacker communities form meritocracies [145, 160], members own different levels of capability, expertise, and influence (to mention a few human factors).

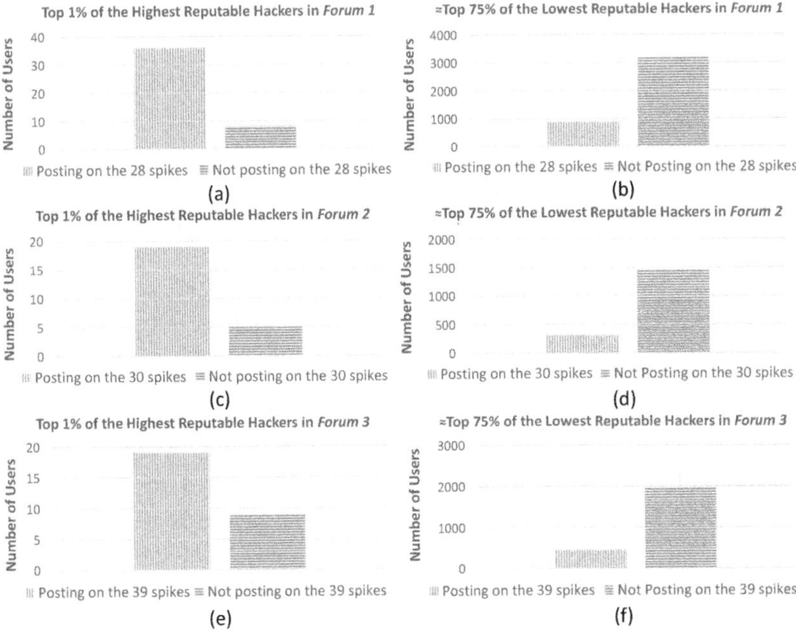


Figure 3.2 Posting pattern of the highest and the lowest reputable hackers on the analyzed hacker forums.

According to [46], those factors are organically consolidated in the user reputation score, which is a metric that codifies users' standing, driving engagement by measuring participation, activity, content quality, content rating, and so on. Zhang et al. [200] showed that malicious hackers who have high reputation are usually linked to emerging cyber-threats, a clear indicator of key cybercriminals.

A case study in our data corroborates with Zhang's et al. assumption. In 2016, Anna Senpai had a high reputation when he released the Mirai botnet source code on a popular hacker forum [177]. His threads generated a high number of responses, especially the one containing the code. Since user reputation is peer assigned, a reputation score mirrors how other forum members evaluate the usefulness of the user's contributions. When we analyze the posting patterns of high- and low-reputation hackers of *Forum 1*, presented in Figure 3.2 (a), we observe that 36 out of the 44 hackers with the highest reputation ($Top_{1\%}$ of all users) are posting on all 28 spikes of user activity (minimum of $4 \times \sigma$ above average), while only 8 of them are not engaged in any of these high-volume conversation threads.

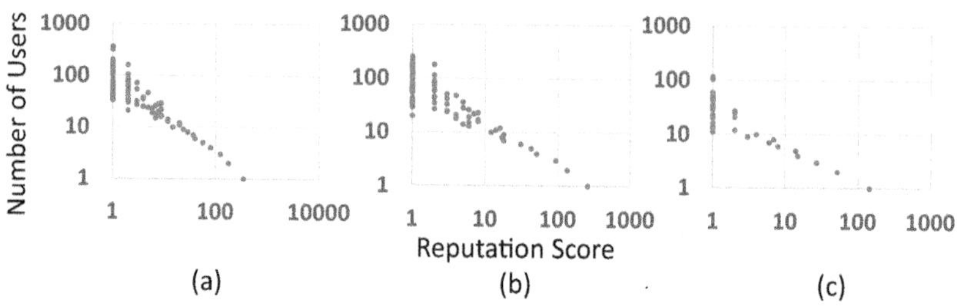


Figure 3.3 Distribution of reputation score in (a) *Forum 1*, (b) *Forum 2*, and (c) *Forum 3* (log-log scale) – these curves fit power-laws with $p_k \approx k^{-0.92}$, $p_k \approx k^{-0.86}$, and $p_k \approx k^{-0.78}$, respectively, where $k$ is the number of users.

On the other hand, Figure 3.2 (b) shows that 870 out of the 4,039 hackers with the lowest reputation ($\approx Top_{75\%}$ of all users) are posting on those spikes, while 3,169 are not engaged in these conversations. A similar pattern is observed for the other two analyzed forums. We investigate those spikes since they promise to offer some insights into possibly interesting topics promoted by skilled and influential hackers on the forums, while confirming the user reputation score as a strong indicator for key-hacker identification.

In this chapter, we also rely on the assumption that users with high reputation form our set of key-hackers, using this metric to obtain ground truth data. Thus, we deliberately select forums that explicitly provide this information, so that the corresponding key-hackers can be identified. Figure 3.3 shows the distribution of the reputation score in (a) *Forum 1*, (b) *Forum 2*, and (c) *Forum 3*, pointing out the existence of a hacking meritocracy. As is observed, only a few users (key-hackers) exhibit high reputation in all the forums, although their corresponding scores vary in magnitude. In addition, although Table 3.1 shows that *Forum 1* and *Forum 2* are closer in terms of reputation distinctness (their scores are formed by 135 and 102 different values, respectively, while *Forum 3* owns only 37), the similar distribution pattern of all three forums informs us that characteristics of the highest-reputation hackers could be similar in all three forums.

## 3.4 Problem Statement

Considering that the highest-reputation hackers form our set of key-hackers, we want to estimate the user reputation score by analyzing features that differentiate standard/lower-level hackers from skilled ones. This would allow us to find key-hackers in forums that do not provide the reputation score or that have a deficient user reputation system.

## 3.5 Feature Engineering

To estimate users' reputations, we design 25 features to mine relevant characteristics and behaviors of key-hackers. From these features, 17 are extracted using content analysis, subdivided into activity (3), expertise (10), and knowledge transfer behavior (4). We subdivide the 10 features related to expertise into involvement quality (7), cyber-criminal assets (1), and specialty lexicons (2). In addition, five features are extracted using social network analysis, subdivided into structural position (3) and influence (2). Finally, three features are extracted using what we denominate seniority analysis, all of them being related to coverage. We analyze users' seniority since it generates indicators of consistent forum involvement over time, checking how much the users continuously contribute to the hacker environments [78, 116, 139]. We believe this set of features comprises a variety of information that differentiates key-hackers from others, contributing to an accurate estimation of the users' reputations. All features have their values normalized to avoid problems with different scales [179]. We detail the features within their corresponding categories in Table 3.3.

Table 3.3 *Feature Engineering*

<table>
<tr><td rowspan="6">Content analysis</td><td colspan="2">Activity</td><td>01. Topics created<br>02. Replies created<br>03. Replies by month</td></tr>
<tr><td rowspan="3">Expertise</td><td>Involvement quality</td><td>04. Length of topics<br>05. Length of replies<br>06. Topic density<br>07. Replies with knowledge provision<br>08. Replies with knowledge acquisition<br>09. Topics with knowledge provision<br>10. Topics with knowledge acquisition</td></tr>
<tr><td>Cyber-criminal assets</td><td>11. Attachments</td></tr>
<tr><td>Specialty lexicons</td><td>12. Technical jargon<br>13. Environment jargon</td></tr>
<tr><td colspan="2">Knowledge transfer behavior</td><td>14. Velocity of knowledge provision pattern in topics<br>15. Velocity of knowledge acquisition pattern in topics<br>16. Velocity of knowledge provision pattern in replies<br>17. Velocity of knowledge acquisition pattern in replies</td></tr>
<tr><td colspan="3"></td></tr>
<tr><td rowspan="2">Social network analysis</td><td colspan="2">Structural position</td><td>18. Degree centrality<br>19. Betweenness centrality<br>20. Closeness centrality</td></tr>
<tr><td colspan="2">Influence</td><td>21. Eigenvector centrality<br>22. PageRank</td></tr>
<tr><td>Seniority analysis</td><td colspan="2">Coverage</td><td>23. Interval btw user's & forum's first posts<br>24. Distinct days of posts<br>25. Interval btw user's & forum's last posts</td></tr>
</table>

### 3.5.1 Activity

The set of features within this category belongs to the content analysis approach and aims to identify how active hackers are in the forums. It includes the three following features.

**Topics created (TOC).** This feature counts how many topics (headers) are initiated by hackers. According to a previous work [199], key-hackers usually create relatively few topics, but with high relevance to the community. We formalize this feature as

$$TOC_{(v)} = \sum_{\theta} g(\langle v, \theta, m, t \rangle). \tag{3.2}$$

where $g(\langle v, \theta, m, t \rangle)$ is defined as

$$g(\langle v, \theta, m, t \rangle) = \begin{cases} 1, \; if \; \langle v, \theta, m, t \rangle \in \mathcal{A} \wedge \nexists \langle v', \theta, m', t' \rangle \in \mathcal{A}, \text{ s.t. } t' < t \\ 0, \; otherwise. \end{cases} \tag{3.3}$$

**Replies created (REC).** This feature counts the number of times users answer the topics in the forums. According to previous work [1, 53, 199, 200], key-hackers usually create a huge quantity of quality replies, offering relevant help to less skilled community members. We formalize this feature as

$$REC_{(v)} = \sum_{\theta} \sum_{m} \sum_{t} |\langle v, \theta, m, t \rangle| - TOC_{(v)}, \text{ s.t. } \langle v, \theta, m, t \rangle \in \mathcal{A}. \tag{3.4}$$

**Replies by month (REM).** This feature averages the replies created by hackers monthly, aiming to estimate how often hackers produce topic answers. Previous work, such as [1], claims that key-hackers usually have a minimum frequency of answers over time to keep the acquired status. We formalize this feature as

$$REM_{(v)} = \frac{REC_{(v)}}{|MA_{(v)}|}. \tag{3.5}$$

where $MA_{(v)}$ is the set of distinct months in which $v$ created at least one topic answer.

### 3.5.2 Expertise

This category of features belongs to the content analysis approach and aims to quantify the users' skills regarding (malicious) hacking. It includes the following ten features.

**Length of topics (LET).** This feature averages the number of words used by hackers to create a topic. Previous work [1] states that key-hackers usually do not create extensive topics, since this is a characteristic of low-skilled hackers. We formalize this feature as

$$LET_{(v)} = \frac{\sum_{\theta} h(\langle v,\theta,m,t\rangle)}{TOC_{(v)}}. \tag{3.6}$$

with $h(\langle v,\theta,m,t\rangle)$ being defined as

$$h(\langle v,\theta,m,t\rangle) = \begin{cases} Length(m),\ if\ \langle v,\theta,m,t\rangle \in \mathcal{A}\ \wedge\ \nexists\langle v',\theta,m',t'\rangle \in \mathcal{A},\ s.t.\ t' < t \\ 0,\ otherwise. \end{cases} \tag{3.7}$$

**Length of replies (LER)**. This feature averages the number of words used by hackers to create a reply. According to previous work [1, 199], key-hackers usually produced detailed answers, as they have interest and knowledge to instruct other community members. We formalize this feature as

$$LER_{(v)} = \frac{\sum_{\theta}\sum_{m}\sum_{t} i(\langle v,\theta,m,t\rangle)}{REC_{(v)}}. \tag{3.8}$$

with $i(\langle v,\theta,m,t\rangle)$ being defined as

$$i(\langle v,\theta,m,t\rangle) = \begin{cases} Length(m),\ if\ \langle v,\theta,m,t\rangle \in \mathcal{A}\ \wedge\ \exists\langle v',\theta,m',t'\rangle \in \mathcal{A},\ s.t.\ t' < t \\ 0,\ otherwise. \end{cases} \tag{3.9}$$

**Topic density (TOD)**. This feature averages the number of users posting in a given topic. As discussions started by key-hackers are more relevant to the community, they often promote higher engagement [200]. We formalize this feature as

$$TOD_{(v)} = \frac{\sum_{\theta} j(\langle v,\theta,m,t\rangle)}{TOC_{(v)}}. \tag{3.10}$$

with $j(\langle v,\theta,m,t\rangle)$ being defined as

$$j(\langle v,\theta,m,t\rangle) = \begin{cases} \sum_{v'}\sum_{m'}\sum_{t'} |\langle v',\theta,m',t'\rangle|,\ if\ \langle v,\theta,m,t\rangle \in \mathcal{A}\ \wedge\ \nexists\langle v',\theta,m',t'\rangle \in \mathcal{A}, \\ \qquad s.t.\ t' < t \\ 0,\ otherwise. \end{cases} \tag{3.11}$$

**Replies with knowledge provision (RKP)**. This feature counts the number of replies containing knowledge provision. Zhang et al. [200] observed a tendency for key-hackers to produce more replies providing versus requesting information. To identify knowledge provision, we apply string matching to a predefined set of keywords. Table 3.4 shows a sample of the keywords that match knowledge provision. We formalize this feature as

$$RKP_{(v)} = \sum_{\theta}\sum_{m}\sum_{t} k(\langle v,\theta,m,t\rangle). \tag{3.12}$$

with $k(\langle v,\theta,m,t\rangle)$ being defined as

$$k(\langle v,\theta,m,t\rangle) = \begin{cases} 1, if\ \exists w \in m \wedge w \in Key_{\{kp\}} \wedge \langle v,\theta,m,t\rangle \in \mathcal{A} \wedge \exists \langle v',\theta,m',t'\rangle \in \mathcal{A}, \\ \hfill s.t.\ t' < t \\ 0,\ otherwise. \end{cases} \tag{3.13}$$

where $Key_{\{kp\}}$ is the predefined set of knowledge provision keywords.

**Replies with knowledge acquisition (RKA).** This feature counts the number of replies indicating knowledge acquisition. Opposing the previous feature (i.e., RKP), Zhang et al. [200] observed a tendency for key-hackers to produce fewer replies acquiring versus providing information. To identify knowledge acquisition, we also apply string matching to a predefined set of keywords illustrated in Table 3.4. We formalize this feature as

$$RKA_{(v)} = \sum_{\theta}\sum_{m}\sum_{t} l(\langle v,\theta,m,t\rangle). \tag{3.14}$$

with $l(\langle v,\theta,m,t\rangle)$ being defined as

$$l(\langle v,\theta,m,t\rangle) = \begin{cases} 1, if\ \exists w \in m \wedge w \in Key_{\{ka\}} \wedge \langle v,\theta,m,t\rangle \in \mathcal{A} \wedge \exists \langle v',\theta,m',t'\rangle \in \mathcal{A}, \\ \hfill s.t.\ t' < t \\ 0,\ otherwise. \end{cases} \tag{3.15}$$

where $Key_{\{ka\}}$ is the predefined set of knowledge acquisition keywords.

**Topics with knowledge provision (TKP).** This feature counts the number of topics containing knowledge provision. It has the same pattern observed for the feature *RKP*, but with a different magnitude. We formalize this feature as

$$TKP_{(v)} = \sum_{\theta} n(\langle v,\theta,m,t\rangle). \tag{3.16}$$

Table 3.4 *Sample of keywords used for string matching*

| Knowledge provision | Knowledge acquisition | Technical jargon | Environment jargon |
|---|---|---|---|
| advice | request | back door | tor |
| suggest | ask | cookie | blockchain |
| guide | doubt | crack | dispute |
| tutorial | whyd́ | dos | bitcoin |
| recommend | how to | dump | escrow |
| follow | need | zero day | honeypot |
| check | want | xss | i2p |
| yourself | troublesome | spyware | freenet |
| easy-to-follow | fail | shell | onion |
| demonstrate | struggling | phishing | pgp |

with $n(\langle v,\theta,m,t\rangle)$ being defined as

$$n(\langle v,\theta,m,t\rangle) = \begin{cases} 1, if \ \exists w \in m \wedge w \in Key_{\{kp\}} \wedge \langle v,\theta,m,t\rangle \in \mathcal{A} \wedge \nexists \langle v',\theta,m',t'\rangle \in \mathcal{A}, \\ \hfill s.t.\ t' < t \\ 0,\ otherwise. \end{cases} \tag{3.17}$$

**Topics with knowledge acquisition (TKA).** This feature counts the number of topics indicating knowledge acquisition. It has the same pattern observed for the feature *RKA*, but with a different magnitude. We formalize this feature as

$$TKA_{(v)} = \sum_{\theta} o(\langle v,\theta,m,t\rangle). \tag{3.18}$$

with $o(\langle v,\theta,m,t\rangle)$ being defined as

$$o(\langle v,\theta,m,t\rangle) = \begin{cases} 1, if \ \exists w \in m \wedge w \in Key_{\{ka\}} \wedge \langle v,\theta,m,t\rangle \in \mathcal{A} \wedge \nexists \langle v',\theta,m',t'\rangle \in \mathcal{A}, \\ \hfill s.t.\ t' < t \\ 0,\ otherwise. \end{cases} \tag{3.19}$$

**Attachments (ATH).** This feature checks for attachments in the posts (topics and replies). According to [1], key-hackers usually provide relevant cyber-criminal assets in the form of attachments. We apply string matching to a predefined set of keywords, such as “href” or “http,” formalizing this feature as

$$ATH_{(v)} = \sum_{\theta}\sum_{m}\sum_{t} p(\langle v,\theta,m,t\rangle). \tag{3.20}$$

with $p(\langle v,\theta,m,t\rangle)$ being defined as

$$p(\langle v,\theta,m,t\rangle) = \begin{cases} 1, if\ \exists w \in m \wedge w \in Key_{\{at\}} \wedge \langle v,\theta,m,t\rangle \in \mathcal{A} \\ 0,\ otherwise. \end{cases} \tag{3.21}$$

where $Key_{\{at\}}$ is the predefined set of keywords related to attachments.

**Technical jargon (TEJ).** This feature checks for technical jargon in the posts. According to [1], key-hackers often use technical jargon to reference some specific hacking technique or tool. To identify technical jargon, we apply string matching to a set of keywords extracted from a predefined dictionary. Table 3.4 shows a sample of the keywords that match technical jargon. We formalize this feature as

$$TEJ_{(v)} = \sum_{\theta}\sum_{m}\sum_{t} q(\langle v,\theta,m,t\rangle). \tag{3.22}$$

with $q(\langle v,\theta,m,t\rangle)$ being defined as

$$q(\langle v,\theta,m,t\rangle) = \begin{cases} 1, if\ \exists w \in m \wedge w \in Key_{\{te\}} \wedge \langle v,\theta,m,t\rangle \in \mathcal{A} \\ 0,\ otherwise. \end{cases} \tag{3.23}$$

where $Key_{\{te\}}$ is the predefined set of keywords related to technical jargon.

**Environment jargon (ENJ).** This feature checks for environment jargon in the posts. According to [1], key-hackers often use environment jargon to reference some specific hacker platform or resource. To identify environment jargon, we apply string matching to a set of keywords extracted from a predefined dictionary. Table 3.4 shows a sample of the keywords that match environment jargon. We formalize this feature as

$$ENJ_{(v)} = \sum_{\theta}\sum_{m}\sum_{t} r(\langle v,\theta,m,t\rangle). \tag{3.24}$$

with $r(\langle v,\theta,m,t\rangle)$ being defined as

$$r(\langle v,\theta,m,t\rangle) = \begin{cases} 1, if\ \exists w \in m \wedge w \in Key_{\{en\}} \wedge \langle v,\theta,m,t\rangle \in \mathcal{A} \\ 0,\ otherwise. \end{cases} \tag{3.25}$$

where $Key_{\{en\}}$ is the predefined set of keywords related to environment jargon.

### 3.5.3 Knowledge Transfer Behavior

The set of features within this category belongs to the content analysis approach and aims to identify the behavioral trend of hackers related to knowledge provision and knowledge acquisition over time. It includes the following four features.

**Velocity of knowledge provision pattern in topics (VPT).** This feature checks how fast the knowledge provision pattern increases or decreases in the topics created by hackers. The idea is inspired by the work conducted in [200], whose authors examined how this pattern changes by analyzing sequential posts. According to this work, key-hackers usually present increasing knowledge provision over time, and this feature measures the velocity of this behavior in the topics. Specifically, for every sequence of 10 topics $i$ where user $v$ engaged, we create a data point $x_i(v)$ and assign the number of topics created by $v$ containing knowledge provision to $y_i(v)$. Then, we analyze all points created using linear regression, checking the slope $a$ of the line generated ($y = ax$). We formalize this feature as

$$VPT_{(v)} = \frac{y_2(v) - y_1(v)}{x_2(v) - x_1(v)} = \frac{y_2(v) - y_1(v)}{2 - 1} = y_2(v) - y_1(v) = a. \quad (3.26)$$

with $y_i(v)$ being defined as

$$y_i(v) = \sum_{\theta \in TOP_{(v)},\, \theta=[(i-1)*10]+1}^{[(i-1)*10]+10} n(\langle v,\theta,m,t \rangle). \quad (3.27)$$

where $TOP_{(v)}$ is the set of sorted topics created by $v$ and $n$ is defined in Equation 3.17.

**Velocity of knowledge acquisition pattern in topics (VAT).** This feature checks how fast the knowledge acquisition pattern increases or decreases in the topics created by hackers. We use the same strategy mentioned for the previous feature, but now considering knowledge acquisition. According to [200], key-hackers usually present decreasing knowledge acquisition over time, and this feature measures the velocity of this behavior in the topics. We formalize this feature as

$$VAT_{(v)} = \frac{y_2(v) - y_1(v)}{x_2(v) - x_1(v)} = \frac{y_2(v) - y_1(v)}{2 - 1} = y_2(v) - y_1(v) = a. \quad (3.28)$$

with $y_i(v)$ being defined as

$$y_i(v) = \sum_{\theta \in TOP_{(v)},\, \theta=[(i-1)*10]+1}^{[(i-1)*10]+10} o(\langle v,\theta,m,t \rangle). \quad (3.29)$$

where $TOP_{(v)}$ is the set of sorted topics created by $v$ and $o$ is defined in Equation 3.19.

**Velocity of knowledge provision pattern in replies (VPR).** This feature checks how fast the knowledge provision pattern increases or decreases in the replies created by hackers. The pattern here should follow the pattern identified by the feature *VPT*, but with different magnitude. We formalize this feature as

$$VPR_{(v)} = \frac{y_2(v) - y_1(v)}{x_2(v) - x_1(v)} = \frac{y_2(v) - y_1(v)}{2 - 1} = y_2(v) - y_1(v) = a. \quad (3.30)$$

with $y_i(v)$ being defined as

$$y_i(v) = \sum_{\theta \in REP_{(v)},\, \theta = [(i-1)*10]+1}^{[(i-1)*10]+10} k(\langle v, \theta, m, t \rangle). \quad (3.31)$$

where $REP_{(v)}$ is the set of sorted replies created by $v$ and $k$ is defined in Equation 3.13.

**Velocity of knowledge acquisition pattern in replies (VAR).** This feature checks how fast the knowledge acquisition pattern increases or decreases in the replies created by hackers. The pattern here should follow the pattern identified by the feature *VAT*, but with different magnitude. We formalize this feature as

$$VAR_{(v)} = \frac{y_2(v) - y_1(v)}{x_2(v) - x_1(v)} = \frac{y_2(v) - y_1(v)}{2 - 1} = y_2(v) - y_1(v) = a. \quad (3.32)$$

with $y_i(v)$ being defined as

$$y_i(v) = \sum_{\theta \in REP_{(v)},\, \theta = [(i-1)*10]+1}^{[(i-1)*10]+10} l(\langle v, \theta, m, t \rangle). \quad (3.33)$$

where $REP_{(v)}$ is the set of sorted replies created by $v$ and $l$ is defined in Equation 3.15.

### 3.5.4 Structural Position

The set of features within this category belongs to the social network analysis approach and aims to define the hackers' relevance based on their structural position in the networks. This category includes the following three features.

**Degree centrality (DEC).** This feature measures the number of direct neighbors connected to a given node [196]. As we deal with directed networks, we defined this measure as the number of outgoing edges [196]. According to [149], key-hackers usually present high degree centralities, since each of their many replies produces an outgoing edge. We formalize this feature as

$$DEC_{(v_i)} = d_i^{out}. \quad (3.34)$$

where $d_i^{out}$ is the out-degree of $v_i$.

**Betweenness centrality (BEC).** This feature measures the number of shortest paths that pass through a given node [196], indicating its importance for the information flow. According to [199], key-hackers usually present high betweenness centralities, since they are very well-connected users who often appear in those corresponding shortest paths. We formalize this feature as

$$BEC_{(v_i)} = \sum_{s \neq t \neq v_i} \frac{\sigma_{st}(v_i)}{\sigma_{st}}. \tag{3.35}$$

where $\sigma_{st}$ is the number of shortest paths from node $s$ to $t$ and $\sigma_{st}(v_i)$ is the number of shortest paths from node $s$ to $t$ that pass through $v_i$.

**Closeness centrality (CLC).** This feature measures how close an individual is to all other individuals in the networks [196]. As key-hackers have a central position in the networks that shrinks their distance to others, these individuals usually present high closeness centralities. We formalize this feature as

$$CLC_{(v_i)} = \frac{1}{\bar{l}_{v_i}}. \tag{3.36}$$

where $\bar{l}_{v_i} = \frac{1}{n-1} \sum_{v_j \neq v_i} l_{i,j}$ is node $v_i$'s average shortest path length to other nodes and $n$ is the number of nodes.

### 3.5.5 Influence

The set of features within this category belongs to the social network analysis approach and aims to identify the level of prestige of hackers. It includes the following two features.

**Eigenvector centrality (EIC).** This feature assigns importance to a node if other important nodes are linked to it [196]. According to [125], key-hackers usually present high eigenvector centralities, since they form connections among themselves. We formalize this feature as

$$EIC_{(v_i)} = \frac{1}{\lambda} \sum_{j=1}^{n} A_{j,i} EIC(v_j). \tag{3.37}$$

where $\lambda$ is a fixed constant, $A_{j,i}$ is the adjacent matrix of the directed graph $G = (V, E)$, and $n$ is the number of nodes.

**PageRank (PAR).** As a variant of *EIC*, this feature checks the quality of the links pointing to a hacker in order to estimate its importance [196]. According to [125], key-hackers usually present high PageRank, since they are likely to receive more links from other key-hackers. We formalize this feature as

$$PAR_{(v_i)} = \alpha \sum_{j=1}^{n} A_{j,i} \frac{PAR(v_j)}{d_j^{out}} + \beta. \tag{3.38}$$

where $\alpha$ and $\beta$ are fixed constants, $A_{j,i}$ is the adjacent matrix of the directed graph $G = (V, E)$, and $n$ is the number of nodes.

### 3.5.6 Coverage

The set of features within this category belongs to the seniority analysis approach and aims to identify the active long-term hackers in the forums. It includes the following three features.

**Interval between user's and forum's first posts (IFP).** This feature checks the time interval between the first post in the forum and the first post of a specific hacker. Previous work [1, 17] argues that founding members are usually key-hackers, being actively involved in the discussions since the beginning. We formalize this feature as

$$IFP(v) = \sum_{\theta}\sum_{m}\sum_{t} s(\langle v,\theta,m,t\rangle) - \sum_{v'}\sum_{\theta'}\sum_{m'}\sum_{t'} u(\langle v',\theta',m',t'\rangle). \tag{3.39}$$

where $s(\langle v,\theta,m,t\rangle)$ and $u(\langle v',\theta',m',t'\rangle)$ are defined as

$$s(\langle v,\theta,m,t\rangle) = \begin{cases} t, if\ \langle v,\theta,m,t\rangle \in \mathcal{A} \wedge \nexists \langle v,\theta'',m'',t''\rangle \in \mathcal{A},\ s.t.\ t'' < t, \\ 0, otherwise, \end{cases} \tag{3.40}$$

$$u(\langle v',\theta',m',t'\rangle) = \begin{cases} t, if\ \langle v',\theta',m',t'\rangle \in \mathcal{A} \wedge \nexists \langle v'',\theta'',m'',t''\rangle \in \mathcal{A},\ s.t.\ t'' < t', \\ 0, otherwise. \end{cases} \tag{3.41}$$

**Distinct days of postings (DDP).** This feature checks the continuity of posts created by hackers. Previous work [17, 200] argues that continuous participants are more likely to be key-hackers, since they are often contributing to the communities' development. We formalize this feature as

$$DDP_{(v)} = |Days_{(v)}|. \tag{3.42}$$

where $Days_{(v)}$ returns the set of distinct days in which $v$ posted.

**Interval between user's and forum's last posts (ILP).** This feature checks the time interval between the last post in the forum and the last post of a specific hacker. Previous work [1, 17] argues that key-hackers are usually active in the communities with no fleeting interests. We formalize this feature as

$$ILP(v) = \sum_{\theta}\sum_{m}\sum_{t} x(\langle v,\theta,m,t\rangle) - \sum_{v'}\sum_{\theta'}\sum_{m'}\sum_{t'} y(\langle v',\theta',m',t'\rangle). \quad (3.43)$$

where $x(\langle v,\theta,m,t\rangle)$ and $y(\langle v',\theta',m',t'\rangle)$ are defined as

$$x(\langle v,\theta,m,t\rangle) = \begin{cases} t, \; if \; \langle v,\theta,m,t\rangle \in \mathcal{A} \land \nexists\langle v,\theta',m',t'\rangle \in \mathcal{A}, \; s.t. \; t' > t, \\ 0, \; otherwise, \end{cases} \quad (3.44)$$

$$y(\langle v',\theta',m',t'\rangle) = \begin{cases} t, \; if \; \langle v',\theta',m',t'\rangle \in \mathcal{A} \land \nexists\langle v'',\theta'',m'',t''\rangle \in \mathcal{A}, \; s.t. \; t'' > t', \\ 0, \; otherwise. \end{cases} \quad (3.45)$$

## 3.6 Supervised Learning Experiments

This section presents our supervised learning experiments to mine key-hackers. We first introduce how we perform training and test using four different algorithms, including an optimization metaheuristic and three machine learning methods. Our intention is to verify which algorithms generalize better when estimating user reputation, using the hackers' characteristics learned in one forum to test on another one. Then, we compare the performance of our model under two conditions: (1) when it is trained/tested using the features related to each approach individually and combined and (2) when it is trained/tested using different ranges for the definition of key-hackers.

### 3.6.1 Training and Testing

We use the 25 engineered features as input to the supervised learning algorithms. We compare the algorithms' performance when they use features of content, social network, and seniority analysis individually and combined. To perform that, we leverage the user reputation score to maximize the overlap of two distinct sets of hackers: the $Top_{10\%}$ found with their Estimated Reputation Score (ERS) and the $Top_{10\%}$ found with their Actual Reputation Score (ARS). The ARS represents the user's reputation informed by the forums, and we use this information as our ground truth. This way, we sort the users according to their reputation in descending order, and the $Top_{10\%}$ will represent the key-hackers – for instance, the $Top_{10\%}$ of *Forum 1* are the 431 hackers with the highest ARS. The ERS is the reputation to be estimated by our algorithms based on the features extracted, and we also want to use the $Top_{10\%}$ to infer who should be the key-hackers. With both metrics in hand, our goal is to maximize the value of $Overlap_{10\%}$ presented in Equation 3.46, which is a metric that provides a measure for user ranking consistency [22]:

$$Overlap_{10\%} = \frac{|ERS_{10\%} \cap ARS_{10\%}|}{|ERS_{10\%} \cup ARS_{10\%}|}. \tag{3.46}$$

We train and test four different supervised learning algorithms. The first one comprises an optimization metaheuristic inspired by the natural selection process: genetic algorithms (GAs) [111]. In the training phase, we use this algorithm to perform a linear combination of our 25 features, calibrating the ERS's feature weights in Equation 3.47 so that $Overlap_{10\%}$ is maximized. As this approach relies on genetic operators such as *selection*, *crossover*, and *mutation* to produce high-quality solutions to optimization problems [111] (we apply the elitist, two-points, and order-changing methods, respectively), we expect it searches through a huge combination of feature weights to find the ones generating the highest value for $Overlap_{10\%}$. Then, we use the calibrated linear system trained in a particular forum to test its performance on a different one, also using the $Overlap_{10\%}$:

$$ERS(v) = \sum_{i=1}^{n} w_i * v_{x_i}. \tag{3.47}$$

where $w_i$ is the weight of feature $i$, $v_{x_i}$ is the value of the feature $i$ for user $v$, and $n$ is the set of considered features.

The second algorithm is a multiple linear regression (MLR) [179]. In the training phase, we model the relationship between our dependent variable (reputation) and our 25 independent variables (features). This relationship is modeled using linear predictor functions, whose parameters are estimated from the data to fit a curve that produces the highest value for $Overlap_{10\%}$. Then, we use this curve fitted to a particular forum to test its performance on a different one, also using the $Overlap_{10\%}$. Note that the correct order of hackers based on reputation is not required, only the presence of the correct individuals in the $Top_{10\%}$. The next two algorithms comprise classifiers: random forests (RFs) and support vector machines (SVM) [179]. Here, we define a binary classification problem to identify the individuals belonging to the positive class (key-hackers). Random forests are an ensemble method that use multiple decision trees for training, outputting the class that is the mode of the classes. Support vector machines (SVM) are a discriminative classifier formally defined by a separating hyperplane that gives the largest minimum distance to the training examples. For both classifiers in the training phase, we want to learn the feature values of the $Top_{10\%}$ reputable hackers of a given forum, in order to apply this knowledge to another forum (testing phase), maximizing the value of $Overlap_{10\%}$.

Figure 3.4 presents the performance of the algorithms when they are trained using Forum 1 and tested using *Forum 2* and *Forum 3*. We detail the performances when the algorithms learn only the features of individual approaches and when they learn all the features combined (hybrid approach).

We observe five cases when the hybrid approach obtains the best performance, while one and two cases are verified for content and seniority analysis, respectively. The highest value for $Overlap_{10\%}$ when testing on *Forum 2* (0.52) is achieved by Genetic Algorithms using the hybrid approach. This result implies that more than half of the $Top_{10\%}$ reputable hackers were identified, which for this forum represents around 121 users. Also, the highest value for $Overlap_{10\%}$ when testing on *Forum 3* (0.33) is achieved by GAs and SVM using the hybrid approach. This result implies that more than one-third of the $Top_{10\%}$ reputable hackers were identified, which for this forum represents around 92 users. Note these performance results correspond to finding only 10% of the hackers (those with the highest reputation), which represents a strict filter of users.

Figure 3.5 presents the performance of the algorithms when they are trained using *Forum 2* and tested using *Forum 1* and *Forum 3*. We observe five cases in which the hybrid approach obtains the best performance, while one case is verified for each of the other approaches. The highest value for $Overlap_{10\%}$ when testing on *Forum 1* (0.43) is achieved by GAs using the hybrid approach. This result implies that almost half of the $Top_{10\%}$ reputable hackers were identified, which for this forum represents around 186 users. In addition, the highest value for $Overlap_{10\%}$ when testing on *Forum 3* (0.32) is achieved by GAs and RFs using the hybrid approach. This result implies that almost one-third of the $Top_{10\%}$ reputable hackers were identified, which for this forum represents around 88 users.

Figure 3.6 presents the algorithms' performance when they are trained using *Forum 3* and tested using *Forum 1* and *Forum 2*. We observe five cases when the hybrid approach obtains the best performance, while one and two cases are verified for content/seniority and social network analysis respectively. The highest value for $Overlap_{10\%}$ when testing on *Forum 1* (0.45) is achieved by GAs using the hybrid approach. This result implies that almost half of the $Top_{10\%}$ reputable hackers were identified, which for this forum represents 194 users. Also, the highest value for $Overlap_{10\%}$ when testing on *Forum 2* (0.5)

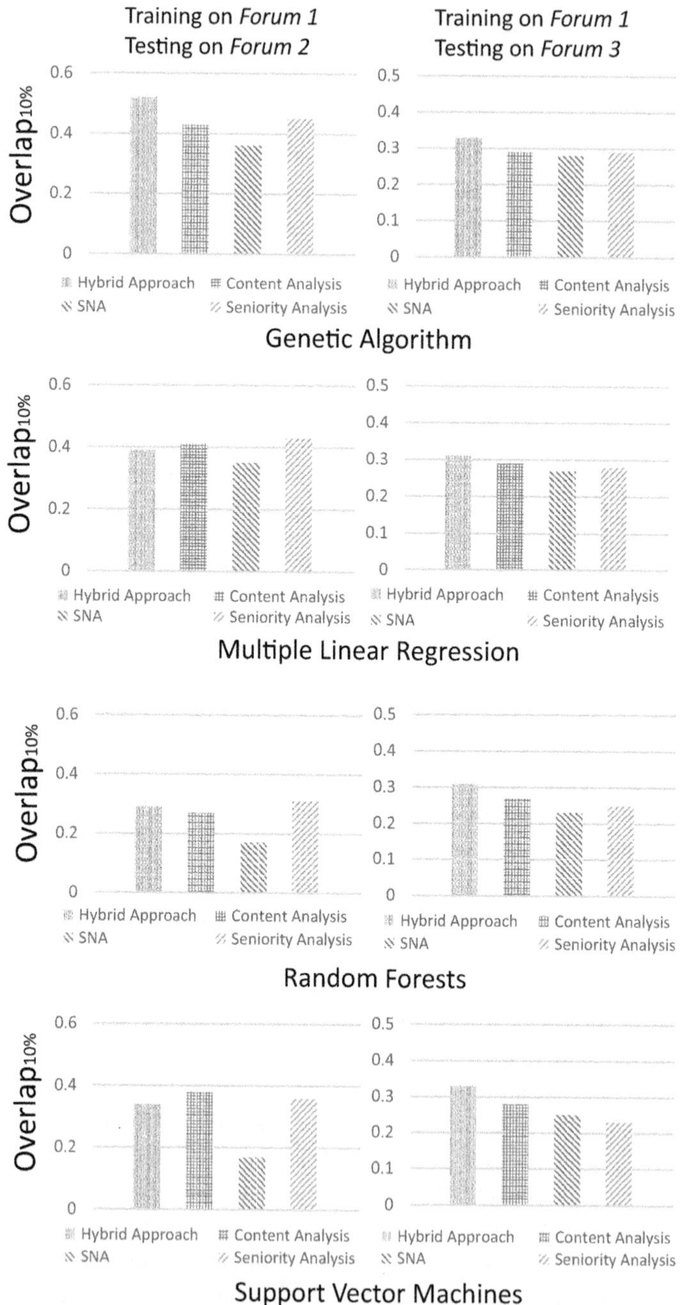


Figure 3.4 Performance when algorithms are trained on *Forum 1* and tested on *Forum 2* and *Forum 3*.

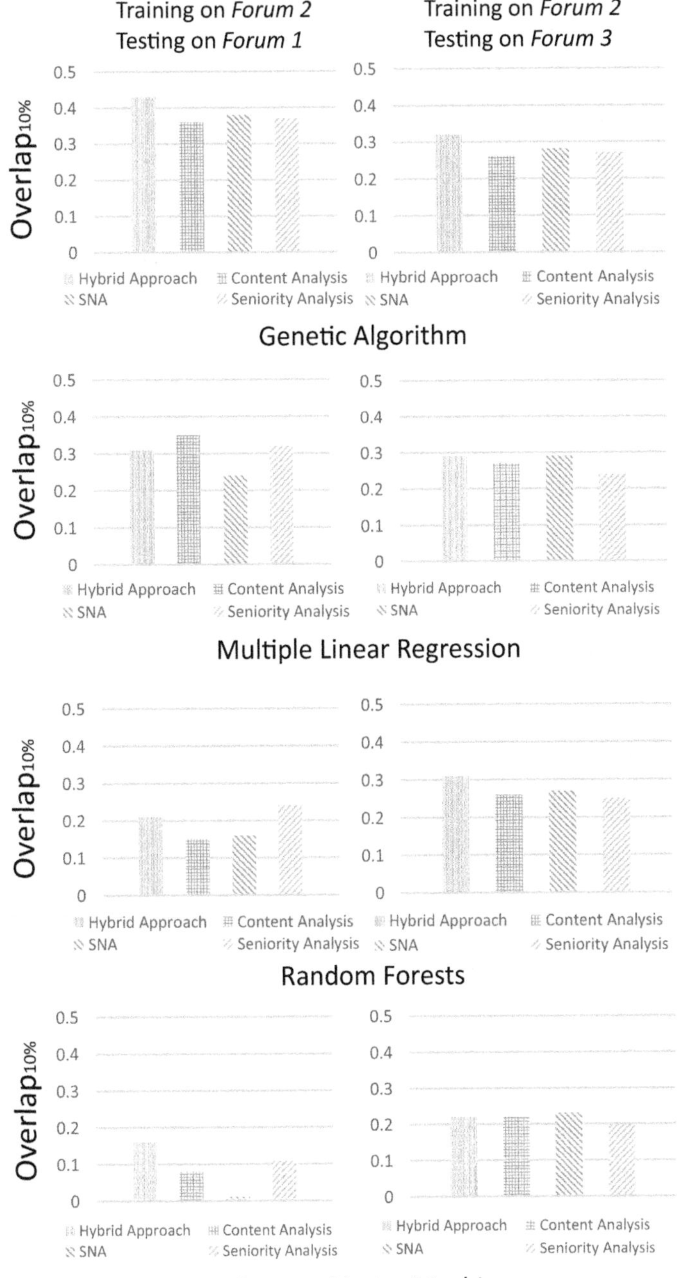


Figure 3.5 Performance when algorithms are trained on *Forum 2* and tested on *Forum 1* and *Forum 3*.

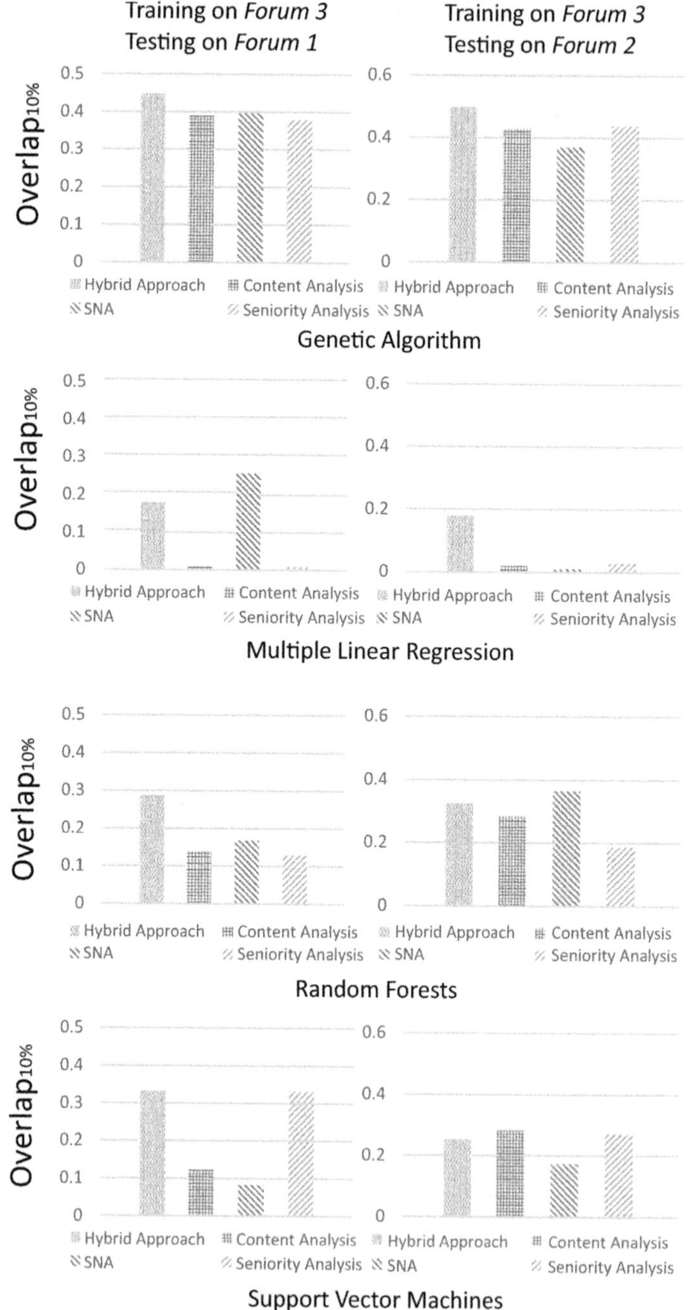


Figure 3.6 Performance when algorithms are trained on *Forum 3* and tested on *Forum 1* and *Forum 2*.

| Train | Test | Genetic Algorithms | | | | Multiple Linear Regression | | | | Random Forests | | | | SVM | | | | Random | | | |
|---|---|---|---|---|---|---|---|---|---|---|---|---|---|---|---|---|---|---|---|---|---|
| | | Top 10 | Top 1% | Top 5% | Top 10% | Top 10 | Top 1% | Top 5% | Top 10% | Top 10 | Top 1% | Top 5% | Top 10% | Top 10 | Top 1% | Top 5% | Top 10% | Top 10 | Top 1% | Top 5% | Top 10% |
| Forum 1 | Forum2 | 0.33 | 0.39 | 0.49 | 0.52 | 0.33 | 0.31 | 0.34 | 0.36 | 0.11 | 0.31 | 0.37 | 0.28 | 0.17 | 0.22 | 0.19 | 0.26 | 0.00 | 0.00 | 0.00 | 0.02 |
| | Forum3 | 0.11 | 0.20 | 0.31 | 0.33 | 0.11 | 0.22 | 0.25 | 0.31 | 0.11 | 0.22 | 0.20 | 0.31 | 0.11 | 0.20 | 0.25 | 0.33 | 0.00 | 0.00 | 0.00 | 0.01 |
| Forum 2 | Forum1 | 0.25 | 0.28 | 0.37 | 0.43 | 0.17 | 0.24 | 0.35 | 0.24 | 0.11 | 0.06 | 0.12 | 0.19 | 0.05 | 0.03 | 0.05 | 0.16 | 0.00 | 0.00 | 0.00 | 0.02 |
| | Forum3 | 0.05 | 0.20 | 0.24 | 0.32 | 0.05 | 0.17 | 0.24 | 0.29 | 0.11 | 0.17 | 0.25 | 0.31 | 0.11 | 0.14 | 0.19 | 0.22 | 0.00 | 0.00 | 0.00 | 0.01 |
| Forum 3 | Forum1 | 0.17 | 0.22 | 0.26 | 0.45 | 0.17 | 0.16 | 0.17 | 0.12 | 0.00 | 0.06 | 0.18 | 0.25 | 0.00 | 0.03 | 0.16 | 0.29 | 0.00 | 0.00 | 0.00 | 0.00 |
| | Forum2 | 0.33 | 0.29 | 0.44 | 0.50 | 0.11 | 0.05 | 0.02 | 0.18 | 0.00 | 0.17 | 0.17 | 0.29 | 0.05 | 0.08 | 0.34 | 0.23 | 0.00 | 0.00 | 0.00 | 0.00 |

Figure 3.7 Analysis of algorithms' performance using different values for $Overlap_{X\%}$.

is achieved by GAs using the hybrid approach. This result implies that half of the $Top_{10\%}$ reputable hackers were identified, which for this forum represents 121 users.

These results show that the hybrid approach is preferable compared to the individual ones, specially if used by GAs. Overall, the generalization of the model is satisfying since we retrieve a considerable portion of the key-hackers in all situations analyzed.

**Varying the overlap**. In order to observe how the results change according to the fraction of users who represent the key-hackers, we test different values for $Overlap_{X\%}$. The idea is to cover different zones for the identification of key-hackers, including $Overlap_{1\%}$, $Overlap_{5\%}$, $Overlap_{10\%}$, and also what we denominate $Overlap_{10}$, which means only the top 10 reputable hackers in the forums. Figure 3.7 presents the performance of the four algorithms with the exact same previous setting, except that we only consider the hybrid approach now. We also include a random key-hacker identification approach for comparison purposes. The highlighted cells correspond to the highest values of $Overlap_{X\%}$ computed among all the algorithms analyzed. We observe that GAs have the best performances in 87.5% of the cases, since they are able to work under very strict search conditions: the number of individuals to be filtered is considerably low, and the search space is very large.

Finally, we show in Figure 3.8 the curves of $Overlap_{X\%}$ for all implemented algorithms, comparing the performances according to the forums used to train and test our model. As verified, GAs produce a superior fit. We believe the characteristic of this strategy – population of candidates searching in multiple directions simultaneously – produces more adapted solutions, avoiding local optima and overfitting. This condition makes this optimization metaheuristic suitable to the key-hacker identification problem, leading opportunities for evolutionary algorithms to be more often considered in cyber-security research.

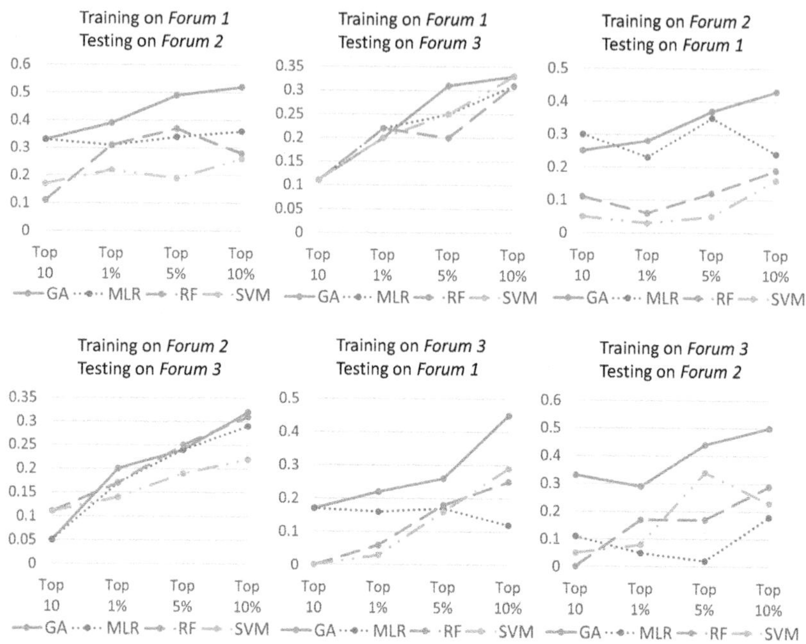


Figure 3.8 Comparison between the $Overlap_{X\%}$ curves.

## 3.7 Related Work

Different works have addressed the key-hacker identification problem in the last years. Abbasi et al. [1] proposed a framework to identify expert hackers in Web forums based on content-mining. First, the authors represented each user with three categories of features: cyber-criminal assets, specialty lexicons, and forum involvement. Then, they profiled the users into four groups based on their specialties: black market activists, founding members, technical enthusiasts, and average users. Analyzing the hackers' interactions, they noted the average users (86% of the total) were participants who did not actively engage in the community, whereas the other groups constituted key-hackers. Later, Zhang et al. [200] also used a content-mining approach on a hacking forum to analyze post orientations regarding knowledge transfer. Knowledge acquisition and knowledge provision were noted as the patterns to construct user profiles, classified by the authors into four ordinal types: guru, casual, learning, and novice hackers. They found that guru hackers act as key knowledgeable and respectable members in the communities, increasingly acting as knowledge providers. In a sequence, Fang et al. [53] developed a framework with a set of topic models for extracting popular topics, tracking topic evolution, and identifying key-hackers with their specialties. Using latent Dirichlet allocation (LDA), dynamic topic model (DTMs), and author topic model (ATMs), the authors identified five major popular topics, trends related to new communication channels, and key-hackers in each area of expertise.

Using a different approach, Seebruck proposed a weighted arc circumplex model to capture hacker motivations [158]. The author created a hacker typology based on five motivations: recreation, prestige, revenge, profit, and ideology, and also based on eight levels of expertise: novices, crowdsourcers, punks, hacktivists, insiders, criminals, coders, and cyber-warriors. Then, the model should determine (as no experiments were performed) the likelihood of an organization being targeted by a certain type of hacker. Samtani and Chen [149] performed social network analysis to identify key-hackers on hacking forums. They analyzed the interactions between users by leveraging metrics such as network diameter and average path length, finding the importance of users to their communities using centrality measures. Also, Zhang and Li performed survival analysis using a Cox proportional hazard regression model to examine what generates a highly reputable hacker on online forums [199]. They found that users should reply with detailed posts and also broaden their interests into multiple topics.

In all these works, we noted the authors did not fully explore a hybrid model to find key-hackers online, considering the advantages of different approaches. In addition, there is still a lack of a validation method, which makes the results of this previous work not comparable. Here, we take the next steps to fill these two gaps, proposing a hybrid model to identify key-hackers on online forums and a systematic method to validate the results.

## 3.8 Conclusion

In this chapter, we addressed the key-hacker identification problem on online hacker forums using a hybrid approach that combines content, social network, and seniority analysis. We started by showing how different algorithms (especially the GAs) perform better when all 25 engineered features are used together, highlighting that a hybridization of approaches improves the results. Then, we demonstrate that our model is able to generalize, learning features in one particular forum that can be applied to another one. This generalization is evaluated by leveraging the user reputation score to systematically cross-validate the key-hackers identified, providing a strategy to find these users in environments that do not offer a reputation system or only a deficient one. Although improvements are necessary in this area, we explored in this chapter some ideas to pave the road – including a comparison between genetic and machine learning algorithms when they use our predictive model to identify the highly skilled and influential users on malicious hacker forums: the key-hackers. These insights offer to security researchers an alternative strategy to aid in the prediction of cyber-attacks: find the key-hackers first and, consequently, their emerging cyber-threats.

# 4
# Reasoning about Hacker Engagement

## 4.1 Introduction

Hacker communities are continually evolving. Due to social influence effects, values are often transmitted from one person to another (see examples in economics [97], psychology [3], sociology [27, 41], business [48], public health [33], and politics [28]), and this behavior is also observed among malicious hackers [56, 99, 115, 137, 168]. Holding acknowledged reputations, key-hackers generally use online platforms to advertise exploits, vulnerabilities, techniques, code samples, and targets and also to recruit individuals for malicious campaigns [16, 78], attracting low-skill-level individuals who aim to improve their hacking skills. Those influential activities not only expand the key-hackers' networks, bringing like-minded collaborators and learners, but also help them to increase their revenue. Therefore, cyber-security can benefit from the study of user adoption behavior online, using it as crowd-sourced sensor to gain insight about future users' activities that may lead to cyber-attacks.

Consider, for instance, the prediction of online hacktivist campaigns [40]. Those malicious activities would be traceable if the users joining a campaign could be predicted, taking into account the hackers' peer influence. Another application of this chapter is the prediction of which hackers will buy a hacking product/service that has been offered in an online forum [84]. As standard hackers, who are often influenced by reputable ones, rely on hacker forums to improve their skills and capabilities [106], the anticipation of this interaction can be accomplished. Finally, adoption behavior can also be used for anticipating an online hacking cascade [72], whose primary goal is to detect an early-stage post with the potential to "go viral," generating subsequent adoptions that signal a pending cyber-attack [145].

In this chapter, we study adoption behavior, trying to predict in which topic of an online hacker forum users will post a message in the near future, given the influence produced by their peers. We formulate our problem as a sequential rule mining task [61], where the goal is to discover user posting rules through sequences of user posts. Then, we use the mined rules to make predictions of users posting in a particular forum topic. In general, sequential rule mining is an important data mining technique that tries to predict event(s) that are likely to follow other event(s) with a given probability, using patterns mined from sequences [60]. Adapting the problem to our context, we make each rule of the form $X \Rightarrow Y$ only contain the users responsible for the posts, being interpreted as "if $X$ (a set of users) engages in a given forum topic, $Y$ (a unique user) is likely to engage in the same topic (or adopt it) with a given confidence afterward, mainly because of the influence of $X$." Additionally, as previous research has demonstrated that social influence continuously decreases over time [69, 104, 105], we only consider rules occurring within defined time windows. We also verify how the precision of our model changes according to two posting time granularities (day and hour). Finally, we compare our results with those produced by the prior probabilities of hackers' posts, showing how our predictions and prediction gains are considerably higher. We summarize the main contributions of this chapter as follows:

1. We collect more than 330,000 posts of a popular online hacker forum to create a sequential rule mining model capable of predicting future posts of hackers.
2. We consider 2 posting time granularities (day and hour) and 10 different time windows for each time granularity.
3. During training, we mine more than 362,617 sequential rules with different sizes (number of users).
4. During testing, we obtain prediction precision results of up to 0.78, while a baseline model reaches up to 0.18.
5. We observe the highest precision gains [785%, 837%] for time windows in [3,5] days, finding the moment from where hacking influence continuously decays over time.

The remainder of this chapter is organized as follows. Section 4.2 presents our forum dataset. Section 4.3 formalizes our sequential rule mining task applied to the hacker adoption prediction problem. Section 4.4 presents our experiments and results. Section 4.5 shows some related work. Finally, Section 4.6 concludes the chapter.

Table 4.1 *Forum X Information*

| Time period | 06/09/2014 : 08/02/2017 |
|---|---|
| Number of users | 4,112 |
| Number of topics | 95 |
| Number of posts | 331,384 |

## 4.2 Dataset

We collect data from a popular online hacker forum (anonymized here as *Forum X*) in our repository (see Chapter 1 for details), showing its statistics in Table 4.1. The discussions consist of a wide range of hacking-related messages posted by the community members.

## 4.3 Sequential Rule Mining Task

Discovering temporal relationships between events stored in large databases is important in many domains (e.g., stock market data, biological data, patient hospital records, and customer data), as it sets a basis for event prediction. Various methods have been proposed for mining these relationships (see a complete survey in [88]), with sequential rule mining being one of the most popular in the field of data mining [58]. Basically, sequential rule mining consists of discovering rules in a single sequence [47], across sequences [44], or common to multiple sequences [58]. These rules are potentially useful for analyzing data in sequential format, indicating that if some event(s) occur, some other event(s) are likely to occur with a given confidence afterward. Sequential rule mining has been applied in several domains, such as stock market analysis [44], where the goal is to predict stock prices going up or down, e-learning [61], where it is used to predict the behavior of learners in educational data, e-commerce [136], aiming to determine the purchase pattern of customers, weather observation [74], where it is used to forecast the weather, and also drought prediction [47], among other applications.

Bringing to our context, we apply sequential rule mining to multiple sequences in order to study the spread of adoption behavior among malicious hackers, where the goal is to predict in which topic of *Forum X* hackers will post in the near future (topic adoption), given the influence produced by their peers. This way, we make each of the 95 topics of the forum analyzed represent a particular sequence, which starts with the oldest post of the topic and ends with the latest one. In the following, we give a detailed formalization of our problem.

### 4.3.1 Problem Formalization

We follow the definitions of [61] to specify a sequence database as a set of topics $\Theta = \{\theta_1, \theta_2 \ldots \theta_k\}$ and a set of users (malicious hackers) $U = \{u_1, u_2, \ldots u_m\}$ posting in these topics. Each topic $\theta_x$ is an ordered list of user sets (set of users) $\theta_x = U_1, U_2, \ldots U_n$ such that $U_1, U_2, \ldots U_n \subseteq U$. Figure 4.1 illustrates a timeline where users are posting on four topics.

Table 4.2 depicts a sequence database encoding the data presented in Figure 4.1. For instance, topic $\theta_1$ states that users $u_1$ and $u_2$ posted at the same particular time point $t_i$, being followed successively by nobody at $t_i + 1$, user $u_3$ at $t_i + 2$, $u_6$ at $t_i + 3$, and so forth.

In our context, a sequential rule $X \Rightarrow Y$ is defined as a relationship between two user sets $X$ (antecedent), $Y$ (consequent) $\subseteq U$ such that $X \cap Y = \varnothing$ and $X, Y \neq \varnothing$. A rule $X \Rightarrow Y$ is said to occur in a topic $\theta_x = U_1, U_2, \ldots U_n$, if there

Table 4.2 *Modeling a forum as a sequence database*

| Topics | Sequences of post users |
|---|---|
| $\theta_1$ | $\{u_1,u_2\},\{\},\{u_3\},\{u_6\},\{\},\{u_7\},\{u_5\}$ |
| $\theta_2$ | $\{u_1,u_4\},\{\},\{u_3\},\{u_2\},\{u_1,u_2,u_5,u_6\}$ |
| $\theta_3$ | $\{u_1\},\{u_2\},\{u_6\},\{u_5\}$ |
| $\theta_4$ | $\{u_3\},\{u_1,u_2\},\{u_5\},\{\},\{\},\{u_6,u_7\}$ |

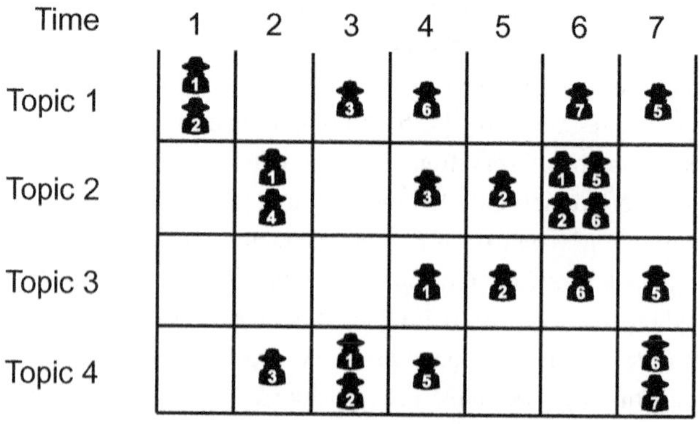

Figure 4.1 Sample timeline of forum topics.

exists an integer $u$ such that $1 \leq u < n, X \subseteq \cup_{i=1}^{u} U_i$, and $Y \subseteq \cup_{i=u+1}^{n} U_i$. For example, the rule $\{u_1, u_2, u_3\} \Rightarrow \{u_5\}$ occurs in the topics $\theta_1$, $\theta_2$, and $\theta_4$ of Table 4.2. According to [61], a rule $X \Rightarrow Y$ is said to be of size $v^*w$ if $|X| = v$ and $|Y| = w$. Thus, the rule $\{u_1, u_5\} \Rightarrow \{u_6\}$ is of size $2^*1$. We only consider sequential rules containing a single user in the rule consequent ($w = 1$), since we want to predict one hacker at a time for the adoption prediction task. Furthermore, a rule of size $f^*g$ is larger than another rule of size $h^*i$ if $f > h$ and $g \geq i$, or if $f \geq h$ and $g > i$ [61].

We leverage two standard measures to evaluate the quality of our rules: the *sequential support*, which is the fraction of topics where all the users of $X$ appear before the user of $Y$ and the *sequential confidence*, which is the number of topics where all the users of $X$ appear before the user of $Y$ divided by the number of topics where all the users of $X$ appear. Therefore, the problem of mining sequential rules consists in finding all rules with support and confidence no less than the respectively user-defined thresholds $minsup$ and $minconf$. Those rules are interpreted as "if the users of $X$ post in a given topic, the user of $Y$ is likely to post in (or adopt) the same topic with a given confidence afterward, mainly because of the influence of $X$." Note that in addition to predicting the next user to post in the near future ($Y$), the rules also provide information about the reason for that post (influence of $X$), allowing easy interpretation. There is also one important point about the non-requirement of ordering restriction between users of $X$. Fournier pointed out that mining sequential rules has the following three drawbacks when a strict ordering is applied between items (our users) of the antecedent or consequent of a rule [59]:

1. **Rules may have many variations:** There are different variations of the rule $\{u_1\}, \{u_3\} \Rightarrow \{u_5\}$, as illustrated with the following rules $r_i, r_{i'}, r_{i''}$. However, all these variations describe the same situation: if users $u_1$ and $u_3$ post in a given topic in any order, then user $u_5$ is likely to post in the same topic after them:

$$r_i : \{u_1\}, \{u_3\} \Rightarrow \{u_5\},$$
$$r_{i'} : \{u_3\}, \{u_1\} \Rightarrow \{u_5\},$$
$$r_{i''} : \{u_1, u_3\} \Rightarrow \{u_5\}.$$

2. **Similar rules are rated very differently:** Considering a strict order, the rules $r_i$ and $r_{i'}$ have support/confidence of 0.5/1.0 and 0.25/0.5, respectively, while the rule $r_{i''}$ does not appear in our sample database. This condition produces a wrong impression about the existing sequential relationships. Taken as a whole, the support of the rule $\{u_1, u_3\} \Rightarrow \{u_5\}$ grows to 0.75.

Table 4.3 *Sample of mined sequential rules from Table 4.2*

| ID | Rule | Support | Confidence |
|---|---|---|---|
| $r_1$ | $\{u_1, u_2, u_3\} \Rightarrow \{u_5\}$ | 0.75 | 1.00 |
| $r_2$ | $\{u_1, u_2, u_6\} \Rightarrow \{u_5\}$ | 0.50 | 0.50 |
| $r_3$ | $\{u_1, u_2\} \Rightarrow \{u_5\}$ | 1.00 | 1.00 |
| $r_4$ | $\{u_2, u_3\} \Rightarrow \{u_6\}$ | 0.75 | 1.00 |
| $r_5$ | $\{u_3\} \Rightarrow \{u_2\}$ | 0.50 | 0.66 |
| $r_6$ | $\{u_1\} \Rightarrow \{u_2\}$ | 0.50 | 0.50 |

3. **Rules are less likely to be useful:** Rules with a strict order are less likely to match with a sequence for adoption predictions. For example, no rule can be retrieved from the sample database to match the sequence $\{u_1\}, \{u_2\}, \{u_3\}$ using this strict order.

In order to avoid these drawbacks of standard sequential rules, we consider in our model partially ordered sequential rules [59]. They define a broader type of sequential rules common to multiple sequences, such that users in the rule antecedent are unordered. However, the requirement of a sequential relationship between the antecedent and consequent of a rule is preserved. According to this partially ordered definition, the rules $r_i, r_{i'}, r_{i''}$ presented before can be represented by a single rule $\{u_1, u_3\} \Rightarrow \{u_5\}$. We show in Table 4.3 some rules found in our sample database (Table 4.2), considering $minsup = 0.5$ and $minconf = 0.5$.

Finally, we only consider in our model rules occurring within a time window ($\Delta_t$), which is a constraint used by many applications that wish to discover relevant sequential patterns within a limited time interval [59, 60, 133, 159]. As research has already demonstrated how social influence decreases over time, we use time windows to discard found patterns irrelevant for social influence. They constitute sequential user posts happening within an interval greater than the one specified by a given time window, bringing spurious information to our model that is not related to influence. This way, we define a time window as a group of consecutive time points in our sequences of hacker posts. Then, we check how many time windows can be generated from the beginning of a forum topic to its end, one time point at a time (defined by [60] as a sliding time window). For example, for $\Delta_t = 3$, there are five different time windows $w_1, w_2, w_3, w_4, w_5$ for the topic $\theta_1$ of Table 4.2 depicted in Figure 4.2.

Formally, we follow the concepts of [61] and define the problem of mining sequential rules with a time window as being the same as the problem of

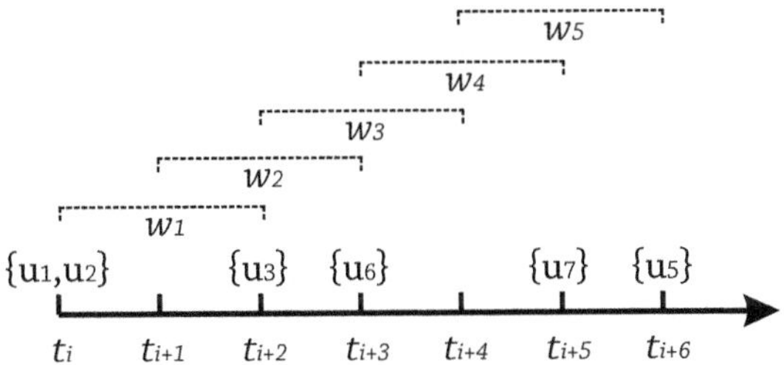


Figure 4.2 Considered time windows when $\Delta_t = 3$ for topic $\theta_1$ of Table 4.2.

mining sequential rules, except that a rule $X \Rightarrow Y$ occurs in a topic $\theta_x = U_1, U_2, \ldots U_n$, if there exist integers $j$, $k$, $m$ such that $1 \leq j \leq k < m \leq n, X \subseteq \cup_{i=j}^{k} U_i$, $Y \subseteq \cup_{i=k+1}^{m} U_i$, and $m - j + 1 \leq \Delta_t$, where $\Delta_t$ is user defined. We also consider the border cases, keeping rules only when $j \leq n - \Delta_t + 1$, so that we always have $\Delta_t$ time points (not less) to find the consequent of a rule. We include the time window constraint to compute the values of the two measures used to evaluate the rules. After defining a time window ($\Delta_t$), the sequential support becomes the fraction of topics where all the users of $X$ appear before the user of $Y$ within $\Delta_t$, while the sequential confidence becomes the number of topics where all the users of $X$ appear before the user of $Y$ within $\Delta_t$ divided by the number of topics where all the users of $X$ appear within $\Delta_t$. We show in Table 4.4 how the sequential support and sequential confidence of the rules presented in the Table 4.3 changes for $\Delta_t$ in [3,4,5].

## 4.4 Experiments and Results

In this section, we present our experiments designed to predict hacker adoption of a particular forum topic, mining sequential rules of hacker posts. We detail how we train and test our model under a variety of conditions and also how we compare our results with a standard baseline.

### 4.4.1 Training

In the training phase, we mine sequential rules from *Forum X*, which contains 95 hacking-related topics. These topics comprise sequences of hacker posts, where each sequence starts with the oldest post of the topic and ends with the latest one. Our goal is to discover the sequential rules that will be used for hacker adoption prediction. As our dataset has approximately 38 months of

Table 4.4 *Sequential rule measures considering different time windows*

| | $\Delta_t = 3$ | | |
|---|---|---|---|
| ID | Rule | Support | Confidence |
| $r_1$ | $\{u_1, u_2, u_3\} \Rightarrow \{u_5\}$ | 0.25 | 0.33 |
| $r_2$ | $\{u_1, u_2, u_6\} \Rightarrow \{u_5\}$ | 0.00 | 0.00 |
| $r_3$ | $\{u_1, u_2\} \Rightarrow \{u_5\}$ | 0.25 | 0.25 |
| $r_4$ | $\{u_2, u_3\} \Rightarrow \{u_6\}$ | 0.25 | 0.33 |
| $r_5$ | $\{u_3\} \Rightarrow \{u_2\}$ | 0.50 | 0.66 |
| $r_6$ | $\{u_1\} \Rightarrow \{u_2\}$ | 0.25 | 0.25 |
| | $\Delta_t = 4$ | | |
| ID | Rule | Support | Confidence |
| $r_1$ | $\{u_1, u_2, u_3\} \Rightarrow \{u_5\}$ | 0.25 | 0.33 |
| $r_2$ | $\{u_1, u_2, u_6\} \Rightarrow \{u_5\}$ | 0.25 | 0.33 |
| $r_3$ | $\{u_1, u_2\} \Rightarrow \{u_5\}$ | 0.50 | 0.50 |
| $r_4$ | $\{u_2, u_3\} \Rightarrow \{u_6\}$ | 0.50 | 0.66 |
| $r_5$ | $\{u_3\} \Rightarrow \{u_2\}$ | 0.50 | 0.66 |
| $r_6$ | $\{u_1\} \Rightarrow \{u_2\}$ | 0.50 | 0.50 |
| | $\Delta_t = 5$ | | |
| ID | Rule | Support | Confidence |
| $r_1$ | $\{u_1, u_2, u_3\} \Rightarrow \{u_5\}$ | 0.50 | 0.66 |
| $r_2$ | $\{u_1, u_2, u_6\} \Rightarrow \{u_5\}$ | 0.25 | 0.25 |
| $r_3$ | $\{u_1, u_2\} \Rightarrow \{u_5\}$ | 0.75 | 0.75 |
| $r_4$ | $\{u_2, u_3\} \Rightarrow \{u_6\}$ | 0.50 | 0.66 |
| $r_5$ | $\{u_3\} \Rightarrow \{u_2\}$ | 0.50 | 0.66 |
| $r_6$ | $\{u_1\} \Rightarrow \{u_2\}$ | 0.50 | 0.50 |

sequential data, we use the first 34 months (≈90% of the period analyzed) to form our training set, which totals 298,245 posts.

Aiming to remove infrequent rules from our training data, since they have a lower chance of reflecting influence, we define $minsup = 0.1$ after analyzing some other possible values. This support means that any found sequential rule must be present in at least 10 out of 95 topics within the defined time window. In addition, to increase the correlation between the antecedent and consequent of the rules during training, we define $minconf = 0.8$ after considering other values. This confidence means that any found sequential rule must have its consequent predicted in 80% of the cases within the defined time window. We also use two granularities (day and hour) to represent the hacker posting

Table 4.5 *Representation of different posting time granularities*

| Time granularity (day) | | | |
|---|---|---|---|
| Topic | User | Original posting time | Representation |
| $\theta_5$ | $u_1$ | 01/01/2017 10:20:18 | 01/01/2017 00:00:00 |
| $\theta_5$ | $u_2$ | 01/01/2017 10:25:32 | 01/01/2017 00:00:00 |
| $\theta_5$ | $u_3$ | 01/01/2017 11:10:55 | 01/01/2017 00:00:00 |
| $\theta_5$ | $u_2$ | 01/02/2017 13:25:12 | 01/02/2017 00:00:00 |
| $\theta_5$ | $u_4$ | 01/02/2017 13:32:19 | 01/02/2017 00:00:00 |
| Time granularity (hour) | | | |
| Topic | User | Original posting time | Representation |
| $\theta_5$ | $u_1$ | 01/01/2017 10:20:18 | 01/01/2017 10:00:00 |
| $\theta_5$ | $u_2$ | 01/01/2017 10:25:32 | 01/01/2017 10:00:00 |
| $\theta_5$ | $u_3$ | 01/01/2017 11:10:55 | 01/01/2017 11:00:00 |
| $\theta_5$ | $u_2$ | 01/02/2017 13:25:12 | 01/02/2017 13:00:00 |
| $\theta_5$ | $u_4$ | 01/02/2017 13:32:19 | 01/02/2017 13:00:00 |

time (granularities commonly used for adoption prediction [104]), aiming to observe whether these granularities affect our prediction results. Table 4.5 illustrates this representation with random sequential data.

As verified in Table 4.5, when the time granularity is defined as "day," the first three posts are assigned to the same time point 01/01/2017 00:00:00, since the hours, minutes, and seconds of these posts are discarded. Following the same idea, the last two posts are assigned to the same time point 01/02/2017 00:00:00. On the other hand, when the time granularity is defined as "hour," only the first two posts are assigned to the time point 01/01/2017 10:00:00, since the hours are not discarded now. Then, the next post is assigned to the time point 01/01/2017 11:00:00, while the last two posts are assigned to the time point 01/02/2017 13:00:00. These two representations produce different sequences of user posts as demonstrated in Figure 4.3, where panel (a) and panel (b) show the sequences created when the time granularity is defined as "day" and "hour," respectively. In panel (a), we observe the existence of only two time points, with the user set $\{u_1, u_2, u_3\}$ being assigned to the time point 01/01/2017 00:00:00 and the user set $\{u_2, u_4\}$ being assigned to the time point 01/02/2017 00:00:00. However, in panel (b), we observe the existence of three time points, being the user set $\{u_1, u_2\}$ assigned to the time point 01/01/2017 10:00:00, the user set $\{u_3\}$ assigned to the time point 01/01/2017 11:00:00, and the user set $\{u_2, u_4\}$ assigned to the time point 01/02/2017 13:00:00. Note

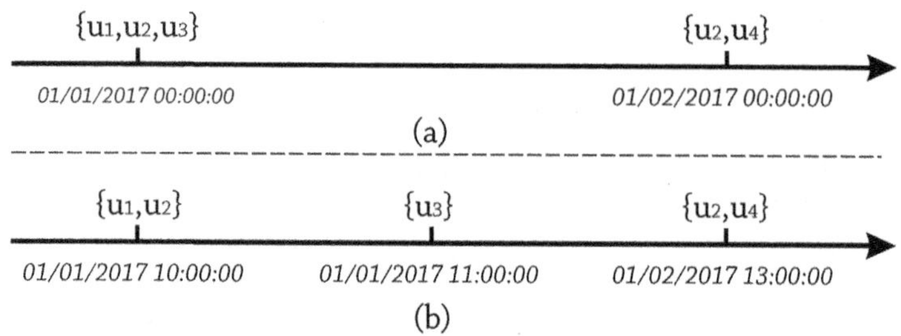


Figure 4.3 Sequential representation of posts using different time granularities.

that only panel (b) includes the sequential rules $\{u_1\} \Rightarrow \{u_3\}$ and $\{u_2\} \Rightarrow \{u_3\}$, which makes the user $u_3$ predictable only for panel (b). Setting the time granularity as "hour" generates more sequences, and we want to investigate whether this implies a higher performance of our model.

We analyze 10 time window values for each time granularity, being $\Delta_t \in (2,3,4,5,6,7,8,15,22,31)$ (sequence $d$) for "days" and $\Delta_t \in (48,72,96,120,145,168,192,360,528,744)$ (sequence $h$) for "hours." We want to vary $\Delta_t$ while generating rules during training in order to check which configuration leads to a better prediction accuracy during testing. Although we change the time window magnitude for the corresponding indices of sequences $d$ and $h$, we maintain the same time interval for all of them (e.g., 2 days = 48 hours, 3 days = 72 hours, 4 days = 96 hours, ...31 days = 744 hours). Our intention is to have a fair comparison between both time granularities when predicting hacker adoption.

**TRuleGrowth algorithm**. To proceed with the generation of rules, we implement an extension of the TRuleGrowth algorithm [60, 61]. This algorithm was originally proposed to discover all partially ordered sequential rules common to several sequences that have a support and confidence higher than $minsup$ and $minconf$ respectively. The algorithm accepts a sliding-window constraint to find rules occurring within a time interval and the specification of the maximum number of items (here posts) that can appear in the antecedent and consequent of a rule. Thus, TRuleGrowth was a natural choice to produce our training data. It allows us to specify all required constraints to our problem, also providing us an optimized performance when compared with other algorithms that address the same sequential rule mining task, such as CMDeo or CMRules [58]. We show in Figure 4.4 the number of rules generated by TRuleGrowth, considering the 10 defined values of $\Delta_t$ for each time granularity and the values assigned for $minsup$ and $mincon$.

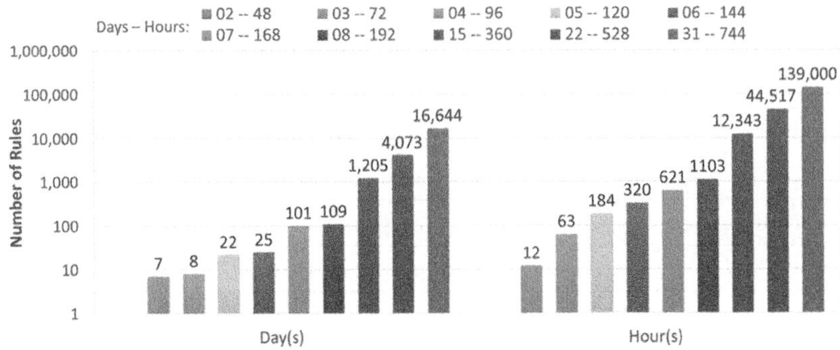


Figure 4.4 Number of rules generated for 10 values of $\Delta_t$ considering each time granularity ($y$-axis is in log-scale to improve visualization).

Note how the number of rules grows as we increase the value of $\Delta_t$, since there is more time to find all users that form a specific rule. Also, we find a considerable difference in the number of generated rules when "hour" is set as the time granularity. Remember we are dealing with partially ordered sequential rules and that TRuleGrowth eliminates antecedent variations of the same rule. For instance, if the algorithm stores the rule $\{u_1, u_2, u_3\} \Rightarrow \{u_4\}$, it will discard rules such as $\{u_2, u_1, u_3\} \Rightarrow \{u_4\}$ or $\{u_3, u_1, u_2\} \Rightarrow \{u_4\}$. However, TRuleGrowth stores all consequent variations of the same rule antecedent, since this condition implies multiple hacker adoptions derived from the influence of the same individuals. For instance, both rules $\{u_1, u_3\} \Rightarrow \{u_5\}$ and $\{u_1, u_3\} \Rightarrow \{u_6\}$ are stored by the algorithm.

As verified, no rule is generated when $\Delta_t = 2$ and $\Delta_t = 48$ for granularities "day" and "hour," respectively. This condition informs that there is no sequence of hacker posts among 2 consecutive days (the consequent is observed one day after the observation of the antecedent) or 48 consecutive hours in our forum data for this particular set up, pointing out that a longer time interval is required for social influence to take place. Actually, many research works claim that social influence gets stronger as the number of "active neighbors" of a given user increases as time goes by (until a threshold is reached), since this user becomes more influenced by all these individuals together [55, 69, 104, 197]. We count in Table 4.6 the number of distinct users present in the antecedent $a_{\Delta_t}$ and in the consequent $c_{\Delta_t}$ of the generated rules for each time granularity and time window ($\Delta_t$). Note how the former is greater than the corresponding number of rules for some cases, which means that rules with different antecedent sizes (more than one person influencing together) are generated. The latter indicates that different consequents (influenced individuals) are predicted by the rules.

Table 4.6 *Number of distinct users in the generated rules*

| Rule antecedent; time granularity (days) | | | | | | | | | |
|---|---|---|---|---|---|---|---|---|---|
| $a_2 = 0$ | $a_3 = 7$ | $a_4 = 8$ | $a_5 = 29$ | $a_6 = 32$ | $a_7 = 68$ | $a_8 = 72$ | $a_{15} = 187$ | $a_{22} = 227$ | $a_{31} = 266$ |
| Rule antecedent; time granularity (hours) | | | | | | | | | |
| $a_{48} = 0$ | $a_{72} = 18$ | $a_{96} = 52$ | $a_{120} = 91$ | $a_{144} = 121$ | $a_{168} = 147$ | $a_{192} = 177$ | $a_{360} = 250$ | $a_{528} = 283$ | $a_{744} = 312$ |
| Rule consequent; time granularity (days) | | | | | | | | | |
| $c_2 = 0$ | $c_3 = 2$ | $c_4 = 3$ | $c_5 = 9$ | $c_6 = 10$ | $c_7 = 13$ | $c_8 = 15$ | $c_{15} = 57$ | $c_{22} = 77$ | $c_{31} = 99$ |
| Rule consequent; time granularity (hours) | | | | | | | | | |
| $c_{48} = 0$ | $c_{72} = 5$ | $c_{96} = 9$ | $c_{120} = 20$ | $c_{144} = 27$ | $c_{168} = 37$ | $c_{192} = 54$ | $c_{360} = 91$ | $c_{528} = 117$ | $c_{744} = 128$ |

Table 4.7 *Significance analysis of the generated rules*

| Time granularity (days) | | | | | | | | | |
|---|---|---|---|---|---|---|---|---|---|
| $\Delta t = 2$<br>%0 | $\Delta t = 3$<br>%531 | $\Delta t = 4$<br>%463 | $\Delta t = 5$<br>%361 | $\Delta t = 6$<br>%319 | $\Delta t = 7$<br>%292 | $\Delta t = 8$<br>%273 | $\Delta t = 15$<br>%204 | $\Delta t = 22$<br>%171 | $\Delta t = 31$<br>%145 |
| Time granularity (hours) | | | | | | | | | |
| $\Delta t = 48$<br>%0 | $\Delta t = 72$<br>%488 | $\Delta t = 96$<br>%410 | $\Delta t = 120$<br>%358 | $\Delta t = 144$<br>%321 | $\Delta t = 168$<br>%293 | $\Delta t = 192$<br>%273 | $\Delta t = 360$<br>%204 | $\Delta t = 528$<br>%172 | $\Delta t = 744$<br>%146 |

**Rule significance analysis.** Finally, we check the significance of the mined rules to determine their utility for adoption prediction. We accomplish that by comparing the conditional probability of the consequents given the antecedents with the prior probability of the consequents, considering each time window and time granularity. We present the results in Table 4.7. This table shows probability gains for all possible cases that vary from 145% to 531%, confirming the utility of those rules for our prediction task.

### 4.4.2 Testing and Performance Analysis

The testing phase consists of generating adoption predictions for each test case that represents a hacker or a sequence of hackers posting in the same topic. We accomplish this task in two steps. First, we identify the rule(s) that match the test case, or the rule(s) whose users in the antecedent are those who form the test case. Then, after selecting those rule(s), we predict the adoption of the topic retrieved from the test case by the users present in the rule(s) consequent. To generate all test cases, we use the posts from the last four months of our sequential data (≈10% of the period analyzed), which totals 33,140 posts. For each time granularity and time window, we retrieve one topic at a time to locate

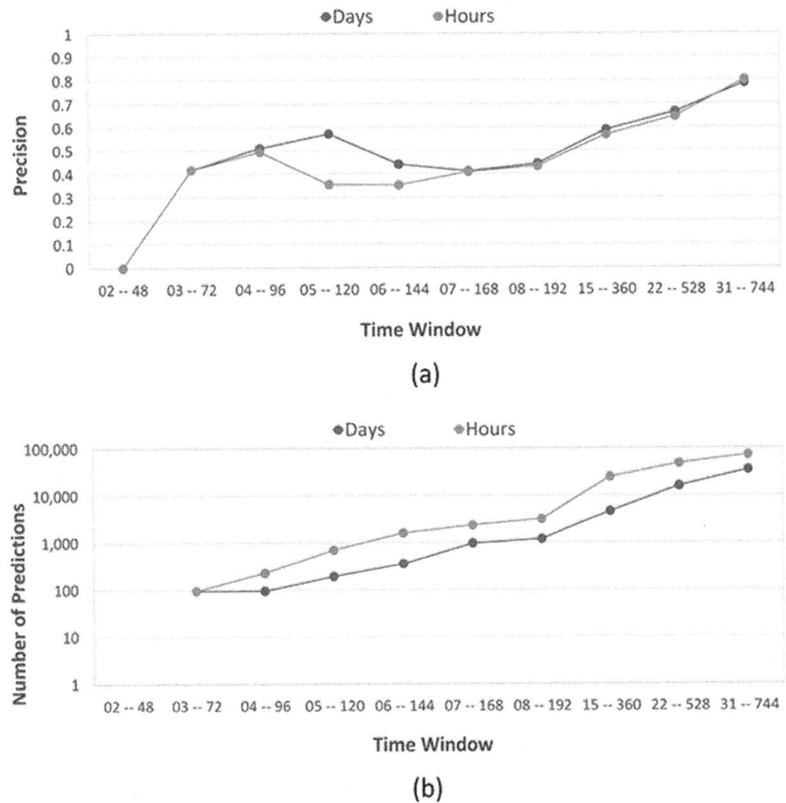


Figure 4.5 Performance of our model when predicting hacker adoption, considering (a) precision and (b) number of predictions ($y$-axis is in log-scale).

possible test cases. We start with test cases with size 1 (one user posting) and then move to locate test cases with size 2 (two users posting), size 3 (three users posting), and so on until we reach the limit size identified for the antecedent of rules in our training set (five users). Figure 4.5 presents the results.

We evaluate our model computing two distinct measures. The first one is precision, which is defined as the number of correct predictions divided by the number of predictions made. The second measure is the number of predictions made, which is higher if the training set (our mined sequential rules) matches more test cases. We observe in panel (a) that, although the two precision curves are similar, our model has slightly higher precision throughout the time windows when we set "days" as the time granularity. For this setting, the precision successively increases when the time window is 3 (0.416), 4 (0.510), and 5 (0.572), successively decreases throughout time windows 6 (0.440) and 7 (0.411), and successively increases again, reaching the highest value in the last time window, following 8 (0.442), 15 (0.588), 22 (0.664), and 31 (0.786).

In addition, panel (b) shows that more predictions are made when we set "hours" as the time granularity, since more test cases are generated. However, the difference in magnitude between the corresponding time windows for both time granularities (2–48, 3–72, ..., 31–744) is not reflected in the growing number of predictions, since this number only doubles in size, on average (96 until 34,923 and 96 until 71,000 when considering "days" and "hours" as time granularity, respectively).

### 4.4.3 Baseline

In this section, we informally explain a baseline predictor that we use to compare with our proposed rule-based approach. A very simple baseline would be predicting user engagement in any forum topic with a probability equal to the multiplication of two terms: the prior probability that a user would post in any time window of length $\Delta_t$ and the average fraction of forum topics on which he or she posts in any time window with length of $\Delta_t$. Such quantities should be learned from the training dataset. However, our baseline is less straightforward, since we assume that users vary in their posting activity. We sought to learn the prior probability of hacker adoption in a time window of length $\Delta_t$, conditioned on the user. Hence, we learn from the training data those prior probabilities and then predict hacker adoption for each test case. Having a prior probability for each user, we can predict adoption in different ways: (1) setting a threshold on prior probability, then predicting hacker adoption if their prior probability is greater than the threshold, and (2) predicting hacker adoption randomly with a chance of being predicted equivalent to the prior probability.[1] With (1), few users would be predicted to post on every single topic at each time point we make predictions – such judgment is not desired; hence we use (2). Clearly, this method is non deterministic. Therefore, we repeat the experiments 10 times and take the average precision of the runs. Figure 4.6 presents the results. The archived precision is much less than the rule-learning approach presented in this chapter.

We observe in panel (a) that both curves are almost identical. They present low precision that successively increases from the first time window until the last one, with values varying in [0.047, 0.180]. Note how the precision value range is much lower than the output of our model, showing we are able to identify patterns of sequential hacker postings among forum topics. Our assumption is that these patterns are a natural consequence of the influence process, which encourages hackers to adopt a topic in a particular time window because of the influential activities of their peers. In panel (b), we observe

[1] We do this by generating a random number in [0,1], sampled from a uniform distribution. If the number falls within the prior probability of a user, we predict his or her adoption; otherwise, we say that user is not going to adopt.

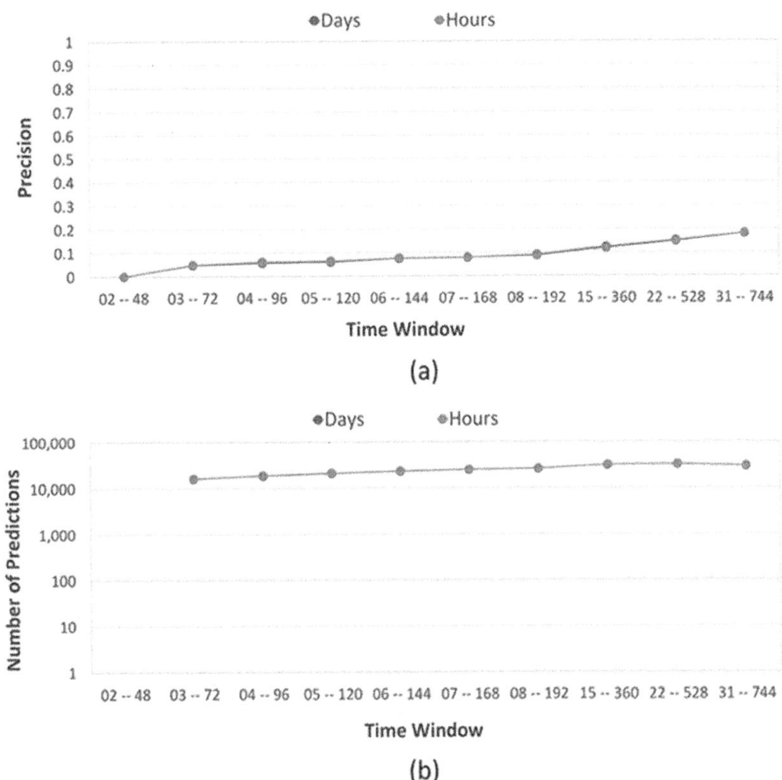


Figure 4.6 Baseline evaluation when predicting hacker adoption, considering (a) precision and (b) number of predictions ($y$-axis is in log-scale).

practically the same number of predictions for both curves (16,302 until 32,260 when considering "days" as time granularity and 16,171 until 32,015 when considering "hours"). Clearly, the variance is lower than the one produced by our model, since the method only considers the prior probabilities throughout the time windows, neglecting other social aspects as peer influence. We verify that, although the number of predictions of our model is relatively small (96–702) for short time windows, when we increase the time windows, the number of predictions grows until eventually passing the one produced by the baseline. From this particular point on, the precision values of our model are relatively high, while the ones produced by the baseline are still very low, which corroborates our influence assumption.

Finally, we analyze the precision gains of our model when compared to the baseline, showing the results in Figure 4.7. We discover a pattern that ratifies the findings relating to the notion of the *Forgettable Span* constraint, previously introduced in [104]. As it is well known that social influence decreases over time, this constraint was proposed to determine the subset of users who should

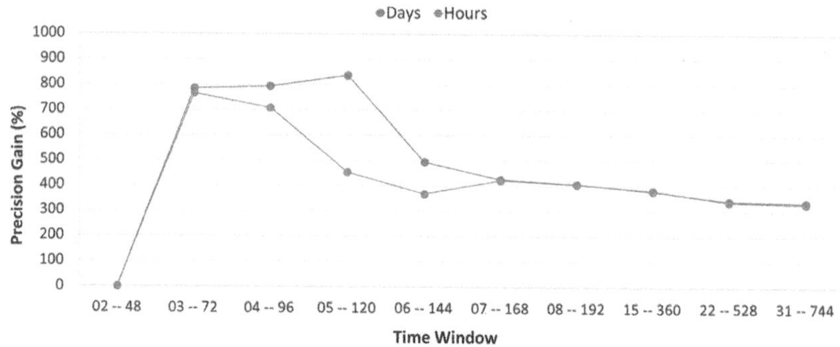


Figure 4.7 Precision gain of our model compared to the baseline.

be predicted to adopt a behavior; it sets a maximum time interval for the adoption of neighbors still be remembered by the influenced users. By running experiments on Twitter, the authors found that when *Forgettable Span* is set as approximately two or three days, the precision of hashtag adoption prediction is maximized, decreasing after that [104, 105]. Looking at Figure 4.7, we note the highest precision gains [785%, 837%] for hacker adoption are obtained for time windows in [3,5] days, successively decreasing for time windows greater than that (a similar pattern can be observed for setting "hours" as time granularity).

Assuming that in most hacker forums, the frequency of user activity is lower than the one observed on Twitter (where strongly ephemeral hashtags are usually observed), we understand that both values are very similar. This finding is relevant since predicting within a short time is considerably more difficult than when a large time interval is given, since the latter allows more time for a post to appear by chance than the former. Thus, we believe our model captures the social influence process on hacking forums throughout the time.

## 4.5 Related Work

To the best of our knowledge, this is the first applied study where adoption prediction is conducted among threat actors on online hacker forums. Even so, we present in the following some studies that could be used to predict opinions, activities, link formation, and also participation of hackers on online forums.

Qiu et al. [138] proposed a model that leveraged user arguments, interactions, and attributes into a collaborative filtering framework for stance prediction on a surface-web forum. Although the model is able to infer public opinion, which could be used for understanding the hackers' reasoning, it cannot estimate where (topic) and when (time) a hacker will post. Glenski et al. [67] tracked the online activity of 186 users of the popular Reddit forum over a year to predict their future interactions. They formulated the task as a multiclass classification, leveraging ranking and semantic features to estimate browse content, browse comments, upvote, downvote, or do-nothing behavior for each post visualized. This technique can be used to predict behaviors with respect to an existing post, but it is not able to anticipate a new one. Pastrana et al. [131] analyzed user activity in a popular underground forum of the surface-web, combining social network analysis, logistic regression, and clustering to first preselect a list of potential key actors (users who have been linked to criminal activities). Then, they filtered key terms used by these individuals in their posts to predict who is actually a key actor. The idea is relevant to profiling skilled hackers, but no predictive method was included to foresee new content. Yang et al. [194] developed a time series methodology for predicting link formation in real-world datasets from massive open online course (MOOC) discussion forums. They leveraged neighborhood, path, and post-based quantities between learners as features to a long-short term memory (LSTM) recurrent neural network (RNN), in order to forecast interactions between two users (link) in a thread. Although this model can be used to predict hacker posts, we identify three main drawbacks here: first, training is costly because of the different natures of the features; second, the prediction is done taking into consideration only one neighbor; finally, the links are bidirectional, making the prediction of user $u_2$ given user $u_1$ also valid for cases in the opposite direction.

## 4.6 Conclusion

In this chapter, we study the adoption behavior among hackers online, aiming to predict their future adoptions of a particular forum topic given the influence produced by their peers. We accomplish this task by leveraging sequential rule mining to discover user posting rules through sequences of user posts, to later use these rules to make the predictions. We analyze the performance of our model when it uses different time granularities to represent the posts and multiple time windows for mining the sequential rules, obtaining results that by far overcome the prior probabilities of hackers' posts. The proposed model provides an alternative strategy that leverages adoption prediction for proactive intelligence-driven security, anticipating the participation of cyber-criminals in hacking-related forum topics. With this insight, organizations can better monitor their networks for threats and exploitable vulnerabilities. They can extend their reach to cover forums where hackers often share valuable information, anticipating collaborators of the ever-expanding networks of key-hackers.

# 5

# Uncovering Communities of Malware and Exploit Vendors

## 5.1 Introduction

Recently, online hacker marketplaces have become a central venue for purchasing of malicious products and services by cyber-criminals, who take advantage of the numerous offerings provided especially by trustful and well-succeeded key-hackers. An example that illustrates this fact is given by Nunes et al. in [126]. An exploit targeting a Microsoft Windows vulnerability was for sale on a darkweb marketplace in March 2015. The corresponding vulnerability was disclosed by Microsoft a month earlier, with no publicly available exploit at that time. Four months after the availability of the exploit, FireEye[1] reported the Dyre banking Trojan, designed to target organizations to steal credit card information, had used the exploit [9].

In this context, consider the importance of finding communities of vendors with similar hacking expertise for surveillance purposes. Many vendors possibly linked to the Dyre banking Trojan could be automatically identified if at least one of them had been already confirmed as offering the exploit online, allowing defenders to anticipate subsequent similar product offerings. In more complex scenarios, those communities might correspond to sets of individuals dealing with similar products or services in some specific subfields of hacking, such as carding, phishing, and keyloggers, which is a feature typically owned by key-hackers [100]. Therefore, early detection of specialized hacker communities becomes another form of discovering who are in the ever-evolving network of key-hackers, helping defenders to anticipate their imminent cyber-criminal activities.

Based on this insight, we explore in this chapter a method built on social network analysis and machine learning techniques to identify and validate

[1] A major cyber-security firm.

communities of malware and exploit vendors on online hacker marketplaces. As there is no direct communication between vendors in those environments, we start by collecting information about their hacking-related product offerings in 20 different markets, from where we produce a similarity matrix of the vendors. To create this matrix, we leverage unsupervised learning to cluster the vendors' products into the 34 main hacking categories proposed by our prior work published at [103]. Then, we quantify the similarity between vendors by analyzing the number of product categories shared between them and also the number of products they have in each product category. Finally, in order to address the lack of ground truth (the existing vendor communities in the markets), we split the marketplaces into two disjoint sets to detect the community overlapping between them. Our results demonstrate how the multiplexity of social ties [107, 108, 189], which makes individuals interact in multiple domains, helps us to validate a considerable part of the mined communities. This chapter makes the following main contributions:

- We cluster around 40,000 hacking-related products using 34 product categories.
- We calculate the similarity of hacking vendors applying different metrics over their products and product categories, inferring the implicit connections among them.
- We perform community finding to detect the communities of hacking-related vendors in two disjoint sets of marketplaces, validating our results by checking the overlap between them. We find that the Adjusted Rand Index (ARI)[2] achieves 0.445 using our method, while randomly assigning individuals to communities yields an ARI of – 0.006.

The remainder of this chapter is organized as follows. Section 5.2 introduces our market dataset. Section 5.3 describes our methodology, detailing its modules, experiments, and results. We discuss related work in Section 5.4. Finally, Section 5.5 concludes the chapter.

## 5.2 Dataset

In this chapter, we select 20 popular online English hacking-related marketplaces from our data repository (see Chapter 1 for details). Table 5.1 shows the number of hacking-related products and the number of vendors in the markets that have been anonymized.

[2] Metric used to calculate the agreements and disagreements of both sets of markets.

Table 5.1 *Hacker marketplace statistics*

| Marketplace | Products | Vendors | Marketplace | Products | Vendors |
|---|---|---|---|---|---|
| *Market 1* | 22,956 | 525 | *Market 11* | 1,136 | 87 |
| *Market 2* | 13,423 | 1,323 | *Market 12* | 1,122 | 63 |
| *Market 3* | 9,936 | 856 | *Market 13* | 995 | 34 |
| *Market 4* | 7,360 | 243 | *Market 14* | 936 | 40 |
| *Market 5* | 3,443 | 1,439 | *Market 15* | 739 | 61 |
| *Market 6* | 3,437 | 1,625 | *Market 16* | 527 | 6 |
| *Market 7* | 3,328 | 266 | *Market 17* | 328 | 18 |
| *Market 8* | 1,358 | 131 | *Market 18* | 302 | 135 |
| *Market 9* | 1,269 | 589 | *Market 19* | 182 | 26 |
| *Market 10* | 1,264 | 106 | *Market 20* | 159 | 32 |

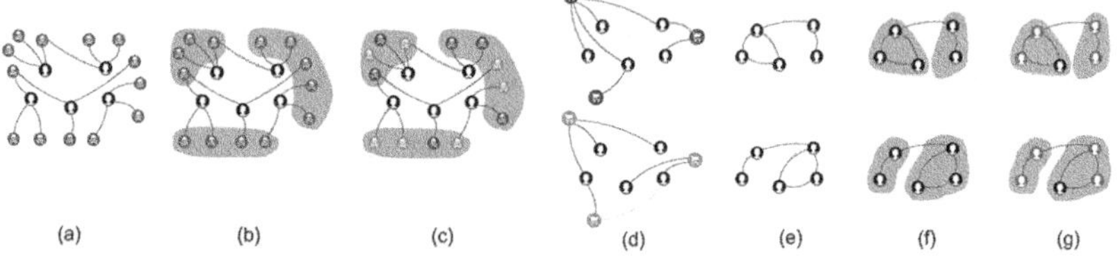


Figure 5.1 Methodology: (a) Creating a bipartite network of vendors and products, (b) clustering the products in product categories, (c) splitting the marketplaces into two disjoint sets (black and white), (d) creating a bipartite network of vendors and product categories, (e) projecting bipartite networks of vendors and product categories into monopartite network of vendors, (f) finding communities of vendors in each set of markets, (g) calculating the community overlapping between the two sets of markets.

## 5.3 Methodology

This section explains the steps of our methodology designed to address the community finding of vendors on online hacker markets, as illustrated in Figure 5.1.

### 5.3.1 Creating a Bipartite Network of Vendors and Products

The first step of our methodology consists of collecting the malicious hacking products offered by each vendor on the marketplaces to generate a bipartite network of vendors and their corresponding products. Therefore, the nodes of this bipartite graph are formed by vendors and products, while the edges are created only between these two type of nodes. We use the vendors' screen

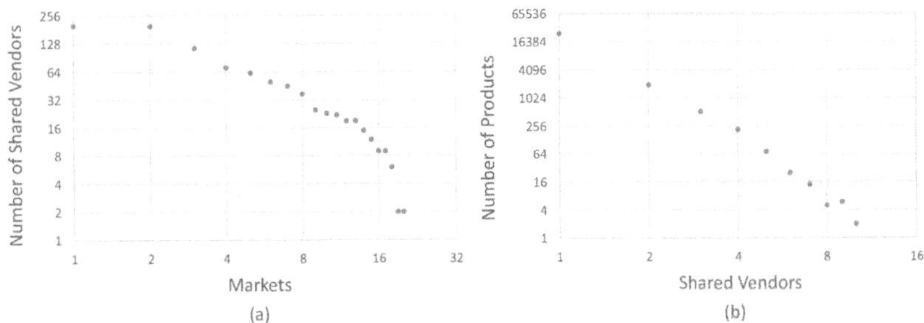


Figure 5.2 Distribution of (a) shared vendors over markets and (b) products over shared vendors (at log-log scale).

Table 5.2 *Scraped data from the online hacker marketplaces*

| Original | | Filtered | |
|---|---|---|---|
| Marketplaces | 20 | Marketplaces | 20 |
| Products (total) | 74,200 | Products (total) | 40,610 |
| Products (distinct) | 51,902 | Products (distinct) | 27,581 |
| Vendors | 7,605 | Vendors | 390 |

names and products' names to uniquely identify vendors and products. By analyzing the vendors' screen names, we note that many products are cross-posted by vendors in multiple sites. This happens since vendors usually adopt the strategy of using the same screen name in different marketplaces to transfer their reputation [126]. As the great majority of screen names are personal and exotic, we believe that applying string matching over them is a reasonable approach to uniquely identifying individuals.[3] Figure 5.2 (a) shows the distribution of vendors who use the same screen name across multiple marketplaces. As observed, there is no exclusive vendor for any marketplace, and two of these environments share almost 200 vendors with other markets.

As our method uses duplicated vendors in different sets of markets to validate the results, we filter our dataset to consider only vendors present in at least two markets, collecting their corresponding products. Table 5.2 shows the size of the original and the filtered datasets. By using this filtered data, we generate a bipartite graph considering the vendors and distinct products as two disjoint sets of nodes and the total number of products as the edges.

[3] We leave other methods of similarity-based comparison to future work.

### 5.3.2 Clustering the Products in Product Categories

As we collect data from different sites, there is inconsistency as to how products are categorized on each site (if a non trivial categorization exists). Furthermore, there is a clear absence of a standardized method for vendors to register their products. As a consequence, the majority of the products are unique when compared with simple matching or regular expression technique. Figure 5.2 (b) presents the distribution of products and the vendors shared between them, showing that around 70% of the distinct products belong to a single vendor.

In order to mitigate this inconsistency, we cluster the products into the 34 hacking categories that we defined in [103]. The idea is to make the vendors share more information, assigning similar products to the same product category. This strategy allows us to generate a more precise matrix of vendors similarity, using their shared product categories and the corresponding products. Following the approach in [103], we apply character n-grams in the range 3–6 over the product names, aiming to engineer features that represent products as vectors. Then, we value all features using term frequency–inverse document frequency (TF-IDF), after eliminating stopping words and executing steaming. Finally, we run k-means[4] using cosine similarity as the distance function (spherical k-means [80]) in the entire dataset (27,581 distinct products). The results are detailed in Table 5.3.

As shown in Table 5.3, "Netflix-related" is the top product category in terms of number of products, following the trend observed in [103]. Nevertheless, other product categories emerged, such as "Virus/Evade AntiVirus," "VPN," "keyloggers," and "Linux-related," followed by the one also pointed to by [103] as very active ("Carding"). We include the number of markets and vendors assigned to each product category. "Exploit Kits" appears as the product category most spread among the 20 markets (19), while "Keyloggers" appears as the one most spread among vendors (221).

### 5.3.3 Splitting the Marketplaces into Two Disjoint Sets

We assume that vendors on hacker marketplaces strive to build social status and trust, and one common way to accomplish that is by using the same screen name in multiple environments. This assumption is common across research work on hacking-related environments [9, 145]. For this reason, we split our

[4] We manually label 400 samples using the 34 product categories (the "k" parameter of k-means), ensuring at least 10 samples for each cluster. Then, we use those samples to determine the initial centroids for each cluster, instead of doing this task randomly.

Table 5.3 *Product categories*

| Rank | Cluster name | Nº of products | Nº of markets | Nº of vendors | Rank | Cluster name | Nº of products | Nº of markets | Nº of vendors |
|---|---|---|---|---|---|---|---|---|---|
| 1 | Netflix-related | 3786 | 16 | 186 | 18 | RDP Servers | 938 | 17 | 130 |
| 2 | Virus/Evade AntiVirus | 3216 | 14 | 61 | 19 | Physical Layer Hacking | 935 | 18 | 122 |
| 3 | VPN | 3064 | 14 | 66 | 20 | Exploit Kits | 858 | 19 | 123 |
| 4 | Keyloggers | 2662 | 18 | 221 | 21 | Smartphone – General | 791 | 17 | 141 |
| 5 | Linux-related | 1875 | 14 | 69 | 22 | Ebay-related | 780 | 16 | 92 |
| 6 | Carding | 1634 | 17 | 171 | 23 | Windows-related | 708 | 17 | 96 |
| 7 | Generic Hacking Tools | 1610 | 15 | 111 | 24 | Password Cracking | 615 | 18 | 113 |
| 8 | PGP | 1609 | 14 | 120 | 25 | Network Security Tools | 615 | 15 | 75 |
| 9 | Facebook-related | 1526 | 15 | 97 | 26 | Botnet | 611 | 18 | 87 |
| 10 | Point of Sale | 1275 | 18 | 131 | 27 | Bitcoin | 595 | 16 | 116 |
| 11 | Dumps – General | 1227 | 16 | 99 | 28 | Phishing | 587 | 16 | 107 |
| 12 | Network Layer Hacking | 1181 | 17 | 134 | 29 | Android-related | 523 | 16 | 69 |
| 13 | PayPal-related | 1148 | 15 | 133 | 30 | Hacking Groups Invites | 473 | 15 | 92 |
| 14 | Cashing Credit Cards | 1134 | 18 | 124 | 31 | Amazon-related | 464 | 16 | 94 |
| 15 | Browser-related | 1038 | 15 | 104 | 32 | Wireless Hacking | 442 | 15 | 77 |
| 16 | Banking | 959 | 15 | 139 | 33 | Links (Lists) | 409 | 12 | 100 |
| 17 | RATs | 940 | 16 | 104 | 34 | Email Hacking Tools | 382 | 16 | 96 |

Table 5.4 *Results of the marketplace split*

| | $M_1$ | $M_2$ |
|---|---|---|
| Number of markets | 10 | 10 |
| Number of products | 13,486 | 27,124 |
| Number of vendor | 345 | 374 |
| Number of duplicated vendors in both sets | 329 | |

dataset into two partitions, using an optimization process to produce a division that maximizes the redundancy of vendors in both partitions. We will leverage this redundancy to check if the communities found in one part of the data are also present in the other one. Formally, we implement an optimization algorithm to produce the best split of all 20 markets (set $M$) into 2 nonempty and disjoint sets. Thus, $M_1 \neq \emptyset$, $M_2 \neq \emptyset$, $M_1 \cap M_2 = \emptyset$, and $M_1 \cup M_2 = M$. The complexity of the algorithm for $n$ markets is $O(2^{(n-1)} - 1)$. Considering $V_{M_1}$ and $V_{M_2}$ as the set of vendors present in $M_1$ and $M_2$, respectively, our objective function seeks to maximize the number of duplicated vendors in both sets, as shown in Equation 5.1:

$$\max f(V_{M_1}, V_{M_2}),\ with\ f(V_{M_1}, V_{M_2}) = |\{V_{M_1} \cap V_{M_2}\}| \qquad (5.1)$$

Table 5.4 presents the results of the data split algorithm, showing that we found 329 duplicated vendors in our two disjoint sets of markets. We will use these individuals to verify if they form similar communities in these two different environments.

### 5.3.4 Creating Bipartite Networks of Vendors and Product Categories

At this point, we are able to connect the vendors to their product categories in a bipartite graph, allowing us to check which categories are shared between them. Figure 5.3 illustrates this process with a subset of the graph within set $M_1$. In panel (a), the vendors are connected to their products, which in turn are connected to their categories. In panel (b), we plot the same graph without the products to better visualize the shared product categories between the vendors. Vendors who were previously disconnected from others (note the nine disconnected components highlighted in panel (a), since the vendors only own exclusive products) are now connected using the shared product categories in panel (b).

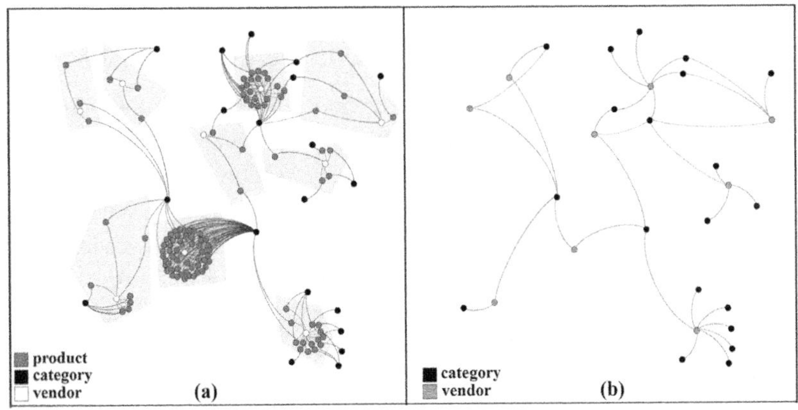


Figure 5.3 (a) Sample of a network of vendors, products, and product categories and (b) the same network without the products.

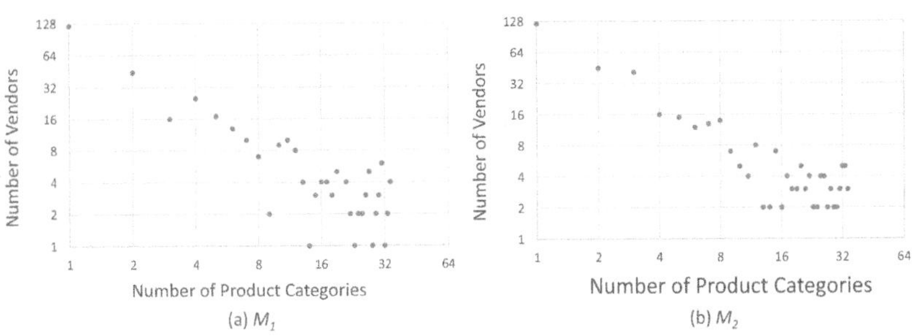


Figure 5.4 Distribution of vendors over product categories in sets (a) $M_1$ and (b) $M_2$.

Figure 5.4 shows the distribution of vendors over product categories in sets (a) $M_1$ and (b) $M_2$. The distributions are similar and point out that the majority of vendors ($\approx 63\%$) are assigned to more than one product category in both sets of marketplaces. This condition increases the probability of creating new connections in the graph, although vendors assigned to a single product category are in most cases sharing it with other individuals. Overall, the number of connections created between vendors and product categories in both subsets of markets is approximately 2,500 (7.5 on average for each one of the 329 duplicated vendors).

### 5.3.5 Projecting Bipartite Networks of Vendors and Product Categories into a Monopartite Network of Vendors

After discovering the shared product categories between vendors, our next challenge is to project the corresponding bipartite graphs of vendors and product categories into a monopartite graph of vendors. This step is crucial here, since the algorithms we will use to find the communities of vendors were designed to work with networks with single-type nodes (such as vendors), and not to work with multimodal networks [21]. To accomplish this task, we create a similarity matrix between vendors using two pieces of information: their product categories and their corresponding products. The former information basically creates a binary matrix connecting vendors and product categories, where "1" means the vendor has a least one product in the product category, and "0" otherwise. The latter information adds magnitude to the product categories owned by vendors, including the number of products vendors have within each product category. We use both pieces of information to create a similarity matrix between vendors, considering an edge between two specific individuals if the corresponding similarity (weight) is greater than a given threshold $\delta$. To calculate this weight, we use four different similarity metrics according to Table 5.5.

The idea of calculating those similarity metrics is to use them to weight the edges of our graphs, since those weights should represent the level of similarity between vendors. We rely on the assumption that vendors with a high product similarity will form a community of interests in the real world. Figure 5.5 illustrates this projection process of a bipartite network of vendors and product categories (panel (a)) to a monopartite network of vendors (panel (b)). The network shown in Figure 5.5 (a) is the one shown in Figure 5.3 (b). Note how we can see the vendors directly connected to each other in a weighed graph in Figure 5.5 (b).

### 5.3.6 Finding Communities of Vendors in Each Set of Markets

After producing the network of vendors, we search for the potential communities existing in both sets of marketplaces. Our method assumes a non overlapping community network structure, which means that every vertex (vendor) belongs to a single community. Algorithms in this context can be broadly grouped into three types: (1) *hierarchical algorithms* construct a tree of communities based on the network topology, being classified as divisive [66] and agglomerative algorithms [38]; (2) *modularity-based algorithms* optimize the modularity objective function to uncover communities in the networks

Table 5.5 *Similarity metrics*

| Metric | Formula |
|---|---|
| Jaccard | $J(V_i,V_j) = \frac{M_{11}}{M_{01}+M_{10}+M_{11}}$, where $V_i$ and $V_j$ are two binary vectors corresponding to the assignment of existing product categories for vendors $i$ and $j$, $M_{11}$ represents the number of product categories where $V_i$ and $V_j$ both have a value of 1, $M_{01}$ represents the number of product categories where the product category of $V_i$ is 0 and the product category of $V_j$ is 1, and $M_{10}$ represents the number of product categories where the product category of $V_i$ is 1 and the product category of $V_j$ is 0. |
| Cosine | $Cos(V_i,V_j) = \frac{V_i \bullet V_j}{\lVert V_i \rVert \lVert V_j \rVert}$, where $V_i$ and $V_j$ are two non binary vectors corresponding to the assignment of the total number of products within each existing product categories that belong to vendors $i$ and $j$. |
| Correlation | $Corr(V_i,V_j) = \frac{cov(V_i,V_j)}{\sigma_{(V_i)} * \sigma_{(V_j)}}$, where $V_i$ and $V_j$ are two binary vectors corresponding to the total number of products within each existing product categories that belong to vendors $i$ and $j$, $cov(V_i,V_j)$ is the covariance of $V_i$ and $V_j$, and $\sigma_{(V_i)}$ is the standard deviation of $V_i$. |
| Tanimoto | $T(V_i,V_j) = \frac{V_i \bullet V_j}{\lVert V_i \rVert^2 + \lVert V_j \rVert^2 - V_i \bullet V_j}$, where $V_i$ and $V_j$ are two non binary vectors corresponding to the assignment of the total number of products within each product category that belongs to vendors $i$ and $j$. |

Note. The concepts of each metric are presented in [179].

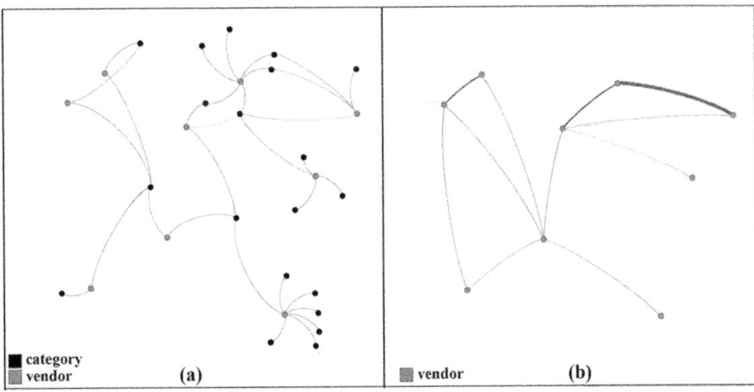


Figure 5.5 Sample of a network (a) of vendors and product categories (b) projected into a network of vendors.

[123], being our choice for this chapter; (3) *other algorithms* include label propagation, spectral methods that use eigenvectors of Laplacian or standard matrix, and methods based on statistical models [57].

In addition, when studying communities, we are interested in detecting either (1) specific members (member-based community detection) or (2) specific forms of communities (group-based community detection) [196]. Here, we work with group-based community detection algorithms, since we are interested in finding communities that own high modularity. Modularity is a measure designed to measure the strength of division of a network into modules (groups), checking how likely the community structure found is created at random [196]. Clearly, community structures should be far from random; therefore, the more distant they are from randomly generated communities, the more structure they exhibit. Modularity defines this distance as a scalar value between $-1$ and 1, and modularity maximization tries to maximize this distance [123]. Networks with high modularity have dense connections between the nodes within modules but sparse connections between nodes in different modules.

Consider an undirected graph $G(V,E), |E| = m$, two nodes $v_i$ and $v_j$, with degrees $d_i$ and $d_j$, respectively, and a partitioning of the graph into $k$ partitions, $P = (P_1, P_2, P_3, ..., P_k)$. For partition $P_x$, this distance can be defined as [196].

$$\sum_{v_i, v_j \in P_x} A_{ij} - \frac{d_i d_j}{2m}. \tag{5.2}$$

Then, this distance can be generalized for partitioning $P$ with $k$ partitions as [196].

$$\sum_{x=1}^{k} \sum_{v_i, v_j \in P_x} A_{ij} - \frac{d_i d_j}{2m}. \tag{5.3}$$

The summation is over all edges $m$, and because all edges are counted twice $(A_{ij} = A_{ji})$, the normalized version of this distance is defined as modularity $Q$ as [123].

$$Q = \frac{1}{2m} \sum_{1}^{k} \sum_{v_i, v_j \in P_x} A_{ij} - \frac{d_i d_j}{2m}. \tag{5.4}$$

Optimizing the value of $Q$ theoretically results in the best possible grouping of the nodes of a given network. However, going through all possible iterations of the nodes into groups is impractical, and heuristic algorithms are used. In this chapter, we use the Louvain heuristic method of community detection [21] to find our communities of vendors. This method iteratively finds small communities by optimizing modularity locally on all nodes, to later group each

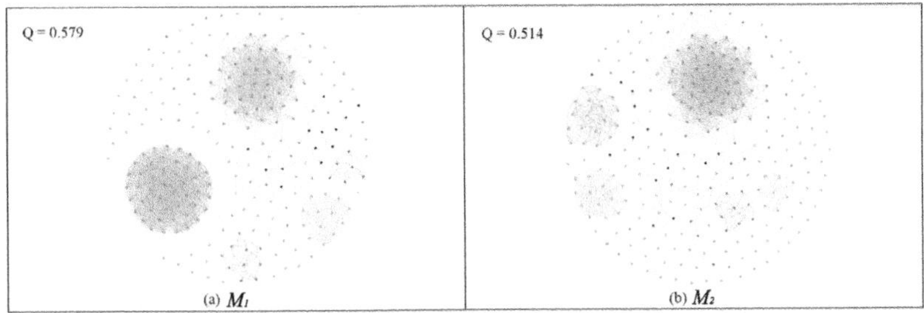


Figure 5.6 Communities found for $\delta = 0.51$ in sets (a) $M_1$ and (b) $M_2$ using Jaccard similarity.

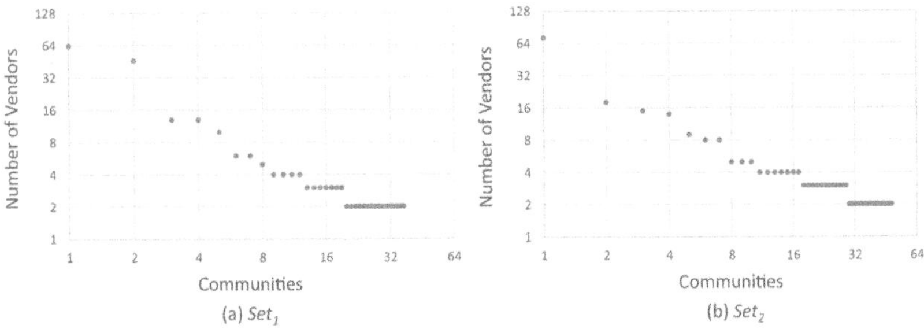


Figure 5.7 Distribution of vendors per community in sets (a) $M_1$ and (b) $M_2$.

small community into one node. It is similar to the original method proposed by Newman [123], connecting communities whose combination produces the largest increase in modularity. Figure 5.6 shows the produced communities and informs the modularity $Q$ found in set $M_1$ (0.579) and in set $M_2$ (0.514) using the Jaccard similarity metric. These values indicate that both networks present a considerable clustering property. The Louvain community detection algorithm found 46 and 37 communities in sets $M_1$ and $M_2$, respectively.

The corresponding distribution of vendors per community is presented in Figure 5.7. Both sets present a similar power law distribution, with most of the communities including few vendors, while a few communities include many individuals.

### 5.3.7 Calculating the Community Overlapping between the Two Sets of Markets

Finally, we move to the final step of our work: the validation of the communities. As mentioned before, we accomplish this task by checking the

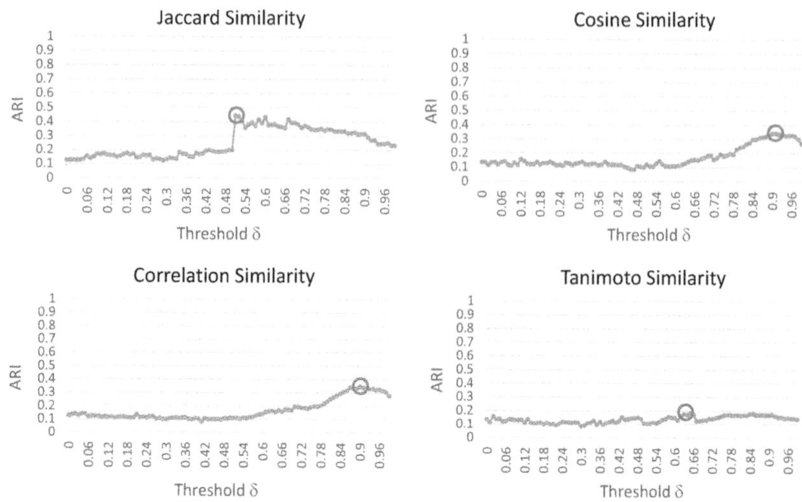


Figure 5.8 Curve of the Adjusted Rand Index (ARI) produced for the networks when we vary the threshold $\delta$.

communities overlapping in both sets. A high agreement here would mean a strong similarity between the vendors and consequently a strong likelihood of them belonging to the same community in the real world. In order to calculate this level of agreement between both sets, we use the Adjusted Rand Index (ARI) proposed in [81]. This metric produces a score range $[-1,1]$ according to the number of agreements and disagreements of the groups produced by two sets. Jointly, we prune the generated networks, varying the threshold $\delta$ in [0,0.99] (considering the step as 0.01), to verify how the ARI changes accordingly. In addition, we also analyze the trade-off between the threshold $\delta$ and the total number of vendors possible to be identified. Figure 5.8 shows the results for our networks of vendors created using the four similarity metrics.

As verified in Figure 5.8, the highest value identified for ARI (0.445) is produced when we use Jaccard similarity to create the network of vendors, and when we set the value of $\delta$ as 0.51. These results show that only the product categories are relevant to create the similarity matrix of vendors (binary matrix), and their magnitude (number of products in each category) should be avoided. We observe that the number of vendors correctly assigned in both sets to the same community is 169, which represents 51.3% of the possible number of vendors that could be matched.

### 5.3.8 Significance Analysis

After identifying the communities of vendors in both sets, we make a final examination of the distribution of vendors per communities shown in Figure 5.7. Our intention is to check if the creation of those agreements between both sets could not be done at random. In order to accomplish that, we get the number of vendors present in each community and apply the same distribution to a randomly community assignment method, carrying out this experiment for both sets. Our results show a value of –0.006 calculated for ARI, which clearly demonstrates a non-randomness property of our method.

## 5.4 Related Work

To the best of our knowledge, this is the first applied study where social network information of malware and exploit vendors is derived from malicious hacker marketplaces. We note that with the exception of our own work [103, 126, 146, 160] – which laid the groundwork for the current study – no previous work has examined malicious hacking marketplaces in this manner. Previous studies examined characteristics of malicious hacking forums, aspects of non malicious hacking markets, or the products for sale in a hacking market. In the following, we will briefly describe some of those studies.

In [91], two topic-based social networks were created, one from the topic creator perspective and the other from the repliers perspective. The authors tried to identify groups of topics as well as groups of key members who created them. Both networks were built over the same database, which consisted of a single darkweb forum monitored for approximately 14 months. Yang et al. [193] used the same dataset with a different approach. They tried to form clusters of users based on their messages' timestamps and then compared user activeness, instead of depending on message content or link analysis. The goal was to discover the specific theme of discussion in each cluster. Anwar et al. [13] treated each post as entity with its own related information (author, timestamp, thread, etc.) and tried to cluster them using agglomerative clustering based on similarities between each pair of entities. This work used surface-web sites, including 58 forums.

Additionally, there have been several studies conducted on malicious hacking forums (i.e., [16, 31, 95, 160, 161, 163, 193, 201]). Unlike our work, the relationships in online hacker forums can be easily extracted from the post/reply activities of users, while in marketplaces there is no explicit communications amongst vendors. Then, inferring those relationships is a significant novel contribution of this chapter.

Our previous work on marketplaces [103, 126, 146] focused on. (1) a game theoretic analysis of a small subset of the data in this chapter; (2) classifying products as malicious hacking related; (3) categorizing the malicious hacking related products for sale; it did not attempt to find any social structure of vendors, such as communities.

## 5.5 Conclusion

In this chapter, we mine communities of malware and exploit vendors on 20 online hacker marketplaces, connecting different vendors based on their product offerings. The multiplexity of social ties allows us to find these hidden communities using two different sets of markets (using social network analysis and machine learning techniques) and then successfully validate the results. We started with a bipartite network of vendors and products and transformed it into a bipartite network of vendors and product categories, to finally project this network into a monopartite network of vendors. To accomplish that, we use a combination of product clustering, similarity functions to connect vendors, and community finding algorithms to identify the community of vendors. Finally, we analyze the overlapping of the communities identified in both sets of markets, observing a reasonable value for this metric. This method can be considered one further step toward comprehending implicit hacker networks formed on online communities, helping law enforcement agencies track suspicious hacking-related organizations and their activities in real time.

# PART II

# Predicting Imminent Cyber-threats

# 6
# Identifying Exploits in the Wild Proactively

## 6.1 Introduction

Software vulnerabilities are weaknesses in software products that can be exploited by attackers to compromise the confidentiality, integrity, or availability of the system hosting these products and thus cause harm [134]. An exploit is a piece of code or a chunk of data that modifies the functionality of a system using an existing vulnerability [62]. Today, vulnerability exploitation is perhaps the most common method of malicious hacking. Defending against vulnerability exploitation is a difficult task that is widely recognized by cybersecurity researchers and practitioners [7, 12, 148]. Part of this comes from the difficulty in keeping pace with the ever-increasing number of vulnerabilities that are publicly disclosed. Moreover, malicious actors continue to smartly target a smaller fraction of the large population of the published vulnerabilities. Therefore, identifying if a vulnerability will likely be exploited by malicious hackers is key to a holistic security defense.

The National Institute of Standards and Technology (NIST)[1] maintains a comprehensive list of publicly disclosed vulnerabilities in the National Vulnerability Database (NVD).[2] The NVD also provides information regarding targeted software products;[3] the Common Vulnerability Scoring System (CVSS),[4] which evaluates the exploitability and impact of vulnerabilities; and the date a vulnerability was published. In 2018 alone, more than 16,500 vulnerabilities were disclosed in the NVD, an increase of over 13% from 2017 and of over 150% from 2016. The rising trend is holding in the past year and a half as of this writing.

[1] https://nist.gov.
[2] https://nvd.nist.gov.
[3] Referred to as common platform enumeration, or CPE, available at https://nvd.nist.gov/cpe.cfm.
[4] https://nvd.nist.gov/vuln-metrics/cvss.

Once vulnerabilities are publicly disclosed, their exploitation likelihood rises drastically [19]. With limited resources, organizations often look to prioritize which vulnerabilities to patch. They do so by assessing the impact on their assets and reputation if vulnerabilities are exploited. In this chapter, the exploits that are used to target systems in real-world attacks are referred to as *real-world exploits*. Differently, a *proof-of-concept exploit* (PoC) is typically developed to verify a reported software flaw in order to reserve a CVE[5] number or illustrate how a vulnerability can be exploited. PoCs generally require additional functionalities to be weaponized and become useful to malicious hackers. While the presence of a PoC is a leverage for hackers, it does not necessarily imply exploitation in real-world attacks.

To be on the safe side, standard risk assessment systems, such as the CVSS score, Microsoft Exploitability Index,[6] and Adobe Priority Rating,[7] report many vulnerabilities to be severe. The foregoing systems are broadly viewed as guidelines to supply vulnerability management teams with tools that help in patch prioritization. One commonality across those systems is that they evaluate the risk of vulnerabilities based on historical attack patterns that are relevant to the technical details of software flaws, neglecting what malicious hackers discuss and circulate in the hacking community platforms. This does little to alleviate the problem since the great majority of the highly rated vulnerabilities will never be exploited [7].

In practice, current methods of patch prioritization appear to fall short of security expectations [7, 186]. Verizon reported that over 99% of breaches are caused by exploits to known vulnerabilities [186]. Cisco also reported that "the gap between the availability and the actual implementation of such patches is giving attackers an opportunity to launch exploits" [37]. For some vulnerabilities, the time window to patch the system is very small. For instance, exploits targeting the Heartbleed[8] vulnerability in the OpenSSL[9] cryptographic software library were detected in the wild twenty-one hours after the vulnerability was publicly disclosed [50]. Hence, organizations need to efficiently assess the likelihood that a vulnerability is going to be exploited in the wild, while keeping the false alarm rate low.

Only a small fraction (less than 3%) of vulnerabilities disclosed in the NVD are exploited in the wild [6, 7, 32, 52, 120, 148] – a result that is confirmed in this chapter. In addition, previous studies have found that the CVSS score

[5] Short for Common Vulnerabilities and Exposures – a dictionary of publicly known software vulnerabilities.
[6] https://technet.microsoft.com/en-us/security/cc998259.aspx.
[7] https://helpx.adobe.com/security/severity-ratings.html.
[8] http://heartbleed.com.
[9] www.openssl.org.

provided by NIST is not an effective predictor of exploitation [7, 12, 148]. It has previously been proposed that other methods, such as the use of social media [112, 148], darkweb markets [5, 103, 150], and certain White-hat[10] websites like Contagio,[11] would be suitable alternatives. However, these approaches have their limitations. For instance, methodological concerns on the use of social media for exploit prediction were recently raised in [26]; and data feeds for exploit and malware were limited to single sites, being used only to provide insights into economic factors of those sites [5, 150]. While other studies demonstrate the viability of data collection, they do not quantify the results of prediction [103, 112].

After reviewing the literature, including (1) studies on data gathered from online hacker communities [7, 79, 103, 116, 160], (2) analysis on data feeds collected from online security sources (e.g., SecurityFocus[12] and Talos[13]), and (3) interviews with professionals working for managed security service providers (MSSPs),[14] firms specializing in cyber-risk assessment, and security specialists working for managed (IT) service providers (MSPs), we identify three data sources that can represent the current threat intelligence used for vulnerability prioritization. The first one is the ExploitDB (EDB),[15] which contains information on PoC exploits for vulnerabilities provided by security researchers from various blogs and security reports. The second one is the Zero Day Initiative (ZDI),[16] which is curated by a commercial firm called TippingPoint and uses reported sources focusing on disclosures by various software vendors and their security researchers. The third data source is a collection of information scraped from more than 120 online hacker sites on different networks. The intuition behind each of these feeds was not only to utilize information that was aggregated over numerous related sources but also to represent feeds commonly used by cyber-security professionals.

This chapter focuses on vulnerabilities that were publicly disclosed in 2015 or 2016, leveraging supervised machine learning techniques using Symantec[17] attack signatures as ground truth. We summarize the main contributions of this chapter as follows:

[10] White-hat is an Internet term that is often used to refer to ethical hackers and/or penetration testers.
[11] http://contagiodump.blogspot.com.
[12] www.securityfocus.com.
[13] www.talosintelligence.com/vulnerability_reports.
[14] An MSSP is a service provider that provides its clients with tools that continuously monitor and manage a wide range of cyber-security-related activities and operations, which may include threat inelegance, virus and spam blocking, and vulnerability and risk assessment.
[15] www.exploit-db.com.
[16] www.zerodayinitiative.com.
[17] www.symantec.com.

- We propose a machine learning model that predicts exploits-in-the-wild, demonstrating its utility with a true positive rate (TPR)[18] of 90% while maintaining a false positive rate (FPR)[19] of less than 15%. In addition, we compare our model to a recent benchmark model that utilized online mentions for exploit prediction [148], showing a significant higher precision while maintaining recall. We also discuss the robustness of our model against various adversarial data manipulation strategies.
- We provide results demonstrating the likelihood of exploitation given vulnerability mention on EDB (9%), ZDI (12%) and online hacker sites (forums and markets) as compared to vulnerabilities only disclosed on the NVD (2.4%). The availability of such information relative to the time an exploit is found in the wild is also studied.
- Exploited vulnerabilities are analyzed based on various other features derived from the three identified data sources, such as the language used. Apparently, vulnerabilities discussed on Russian-language platforms are 19 times more likely to be exploited than vulnerabilities described on websites in any of the other languages analyzed. Additionally, the probability of exploitation is investigated in terms of both data source and software vendor.

The remainder of this chapter is organized as follows. Section 6.2 outlines challenges related to the problem addressed in this study. Section 6.3 provides an overview of the presented exploit prediction model and describes the data sources used. We discuss vulnerability analysis in Section 6.4. In Section 6.5, we provide experimental results for predicting the likelihood of vulnerability exploitation. The robustness of the proposed model against adversarial data manipulation is demonstrated in Section 6.6. In Section 6.7, we discuss the viability of the proposed model and provide the cost of misclassification. Section 6.8 discusses some related work. Finally, Section 6.9 concludes the chapter.

## 6.2 Challenges

Previous work has pointed out methodological issues with exploit prediction studies [26]. We also note that there is a balance between ensuring an

[18] A metric that measures the proportion of exploited vulnerabilities that are correctly predicted from all exploited vulnerabilities.
[19] A metric that measures the proportion of non exploited vulnerabilities that are incorrectly predicted as being exploited from the total number of all non exploited vulnerabilities.

evaluation is conducted under real-world conditions and conducting an evaluation on an adequate sample size. Some of those challenges are reviewed below.

**Class imbalance**. As mentioned earlier, evidence of real-world exploits is found for only around 2.4% of the reported vulnerabilities. This skews the distribution towards one class in the prediction problem (i.e., *not exploited*). In such cases, standard machine learning approaches favor the majority class, leading to poor performance on the minority class. Some of the prior work in predicting the likelihood of exploitation considered the existence of PoCs as an indicator of real-world exploit weaponization, which substantially increases the number of exploited vulnerabilities in the studies adopting this assumption [23, 26, 52]. However, out of the PoC exploits that are identified, only a small fraction are ever used in real-world attacks [120] (e.g., only about 4.5% of the vulnerabilities having PoCs were subsequently exploited in the wild.) Other prior work used class-balancing techniques on both training and testing datasets and reported the performance achieved using metrics like TPR, FPR, and accuracy [92, 170].[20] Resampling the data to balance both classes in the dataset leads to training the classifier on a data distribution that is highly different from the underlying distribution. The impact of this manipulation, whether positive or negative, cannot be observed when testing the same classifier on a manipulated dataset, for example, a testing set with the same rebalancing ratio. Hence, the prediction performance of those models in deployed, real-world settings is questionable. In this chapter, we examine oversampling techniques (in particular SMOTE [30]) to confirm the impact of a highly imbalanced dataset used on the machine learning models. Note that the testing dataset is not manipulated because we aim to observe a performance that can be reproduced under the settings of a model running on real-world deployment (e.g., streaming predictions). Thus, only marginal improvement is observed for some classifiers, as reported in Section 6.5.2, while other classifiers have shown a slightly negative impact when they are trained on an oversampled dataset.

**Evaluating models on temporal data**. Machine learning models are evaluated by training the model on one set of data and then testing the model on another set that is assumed to be drawn from the same distribution. The data split can be done randomly or in a stratified manner, where the class ratio is maintained in both training and testing. A key aspect of the exploit prediction task is that it is time-dependent [26, 32]. Randomly splitting data violates this aspect

[20] Note that these metrics are sensitive to the underlying class distribution and sensitive to the ratio of class rebalancing.

because events that happen in the future would be used to predict events that happened in the past. Prior research has ignored this aspect while designing their experiments [23, 148]. In this chapter, we avoid this temporal mixing in most experiments. However, experiments with a very small sample size, in which temporal mixing is not controlled, are included (this is because one of the used ground truth sources does not have date/time information). It is explicitly noted when this is the case.

**Limitations of ground truth**. As mentioned, we use attack signatures reported by Symantec as the ground truth of the exploited vulnerabilities, similar to previous work [7, 148]. This ground truth is not comprehensive; that is, vulnerabilities that affect Microsoft products have a good coverage compared to products of other OS vendors. Although this source is limited in terms of coverage [148], it is still the most reliable source for labeling exploited vulnerabilities because it reports attack signatures of exploits detected in the wild for known vulnerabilities. Other sources either report whether a piece of software is malicious without proper mapping to the exploited CVE number (e.g., VirusTotal[21]) or rely on online blogs and social media sites to identify exploited vulnerabilities (e.g., SecurityFocus). To avoid overfitting the machine learning model on this not-so-representative ground truth, we omit the software vendor from the set of examined features.

## 6.3 Exploit Prediction Model

Using machine learning models to predict exploits in the wild has interesting security implications in terms of prioritizing which vulnerabilities need to be patched first to minimize the risk of cyber-attacks. Figure 6.1 gives an overview of the proposed exploit prediction model. It consists of the following phases:

- **Data collection:** We use three data sources in addition to the NVD. These data sources are EDB (ExploitDB), ZDI (Zero Day Initiative), and online markets and forums that focus on content around malicious hacking. Ground truth is assigned to the binary classification problem addressed in this chapter using Symantec attack signatures of exploits detected in the wild. The data sources are discussed in Section 6.3.1.
- **Feature extraction:** We extract features from each of the data sources. They include, for instance, bag-of-words features for vulnerability description and for hacker discussion content, binary features that check for

[21] www.virustotal.com

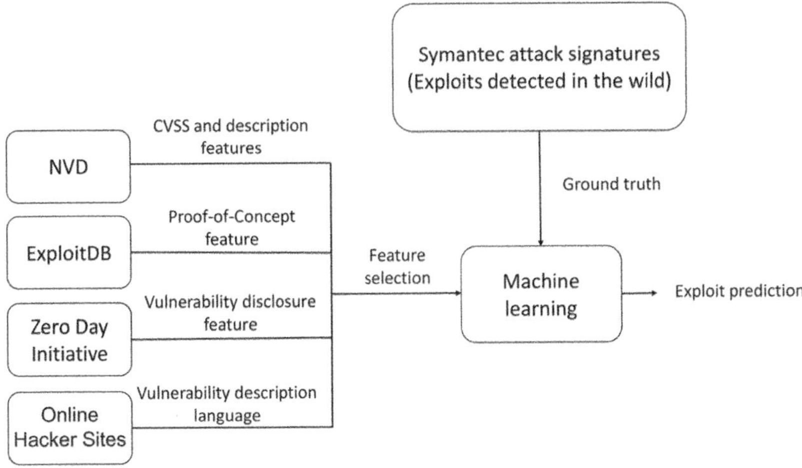


Figure 6.1 Exploit prediction model.

the presence of PoC exploits in EDB, and vulnerability disclosures in ZDI and in online hacker platforms. Additional features are also from the NVD, including CVSS score and CVSS vector.

- **Prediction:** We perform binary classification to determine whether the vulnerability will likely be exploited or not. To address this classification problem, several standard supervised machine learning approaches are evaluated.

### 6.3.1 Data Sources

Our analysis combines vulnerability and exploit information from multiple open source databases, namely, the NVD, EDB, ZDI, as well as our proprietary collection of online hacker sites. Our experiments cover vulnerabilities that were published in 2015 or 2016. Table 6.1 shows the vulnerabilities identified from each of the data sources between 2015 and 2016 as well as the number of vulnerabilities that were exploited in real-world attacks. A brief overview of each of the data sources, including ground truth, is provided below.

**NVD**. The National Vulnerability Database maintains a database of publicly disclosed vulnerabilities. Each vulnerability is identified using a unique CVE identification number. The dataset used for this chapter contains 12,598 vulnerabilities. Figure 6.2 shows the disclosure of vulnerabilities per month. At the time of data collection, there were only 30 vulnerabilities disclosed

Table 6.1 *Number of vulnerabilities (2015–2016)*

| Database | Vulnerabilities | Exploited | % Exploited |
|---|---|---|---|
| NVD | 12,598 | 306 | 2.4% |
| EDB | 799 | 74 | 9.2% |
| ZDI | 824 | 95 | 11.5% |
| Online hacker sites | 378 | 52 | 13.8% |

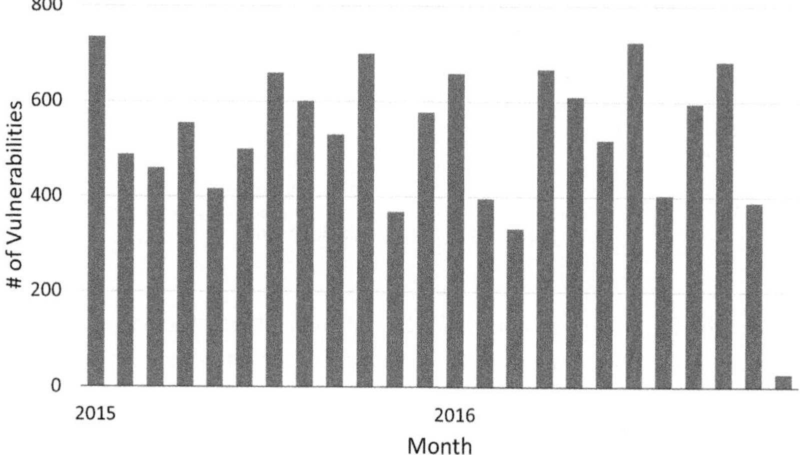


Figure 6.2 Vulnerabilities disclosed per month.

in December 2016, hence the small bar at the end of 2016. For each vulnerability, the description, the CVSS score and vector, and the publication date are collected. Organizations often use the CVSS score to prioritize which vulnerabilities to patch. The CVSS vector lists the components from which the score is computed. More details about CVSS components are provided in Section 6.3.2.

**EDB (White-hat community)**. The Exploit Database is an archive of PoC exploits maintained by Offensive Security.[22] PoC exploits for known vulnerabilities are reported with CVE numbers of target vulnerabilities. By using the unique CVE numbers from the NVD for the period between 2015 and 2016, we query EDB to find out whether a PoC exploit is available, observing the existence of PoCs for 799 of the vulnerabilities studied. The availability date of PoCs has also been recorded.

[22] www.offensive-security.com.

**ZDI (a bug bounty program)**. Zero Day Initiative maintains a database of vulnerabilities that are identified and reported by security researchers. Reported software flaws are first verified by ZDI before disclosure. Monetary incentives are provided to researchers who report valid vulnerabilities. Before ZDI publicly discloses a vulnerability, the software vendors of the target products are notified and allowed time to implement patches. We query the ZDI database for the vulnerabilities finding 824 common CVE numbers between the NVD and ZDI. The publication date has also been noted.

**Online hacker sites**. Online vendors advertise and sell their products on marketplaces that provide a new avenue to gather information about vulnerabilities and exploits. Differently, forums feature discussions on newly discovered vulnerabilities and exploit kits. Based on that, we query our hacker data repository, described in Chapter 1, to extract all items with CVE mentions, since not all exploits or vulnerability items extracted have CVE numbers associated with them. Some vulnerabilities are mentioned in this collection using Microsoft Security Bulletin Number[23] (e.g., MS16-006), which was mapped to its corresponding CVE number, making ground truth assignment easy. These items can be products sold on markets or posts extracted from forums discussing topics relating to malicious hacking. We found 378 unique CVE mentions between 2015 and 2016 on more than 120 websites, much more than what a previous work discovered [7]. We also collect the posting date and descriptions associated with all CVE mentions, including product title and description, vendor information, entire discussion with the CVE mention, author of the posts, and the topic of the discussion.

**Attack signatures (ground truth)**. For our ground truth, we identify vulnerabilities that were exploited in the wild by using Symantec anti-virus attack signatures[24] and intrusion detection systems (IDS) attack signatures.[25] The attack signatures are associated with the CVE number of the vulnerability that was exploited. We map these CVEs to the CVEs mined from the NVD, EDB, ZDI, and online hacker sites. This ground truth indicates actual exploits that were used in the wild and are not just PoC exploits. For the NVD, around 2.4% of the disclosed vulnerabilities were exploited, which is consistent with previous studies. We do not have data regarding the volume and frequency of attacks leveraging the detected exploits; hence we consider all exploited vulnerabilities to have equal importance. This assumption has been adopted by previous work as well [7, 148]. Additionally, we define the *exploitation date*

[23] https://technet.microsoft.com/en-us/security/bulletins.aspx.
[24] www.symantec.com/security_response/landing/azlisting.jsp.
[25] www.symantec.com/security_response/attacksignatures.

Table 6.2 *Summary of features*

| Feature | Type |
|---|---|
| NVD and online hacker sites description | TF-IDF on bag of words |
| CVSS | Numeric and categorical |
| Online hacker sites language | Categorical |
| Presence of PoC | Binary |
| Vulnerability mention on ZDI | Binary |
| Vulnerability mention on online hacker sites | Binary |

of a vulnerability as the date it was first detected in the wild. Symantec IDS attack signatures are reported without recording the dates when they were first detected, but its anti-virus attack signatures are reported with their *exploitation date*. Between 2015 and 2016, 112 attack signatures were reported without and 194 with their exploitation dates.

### 6.3.2 Feature Description

We combine features from all the data sources discussed in Section 6.3.1. Table 6.2 gives a summary of these features. We now discuss each of them.

**NVD and online hacker sites description**. The NVD description provides information on the vulnerability and what it allows hackers to do when they exploit it. Online hacker sites description often provides rich context on what the discussion is about, and is synthesized from forums rather than marketplaces since items are described in fewer words. Patterns can be learned based on this textual content. We obtain the description of published vulnerabilities from the NVD, and we query our hacker data repository for CVE mentions between 2015 and 2016. This description was appended to the NVD description with the corresponding CVE. We observe that some content on hacker sites is produced in foreign languages, as discussed in Section 6.4. The foreign text is translated to English using the Google Translate API.[26] We then vectorize the text features using the *term frequency–inverse document frequency* (TF-IDF) model that is learned from the training set and used to vectorize the testing set. TF-IDF creates a vocabulary of all the words in the description. The importance of a word feature increases with the number of times it occurs but is normalized by the total number of words in the description. This eliminates common words from being important features. We limit our TF-IDF model to the 1,000 most frequent words (using more word

[26] https://cloud.google.com/translate/docs.

features has no benefit in terms of performance, however, it would increase the computational cost).

**CVSS**. The NVD provides the CVSS score and the CVSS vector from which the score is computed, indicating the severity of each disclosed vulnerability. We use the CVSS base metric version 2.0 rather than version 3.0 since the latter is only present for a fraction of the studied vulnerabilities. The components of the CVSS vector include access complexity, authentication, confidentiality, integrity, and availability. Access complexity indicates how difficult it is to exploit the vulnerability once the attacker has gained access. It is defined in terms of three levels: high, medium, and low. Authentication indicates whether authentication is required by the attacker to exploit the vulnerability. It is a binary identifier taking the values required and not required. Confidentiality, integrity, and availability indicate what loss the system would incur if the vulnerability were exploited. They take the values none, partial, and complete. We engineer features by building a vector with all possible CVSS vector categories, assigning "1" if that category is present or "0" otherwise.

**Language**. Although online hacker content is posted in multiple languages, we found four languages that primarily reference vulnerabilities–English, Chinese, Russian, and Swedish. Since there is a limited number of non-English-language postings, giving the model little chance to learn proper representation for each language, we opt to use the text translation as described. We believe translation can result in a loss of important information, although we can retain the impact of knowing the language by using it as a feature. We show analysis on the hacker discussion languages and their variation in the exploitation rate in Section 6.4.

**Presence of proof-of-concept**. The presence of PoC exploits in EDB increases the likelihood of a vulnerability being exploited. We treat it as a binary feature indicating whether a PoC is present for a vulnerability or not.

**Vulnerability mention on ZDI**. ZDI acts similarly to the NVD; that is, both disclose software vulnerabilities. Given that a vulnerability is disclosed on ZDI, its exploitation likelihood raises. Similar to the presence of PoCs, we use a binary feature to denote whether a vulnerability was disclosed in ZDI before it is exploited.

**Vulnerability mention on online hacker sites**. We use a binary feature indicating whether a vulnerability is mentioned in our hacker data repository.

## 6.4 Vulnerability and Exploit Analysis

To assess the importance of aggregating different data sources for early identification of threatened vulnerabilities, we first analyze the likelihood of exploitation given that a vulnerability is mentioned on each data source. Time-based analysis is then provided for the exploited vulnerabilities that have reported *exploitation dates* ($n = 194$) to show the difference in days between when vulnerabilities are exploited and when they are mentioned online. In our time-based analysis, we ignore the exploited vulnerabilities without reported dates because we cannot make any assumptions regarding their exploitation dates. Furthermore, we analyze our ground truth and compare it to other sources to identify the vendors of highly vulnerable software and systems. As described by previous work, Symantec reports attack signatures for vulnerabilities of certain products [7, 148]. We study the distribution of affected software vendors by vulnerabilities from each data source. We base this analysis on the vendor mentions by CPE, which is a list of software programs provided by NVD that are vulnerable to a given CVE. Finally, we illustrate how the likelihood of exploitation significantly increases when vulnerabilities are discussed in certain languages.

**Likelihood of exploitation**. Table 6.3 shows the exploitation probability for the vulnerabilities mentioned in each data source. This analysis emphasizes the value of open data sources in supplementing the NVD data. As mentioned in Section 6.3.1, about 2.4% of the vulnerabilities in NVD are exploited in the wild. Hence, including other sources can increase the likelihood of correctly identifying the vulnerabilities that will be exploited.

**Time-based analysis**. Most software systems are attacked after exploits targeting the corresponding vulnerabilities are detected in the wild [8]. Actually,

Table 6.3 *Number of vulnerabilities, number of exploited vulnerabilities, percentage of exploited vulnerabilities that appeared in each source, and percentage of total vulnerabilities that appeared in each source*

| | EDB | ZDI | OHS* | ZDI ∨ OHS* | EDB ∨ ZDI ∨ OHS* |
|---|---|---|---|---|---|
| **Number of vulnerabilities** | 799 | 824 | 378 | 1,180 | 1,791 |
| **Number of exploited vulnerabilities** | 74 | 95 | 52 | 140 | 164 |
| **Percentage of exploited vulnerabilities** | 21% | 31% | 17% | 46% | 54% |
| **Percentage of total vulnerabilities** | 6.3% | 6.5% | 3.0% | 9.3% | 14.2% |

*Online hacker sites.

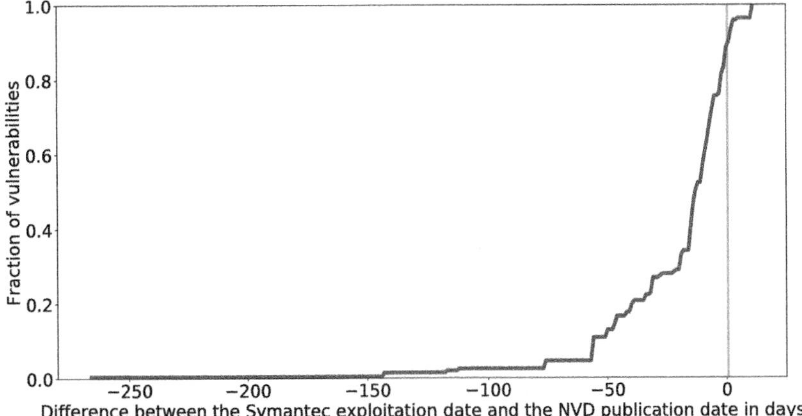


Figure 6.3 Day difference between CVE first published in the NVD and the Symantec attack signature date versus the fraction of exploited CVEs on the NVD reported (cumulative).

vulnerabilities may take a long time between the date they are disclosed and the date they are patched. Here, we only analyze the population of exploited vulnerabilities that are reported with the date when they are first detected (194 vulnerabilities). Figure 6.3 shows that more than 93% of the vulnerabilities are exploited in real-world attacks after being disclosed by NIST.

In the other few cases, attacks were detected in the wild before NIST published the vulnerabilities (i.e., zero-day attacks). This could be caused by many reasons: (1) the vulnerability information is sometimes leaked before the disclosure; (2) by the time NIST disclosed a vulnerability in the NVD, other sources have already validated and published it, giving malicious hackers valuable source of information ahead of time; (3) the attacker knew that what they were doing was successful and continued to exploit their targets until discovered [19], or (4) the vulnerability information was available but undisclosed and allowed the private development of exploits, for example, within exploit vendor companies. Additionally, ZDI and NVD have limited variation on the vulnerability disclosure dates (median is 0 days). It is important to note that because ZDI disclosures come from the industry, reserved CVE numbers are shown earlier here than in other sources.

In the case of the EDB database, almost all of the exploited vulnerabilities that have PoCs archived there were found in the wild within the first 100 days of the PoCs' availability. Such a short period between the availability of PoCs and actual attacks in the real world indicates that having a template for exploits

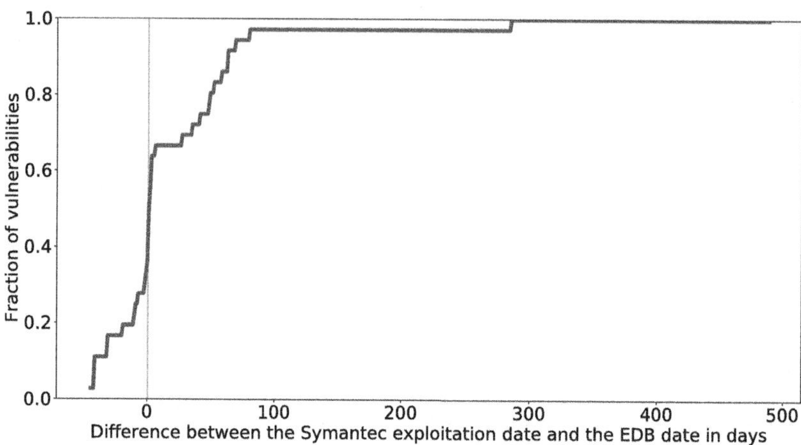


Figure 6.4 Day difference between the date of availability of PoC on EDB and the Symantec attack signature date versus the fraction of exploited CVEs with PoCs on EDB reported (cumulative).

(in this case, PoCs) makes it easy for hackers to configure and use in real-world attacks. Figure 6.4 shows the difference in days between the availability of PoCs and *exploitation dates*.

In the case of our online hacker data, more than 60% of the first-time mentions to the exploited vulnerabilities are within 100 days before or after the *exploitation dates*. The remaining mentions are within the 18-month time frame after the vulnerability *exploitation date* (see Figure 6.5).

**Vendor/system-based analysis**. As noted, Symantec reports vulnerabilities that exist in the systems and software configurations used by its customers. For the vulnerabilities we studied, more than 84% and 36% of the exploited vulnerabilities reported by Symantec exist in products solely from, or run on, Microsoft and Adobe products, respectively, whereas less than 16% and 8% of vulnerabilities published in the NVD are related to Microsoft and Adobe, respectively. Figure 6.6 shows the percentage from the exploited vulnerabilities that can affect each of the top five vendors in every data source. It is important to note that a vulnerability may affect more than one vendor (e.g., CVE-2016-4272 exists in Adobe Flash Player,[27] and it allows attackers to execute arbitrary code via unspecified vectors and can affect products from all five vendors). This explains why some operating systems (e.g., Linux) with less coverage from Symantec data are targeted by vulnerabilities reported by Symantec.

[27] www.adobe.com/products/flashplayer.html.

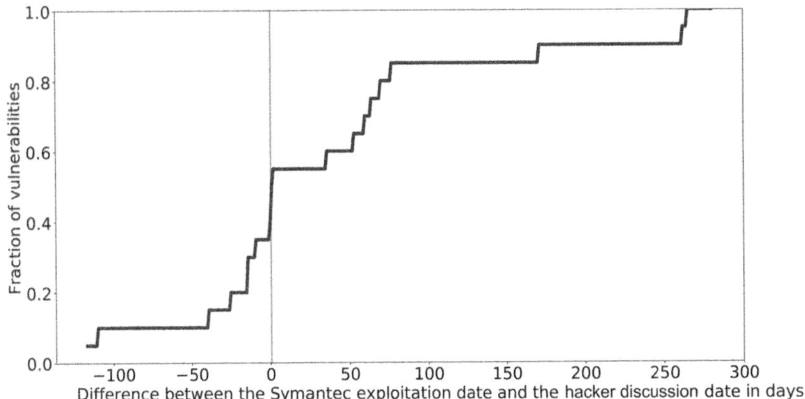


Figure 6.5 Day difference between CVE first mentioned in online hacker sites and Symantec attack signature date versus the fraction of exploited CVEs on online hacker sites reported (cumulative).

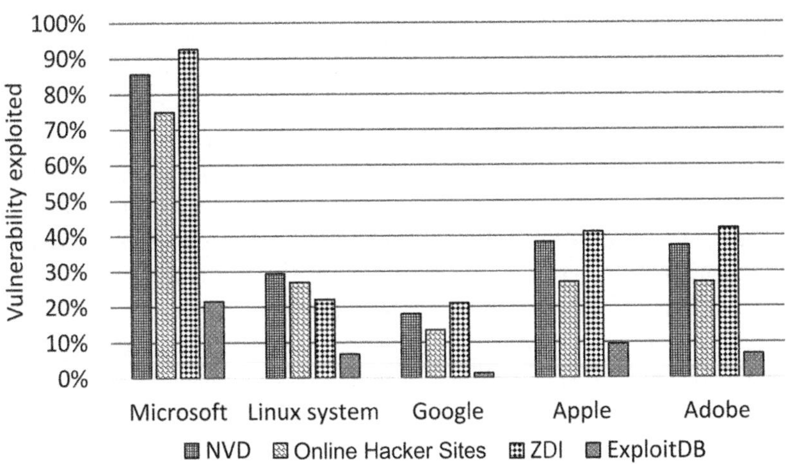


Figure 6.6 Most exploited vendors/systems in each data source.

In addition, online hacker discussions appear to have more uniform user coverage. Only 30% and 6.2% of the vulnerabilities mentioned in the forums and markets during the period we study are related to Microsoft and Adobe, respectively. Additionally, ZDI favors products from these two vendors (57.8% for Microsoft and 35.2% for Adobe). This provides evidence that each data source covers vulnerabilities targeting different sets of software vendors.

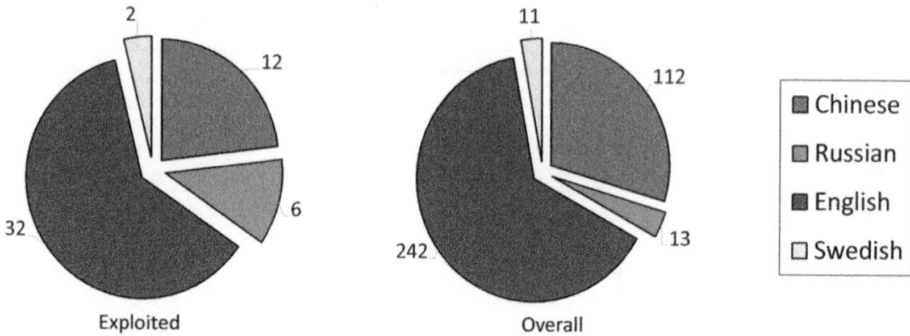


Figure 6.7 (left) Number of *exploited* vulnerabilities mentioned by each language and (right) number of vulnerabilities mentions in each language.

**Language-based analysis**. Interestingly, we found notable variations on the exploitation likelihood depending on the language used on hacker posts that reference CVEs. In online hacker sites, four languages are detected with different vulnerability post and item distributions. Not surprisingly, English and Chinese have far more vulnerability mentions (242 and 112, respectively) than Russian and Swedish (13 and 11, respectively). However, vulnerabilities mentioned in Chinese-language postings are characterized by the lowest exploitation rate. For example, of those vulnerabilities, only 12 are exploited (about 10%), while 32 of the vulnerabilities mentioned in English-language postings are exploited (about 13%). Although vulnerability mentions in Russian- or Swedish-language postings are few, these vulnerabilities have very high exploitation rates: about 46% and 19% of the vulnerabilities mentioned in Russian (6) and Swedish (2) were exploited, respectively. Figure 6.7 shows the number of vulnerability mentions by each language as well as the number of *exploited* vulnerabilities mentioned by each language.

## 6.5 Experimental Setup

We perform a series of experiments to evaluate our model, comparing it to a benchmark work presented in [148] in our first experiment. For our model, we found that random forests (RFs) give us the best performance. We use RFs that combine bagging [25] for each tree with random feature selection [24] at each node to split the data. The final result is an ensemble of decision trees, each having its own independent opinion on class labels (i.e., *exploited* or *not exploited* for a given disclosed vulnerability). Thus, a new vulnerability is classified independently by each tree and assigned a class label that best fits it. Multiple decision trees may result in having multiple class labels for the same data sample; hence, a majority vote is taken and the class label with most votes is assigned to the vulnerability. In [148], the authors temporally mix their samples; that is, vulnerabilities exploited in the future are used to predict vulnerabilities exploited in the past, a practice that is discussed in [26]. Additionally, to account for the severe class imbalance, only vulnerabilities that occur in Microsoft or Adobe products were used in training and testing (477 vulnerabilities, 41 of which were exploited). We compare our model to [148] under the same conditions.

For the second experiment, we restrict the training samples to the vulnerabilities published before any of the vulnerabilities in the testing samples. Also, we only use data feeds that are present before the *exploitation date*. Thus, we guarantee that our experimental settings resemble the real-world case. Since we cannot make any assumptions regarding the sequence of events for the exploited vulnerabilities reported by Symantec without the *exploitation date* ($n = 112$), we remove these vulnerabilities from our experiments. The percentage of exploited vulnerabilities becomes 1.2%. We compare the performance of our model to the CVSS score.

The goal for exploit prediction is to predict whether a disclosed vulnerability will likely be exploited in the future. Few vulnerabilities are exploited before they are published [19]. Predicting such vulnerabilities does not add any value to the goal of the prediction task, considering that they had already been exploited by the time they were revealed. That being said, knowing which unpublished vulnerabilities were exploited in the wild can help organizations with their cyber-defense strategies, but this is outside the scope of this chapter.

### 6.5.1 Performance Evaluation

We evaluate our classifiers based on two classes of metrics that have been used in previous work. The first class is used to demonstrate the performance achieved in the minority class (in our case, 1.2%). The metrics under this class are *precision* and *recall*. They are computed as reported in Table 6.4. *Precision* is defined as the fraction of vulnerabilities that were exploited from all vulnerabilities predicted to be exploited by our model. It highlights the effect of mistakingly flagging non-exploited vulnerabilities. *Recall* is defined as the fraction of correctly predicted exploited vulnerabilities from the total number of exploited vulnerabilities. It highlights the effect of unflagging important vulnerabilities that were used later in attacks. For highly imbalanced data, these metrics give us an intuition regarding how well the classifier performed on the minority class (i.e., exploited vulnerabilities). The *F1* score

Table 6.4 *Evaluation metrics*

| Metric | Formula |
|---|---|
| Precision | $\frac{TP}{TP+FP}$ |
| TPR (recall in case of binary classification) | $\frac{TP}{TP+FN}$ |
| F1 score | $2 * \frac{precision*recall}{precision+recall}$ |
| FPR | $\frac{FP}{FP+TN}$ |

Note. TP: true positive, FP: false positive, FN: false negative, and TN: true negative.

is the harmonic mean of precision and recall. It summarizes precision and recall in a common metric. The F1 score can vary based on the trade-off between precision and recall. This trade-off is dependent on the priority of the applications. If keeping the number of incorrectly flagged vulnerabilities to a minimum is a priority, then high precision is desired. To keep the number of undetected vulnerabilities that are later exploited to a minimum, high recall is desired. We further report the *receiver operating characteristics* (ROC) curve as well as the *area under the curve* (AUC) of the classifier. ROC graphically illustrates the performance of our classifier by plotting the true positive against the false positive at various thresholds of the confidence scores the classifier outputs. In binary classification problems, the overall TPR is always equivalent to recall for the positive class, while FPR is the number of *not exploited* vulnerabilities that are incorrectly classified as *exploited* from all *non exploited* samples. ROC is a curve; thus, AUC is the area under ROC. The higher the AUC value, the closer the model to perfection (i.e., a classifier with an AUC of 1 is a perfect classifier).

### 6.5.2 Results

We utilize and compare the performance of several standard supervised machine learning approaches for exploit prediction. Parameters for all approaches were set in a way to provide the best performance. We use the *scikit-learn* Python package [132].

**Examining classifiers**. We maintain the temporal information for all the classifiers. The vulnerabilities are sorted according to the date they were posted on the NVD. The first 70% are reserved for training, along with the features that are available by the end of the training period. The remaining

Table 6.5 *Performance of RF, SVM, LOG-REG, DT, and NB to predict whether a vulnerability will be exploited*

| Classifier | Precision | Recall | F1 score |
|---|---|---|---|
| RF | **0.45** | 0.35 | **0.40** |
| BN | 0.31 | 0.38 | 0.34 |
| SVM | 0.28 | 0.42 | 0.34 |
| LOG-REG | 0.28 | 0.4 | 0.33 |
| DT | 0.25 | 0.24 | 0.25 |
| NB | 0.17 | **0.76** | 0.27 |

vulnerabilities are used for testing. Table 6.5 shows a comparison between the classifiers with respect to precision, recall, and F1 score. Random forests perform the best with F1 score of 0.4 as compared to support vector machines (SVM), 0.34; Bayesian network[28] (BN), 0.34; logistic regression[29] (LOG-REG), 0.33; decision tree[30] (DT), 0.25; and naïve Bayes[31] (NB), 0.27. Note that even though RF have the best F1 score, they do not have the best recall – NB does. We choose RF with high precision, which makes the model reliable, as compared to low precision, which results in many false positives.

**Benchmark test**. We compare our model to a work that uses vulnerability mentions on Twitter to predict the likelihood of exploitation [148]. The authors use SVM as their classifier, while our model works best with a random forest classifier. Although it would be straightforward to think that our approach would achieve better performance than the work proposed in [148], we only compare to this work because; (1) to the best of our knowledge, there is no existing work on predicting exploits in the wild using online hacker data, and (2) we compare all major approaches, and currently, using feed from social media is the best one.

In [148], the authors restrict the training and evaluation of their classifier to vulnerabilities targeting Microsoft and Adobe products, because other vendors are under represented in the Symantec data. They perform a 10-fold stratified cross-validation, where the data are partitioned into 10 parts

[28] Bayesian network is a probabilistic classifier that does not assume independence among features. Instead, they are modeled in a graph learned from the training data.
[29] Logistic regression classifies samples by computing the odds ratio. The odds ratio gives the strength of the association between the attributes and the class.
[30] Decision tree is a recursive partitioning algorithm that builds a tree-like model of decisions by finding the best split attribute, that is, the attribute that maximizes the information gain at each split of a node.
[31] Naïve Bayes is a probabilistic classifier that uses Bayes theorem with independent attribute assumption.

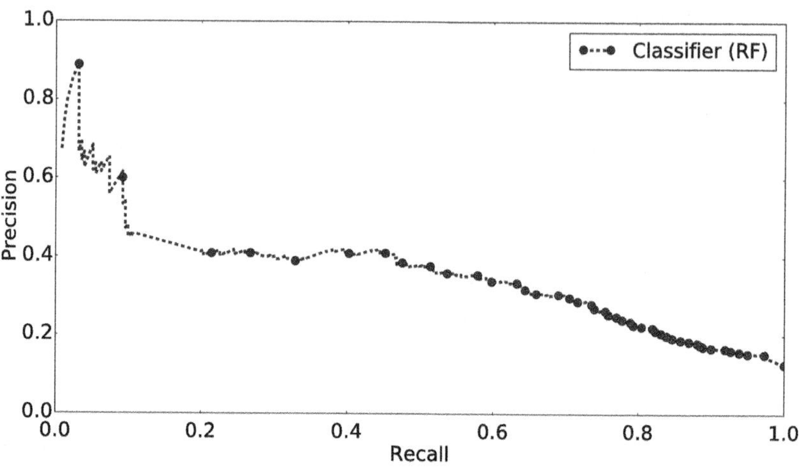


Figure 6.8 Precision-recall curve for proposed features of Microsoft/Adobe vulnerabilities (RF).

while maintaining the class ratio in each part. Models are trained on nine parts and tested on the remaining one. The experiment is repeated for all 10 parts. Hence, each sample is tested once. For comparison, we also perform the same experiment, under highly similar assumptions. We use all exploited vulnerabilities regardless of whether the date is reported by Symantec. In our case, we have 2,056 vulnerabilities targeting Microsoft and Adobe products. Out of 2,056 vulnerabilities, 261 are exploited, a fraction that is consistent with previous work. We perform a 10-fold stratified cross-validation. We plot the precision-recall curve for our model (see Figure 6.8).

The precision-recall curve shows us the trade-off between precision and recall for different thresholds. Since the F1 score is not reported in [148], we use the precision-recall curve reported for comparison. By maintaining the recall value constant, we compare how precision varies. Table 6.6 shows the performance of the two models by comparing precision for different values of recall. For a threshold of 0.5, we get an F1 score of 0.44 with precision 0.53 and recall 0.3. Maintaining recall, the precision value displayed in the graph in [148] is 0.3, significantly lower than 0.4. We perform the same experiment on different recall values to compare precision. At each point, we obtain higher precision than the previous approach.

**Baseline comparison**. In [26], the authors argue that the problem of predicting the likelihood of exploitation is sensitive to the sequence of vulnerability-related events. Temporally mixing such events leads to future events being

Table 6.6 *Precision comparison between [148] and the proposed model while maintaining recall*

| Recall | Precision[a] | Precision (our work) |
|---|---|---|
| 0.20 | 0.30 | **0.41** |
| 0.40 | 0.18 | **0.40** |
| 0.70 | 0.10 | **0.29** |

[a]Numbers derived from Figure 6.a from [148].

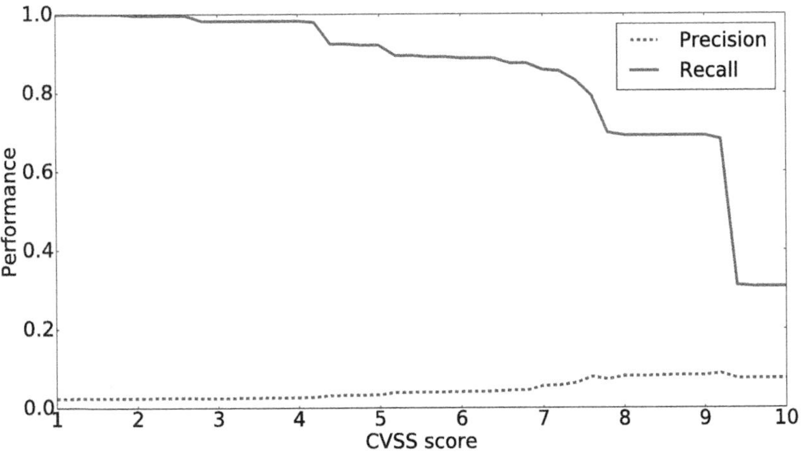


Figure 6.9 Precision and recall for classification based on CVSS base score version 2.0 threshold.

used to predict past ones, resulting in inaccurate prediction results. To avoid that, we create time-based splits, as described in this section. For a baseline comparison, we use the CVSS version 2.0 base score to classify whether a vulnerability will be exploited based on the severity score assigned to it. CVSS score has been used as a baseline in previous studies [7, 148]. CVSS tends to be highly cautious; that is it, tends to assign high scores to many vulnerabilities, resulting in many false positives. Figure 6.9 shows the precision-recall curve for the CVSS score. It is computed by varying the decision threshold ($x$-axis), on which we determine the class label of each vulnerability. CVSS gives high recall with very low precision, which is not desired for real-world patch prioritization tasks. The best F1 score that could be obtained is 0.15.

Figure 6.10 shows the performance comparison between our proposed RF model and the CVSS-based model that yields the highest F1 score. Our model outperforms the baseline with an F1 score of 0.4, a precision of 0.45, and a

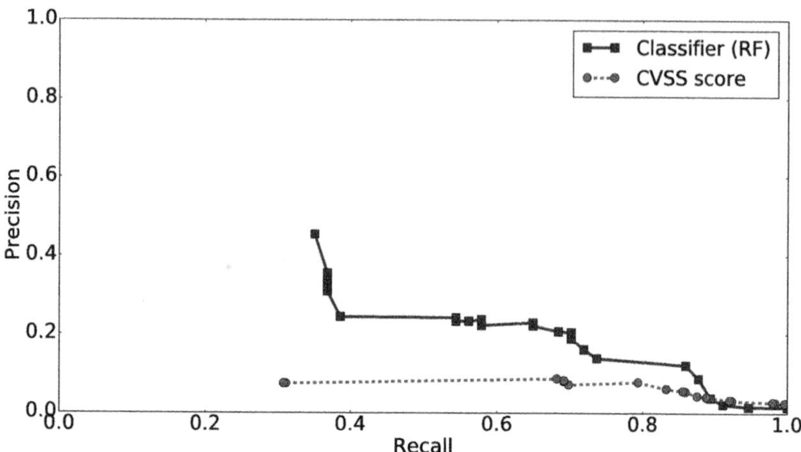


Figure 6.10 Precision-recall curve for classification based on CVSS score threshold (RF).

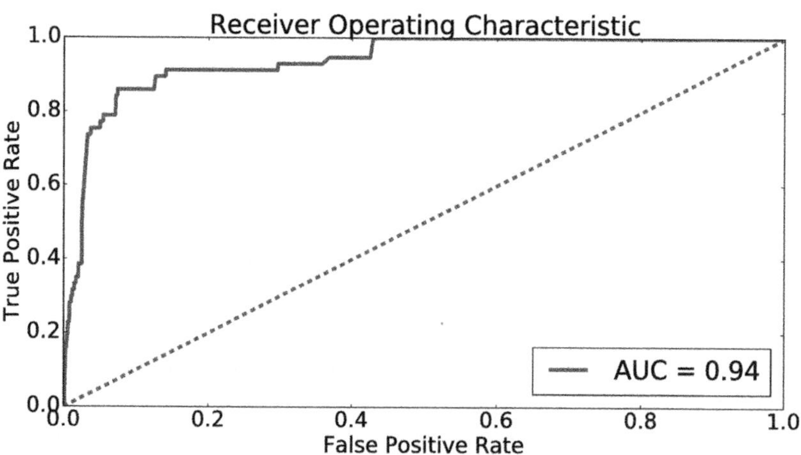


Figure 6.11 ROC curve for classification based on random forests classifier.

recall of 0.35. Additionally, our classifier shows very high TPR (90%) at low FPR (13%), with an AUC of 94%, as depicted in Figure 6.11.

**Evaluation with individual data sources.** We study what effect introducing each data source has on the prediction of vulnerabilities mentioned in that source. We find that the time-based split used in the previous experiments leaves very few vulnerabilities mentioned in these data sources in the test set (ZDI, 18; OHS, 4; EDB, 2). Hence, we increase the numbers by (1) performing

Table 6.7 *Precision, recall, F1 score for vulnerabilities mentioned on OHS, ZDI, and EDB*

| Source | Case | Precision | Recall | F1 score |
|---|---|---|---|---|
| OHS[a] | NVD | 0.23 | 0.38 | 0.27 |
| | NVD + OHS[a] | 0.67 | 0.375 | 0.48 |
| ZDI | NVD | 0.16 | 0.54 | 0.25 |
| | NVD + ZDI | 0.49 | 0.24 | 0.32 |
| EDB | NVD | 0.15 | 0.56 | 0.24 |
| | NVD + EDB | 0.31 | 0.40 | 0.35 |

[a]Online hacker sites.

a 10-fold cross-validation without sorting the vulnerabilities and (2) increasing the ground truth by considering the exploited vulnerabilities that did not have exploitation dates (these were removed from earlier experiments because it was not clear when they were exploited). Using these two techniques, we have 84 vulnerabilities mentioned in ZDI that have been exploited, 57 in EDB, and 32 in OHS. We report the results (precision, recall, and F1) for the vulnerabilities mentioned in each data source. Also, we mention the prediction of these vulnerabilities by using only the NVD features. For the vulnerabilities mentioned in OHS, we only consider the OHS features along with the NVD features. The model predicts 12 vulnerabilities as exploited with a precision of 0.67 and a recall of 0.38. By only considering the NVD features, the model predicts 12 vulnerabilities as exploited with a precision of 0.23 and a recall of 0.38. Consequently, using the OHS features, the precision improved significantly from 0.23 to 0.67. Table 6.7 shows the precision-recall with corresponding F1 score. OHS information was thus able to correctly identify positive samples mentioned in the content with higher precision.

For ZDI, we have 84 vulnerabilities mentioned. By just utilizing the NVD features, we get an F1 score of 0.25 (precision, 0.16; recall, 0.54) as compared to adding the ZDI feature with F1 score of 0.32 (precision, 0.49; recall, 0.24) – a significant improvement in precision. Table 6.7 also shows the precision-recall with corresponding F1 score for samples mentioned on ZDI.

We perform a similar analysis for the vulnerabilities that have PoCs available on EDB. For EDB, there are 57 vulnerabilities with PoCs. With only the NVD features, the model scores an F1 score of 0.24 (precision, 0.15; recall, 0.56); while adding the EDB feature boosts the F1 score to 0.35 (precision, 0.31; recall, 0.40) – a significant improvement in precision, as shown in Table 6.7.

Table 6.8 *Performance improvement attained by Applying SMOTE for the BN classifier using different oversampling for the exploited samples*

| Oversampling percentage | Precision | Recall | F1 score |
|---|---|---|---|
| 100% | 0.37 | 0.42 | 0.39 |
| 200% | 0.40 | **0.44** | **0.42** |
| 300% | **0.41** | 0.40 | 0.40 |
| 400% | 0.31 | 0.40 | 0.35 |

**Feature importance.** To better explain our choices of the features, we examine and provide an understanding on from where our prediction power primarily derives. We report the features that most contribute to the prediction performance. A feature vector for a sample has 28 features computed from the non-textual data (summarized in Table 6.2) as well as the textual features – TF-IDF computed from the bag of words for the 1,000 words that have the highest frequency in the NVD description and the online hacker data. For each of the features, we compute the mutual information (MI) [71], which expresses how much a variable (here a feature $x_i$) tells about another variable (here the class label $y \in$ {*exploited, not exploited*}). The features that contribute the most from the non-textual data are {*language_Russian = true, has_hacker_data = true, has_PoC = false*}. In addition, the features that contribute the most from the textual data are the words {*demonstrate, launch, network, xen, zdi, binary, attempt*}. All of these features received MI scores greater than 0.02.

**Addressing class imbalance.** The problem of class imbalance has gained a lot of research interest (see [63] for a survey). Since our dataset is highly imbalanced, we use SMOTE [30] and measure the improvement in classification performance. SMOTE oversamples the minority class by creating synthetic samples with features similar to those of the exploited vulnerabilities. This data manipulation is only applied to the training set. Using SMOTE, no performance improvement is achieved for our RF classifier. However, SMOTE introduces a considerable improvement with a Bayesian network (BN) classifier. Table 6.8 reports different oversampling ratios and the change in performance. The best oversampling ratio is experimentally determined; that is, high oversampling ratios lead the model to learn from a distribution that differs significantly from the real distribution.

## 6.6 Adversarial Data Manipulation

We study the effects of adversarial data manipulation only on hacker platforms. For the presence of PoCs, we only consider PoCs that are verified by EDB. Adversaries need to hack into EDB to add noise or remove PoCs from the EDB database. Here, we assume such action cannot be taken by adversaries. Similarly, ZDI publishes only vulnerabilities that are verified by its researchers; hence there is a very small chance of manipulating these data sources.

On the other hand, the semi public nature of online marketplaces and forums gives adversaries the ability to poison the data used by the classifier. They can achieve this by adding vulnerability discussions on these platforms with the intent of fooling the classifier to make it produce high false positives. Previous work discusses how adversaries can influence a classifier by manipulating the training data [14, 15, 18].

In our prediction model, we use the presence of the vulnerability in online hacker sources, the language of the market or forum on which it was mentioned, and the vulnerability description as features. Adversaries could easily post discussions regarding vulnerabilities that they not intend to exploit, nor expect these vulnerabilities to be exploited. To study the influence of such noise on the performance of the model, we experiment with two strategies:

**1. Adversary adding random vulnerability discussions:** In this strategy, the adversary initiates random vulnerability discussions online and reposts them with different CVE numbers, so the number of CVE mentions on hacker platforms increases. For our experiment, we consider two cases with different amounts of noise added. In case 1, we assume that the noise is present in both the training and the testing data. We consider varying fractions of noise (5%, 10%, 20% of the total data samples) randomly distributed in training and testing data. The experimental setup follows conditions discussed in Section 6.5. Vulnerabilities are first sorted according to time, and the first 70% are reserved for training and the remaining for testing. Figure 6.12 shows the ROC curve including the false positive rate (FPR) versus the true positive rate (TPR). For different amounts of noise introduced, our model still maintains a high TPR with low FPR and AUC of at least 0.94, a performance similar to the experiment without adding noise. This shows that the model is highly robust against noise such that it learns a good representation of the noise during training and can distinguish it during testing.

For case 2, we randomly add vulnerability discussion found online with different CVE numbers to only the test data and repeat the same experiment.

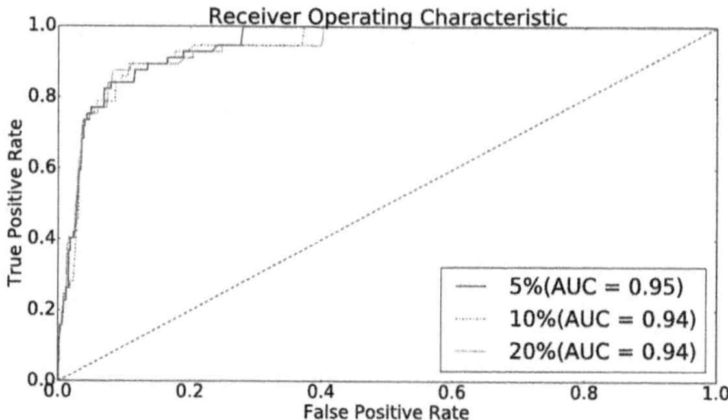


Figure 6.12 ROC curves for adversary adding noise to both the training and the testing data.

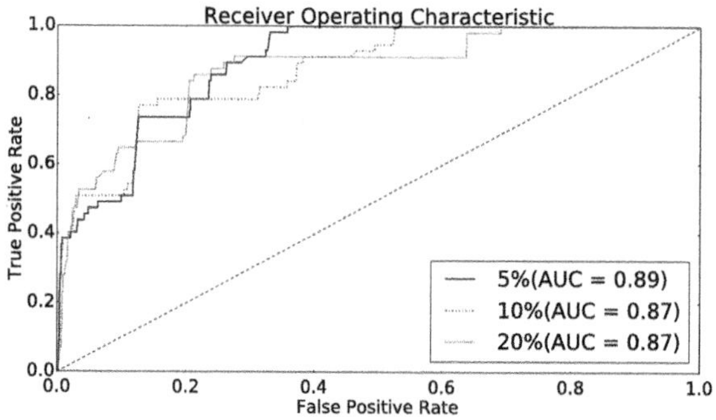


Figure 6.13 ROC curves for adversary adding noise to only the testing data.

Figure 6.13 shows the ROC plot. In this case, even though there is a slight increase in the FPR, the performance is still on par with the experiment without noise (AUC of 0.87 or more). Hence, noisy samples affect the prediction model slightly if they are not introduced in the training data.

**2. Adversaries adding vulnerability discussion similar to the NVD description:** In the previous strategy, the adversary adds vulnerability discussions randomly without taking into account the actual capability of the vulnerability. For instance, CVE-2016-3350 is a vulnerability in Microsoft Edge as reported by the NVD. If the vulnerability is mentioned online but targeting Google Chrome, then it might be easy for the prediction model to detect it, as seen before. But what if the adversary crafts the vulnerability discussion such that it is a copy of the NVD description or consistent with the NVD description? In this strategy, the adversary posts the NVD description with the CVE number online. For case 1, we consider this noise to be randomly distributed in both

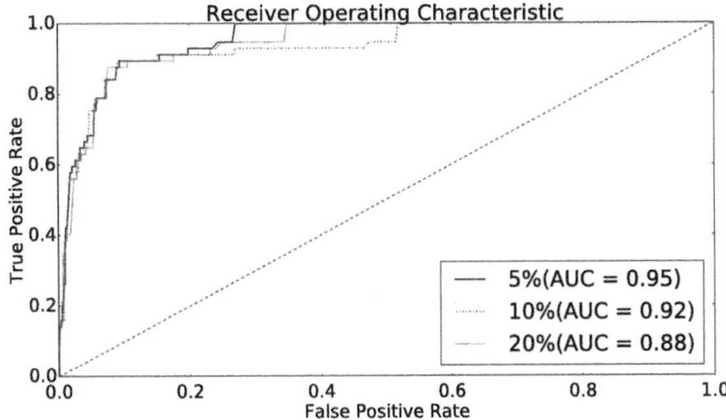


Figure 6.14 ROC curves for adversary adding noise to both the training and the testing data.

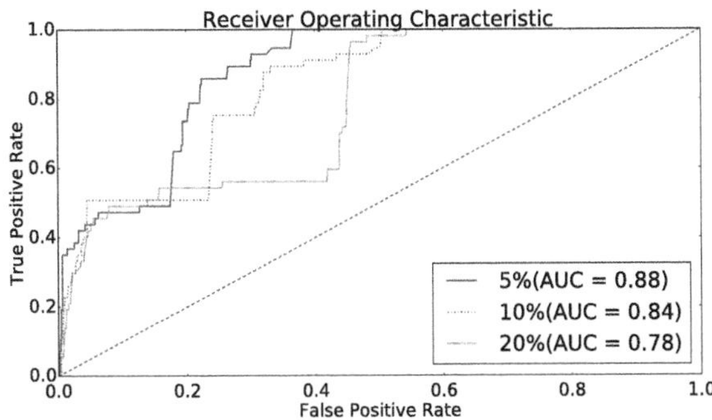


Figure 6.15 ROC curves for adversary only adding noise to the testing data.

training and testing. Figure 6.14 shows the ROC curves for different levels of noise. The performance decreases as the number of noisy samples increases, with no significant decline (AUC of 0.88 or more).

We repeat the experiment by adding noise only in the test data for case 2. In this experiment, we observe that the biggest drop in performance results in an AUC of 0.78 when 20% of the samples are noise (see Figure 6.15). This shows that adding correct vulnerability discussions does affect the prediction model, except if a large number of such samples are used. Also, the effect can be countered by also adding such noisy samples to the training data for the model to learn from.

Note that an adversary would need to add a large number of noisy samples to lower the performance of the prediction model. Previous research on using data feeds like Twitter for exploit prediction mentions that adversaries can register a large number of Twitter accounts and flood Twitter with vulnerability mentions [148]. In online markets and forums, the creation of accounts needs verification and, in some cases, technical demonstration of skills. While fake accounts are often themselves sold on the darkweb, it is difficult to purchase and maintain thousands of such fake accounts to post with them. Also, if one person is posting a large volume of discussions with CVE mentions, he or she can be identified by *username* or can be removed from the market/forum if many of his or her posts get downvoted for being irrelevant. As we detail in Chapter 3, such forums also function as a meritocracy [160], where users who contribute more are held in higher regard given their high reputation (which also makes it difficult to flood discussions with such information).

## 6.7 Discussion

**Viability of the model and cost of misclassification**. The performance achieved by our model as a first-line defense layer is very promising. Recall that a random forest classifier outputs a confidence score for every testing sample. A threshold can be set to identify the decision boundary. We shall note that all the results we report in this chapter are achieved based on hard-cut thresholds, such that all samples that are assigned confidence scores greater than a threshold $thr$ are predicted as to be exploited. Relying solely on a hard-cut threshold may not be good practice in real-world threat assessments; rather, $thr$ should be varied in accordance to other variables within an organization such that different thresholds can be set to different vendors (i.e., $thr_{ven1}$, $thr_{ven2}$) or information systems (i.e., $thr_{sys1}$, $thr_{sys2}$). For instance, if an organization hosts an important website on an Apache server, and the availability of this site is of top priority, then any vulnerability of the Apache server should receive high attention. The organization should put forward remediation plans regardless of additional vulnerabilities that may exist in other used systems.

Since it is very expensive to be responsive to that many security advisories (e.g., some patches may be unavailable, some systems may need to be taken offline to apply patches), assessing the likelihood of exploitation can help in quantifying risk and planning mitigation. Risk is always thought of as a function of likelihood (exploitation) and impact. The cost of classifying negative samples as *exploited* is the effort made to have them fixed. This involves patching or other remediation, such as controlling access or blocking network ports. Similarly, the cost of falsely classifying threatened vulnerability as *not to be exploited* depends on the impact it will cause if exploited. For example, if two companies run the same database management system, and one hosts a database with data about all business transactions, while the other hosts a database with data that are of little value to the company, the resulting costs of a data breach would be significantly different.

**Model success and failure cases.** By analyzing the false negatives and false positives, we gain an understanding of why and where our model performs well and where it is ineffective. We first look into false negatives. The 10 exploited vulnerabilities (about 18% of the exploited samples in the testing dataset) that received the lowest confidence scores seem to have common features. For example, nine of these appear in Adobe products, namely, Flash Player (five vulnerabilities) and Acrobat Reader (four vulnerabilities). Flash Player vulnerabilities seem to have very similar descriptions from the NVD. The same is observed for Acrobat Reader. We also observe that they were assigned CVE numbers on the same day (April 27, 2016), and seven out of these nine were published on the same day as well (July 12, 2016) and assigned a CVSS base score of 10.0 (except for one, assigned 7.0). The other vulnerability exists in the Windows Azure Active Directory (CVSS score of 4.3). Out of these 10 vulnerabilities, 1 had a verified PoC archived on EDB before it was detected in the wild, and another had a ZDI mention, while none were mentioned in our online hacker collection. We attribute misclassifying these vulnerabilities to the limited representation of these samples in the training dataset. Moreover, this observation signifies the importance of avoiding experiments on time-intermixed data, a point discussed in Section 6.2. We also study false positive samples that received high confidence scores – samples our model predicted as exploited, while they were not. For our random forest classifier, all false positives we examine affect Microsoft products, although we do not use vendor as a feature. Our model is able to infer the vendor from other textual features. We assume that this level of overfitting is unavoidable and marginal, and we attribute this largely to the limitations on our ground truth. The model is highly generalizable though. We find examples of vulnerabilities from other vendors with confidence scores close to the $thr$ we set; however, we cannot assume that they were exploited.

## 6.8 Related Work

Predicting cyber-security events is one of those domains that have recently received growing attention [11, 23, 52, 92, 170]. While important for prioritizing defense measures, only little work in this line of research has been proposed so far, compared to work proposed on detecting cyber-threats that are already present in an organization's network. Previous studies have attempted to address this problem using both standard scoring systems (in particular, the CVSS base score) and machine learning techniques. An approach to predict the likelihood that a software product contains a yet-to-be-discovered vulnerability was proposed in [198]. In this study, data feeds from the NVD were leveraged to predict the next time a vulnerability will be discovered in a given software product. The results showed a poor predictive capability of the NVD data. The CVSS version 2.0 is a poor indicator of predicting whether a vulnerability will be exploited, as demonstrated by [7]. The authors' analysis showed that deciding to patch a vulnerability because of a high CVSS score is equivalent to randomly guessing which vulnerability to patch. Yet, integrating information about whether a PoC exploit is available should significantly improve the accuracy of such a decision [7].

Our approach closely resembles previous work on using publicly disclosed vulnerability information as features to train machine learning models to predict whether a given vulnerability will be exploited. Bozorgi et al. [23] proposed a model that engineered features from two online sources, namely, the Open Source Vulnerability Database (OSVDB)[32] and the NVD, to predict whether PoCs will be developed for a particular vulnerability. In their data, 73% of the vulnerabilities are labeled as exploited, a percentage that is orders of magnitude higher than what is reported in recent literature (less than 3%) [7, 52, 120, 148] – a result confirmed in this chapter. The reason behind this is that the authors considered the existence of PoC as weaponized exploitation, which is incorrect for most cases. Using this assumption and a support vector machine classifier, their approach predicts whether vulnerabilities will have PoCs available, a problem that is different from the one studied in this chapter. A similar technique was employed by [52] using the NVD as the data source. They used ExploitDB as ground truth, with 27% of vulnerabilities labeled as exploited (having PoC exploits). High accuracy was achieved on a balanced dataset. Our analysis aims to predict vulnerabilities that will be weaponized for real-world attacks and not just have PoC exploits available.

Building on the work that leverages publicly disclosed vulnerabilities, Sabottle et al. [148] looked into predicting exploitation of vulnerabilities discussed on Twitter.[33] In this study, Twitter short posts, called tweets,[34] that had references to CVE numbers were collected. A linear SVM classifier is trained for prediction. As the source of ground truth data, Symantec attack signatures are used to label positive samples. Comparing to previous predictive studies, even though the authors of [148] maintained the class ratio of 1.3%

[32] https://blog.osvdb.org.
[33] https://twitter.com.
[34] On the Twitter platform, a post is called a *tweet*, and each tweet is limited to 280 characters.

vulnerabilities exploited, they used a resampled and balanced dataset to report the results. Additionally, the temporal aspect (training data should precede testing) of the tweets is not maintained while performing the experiments. This temporal intermixing causes future events to influence the prediction of past events, a practice that is shown to lead to unrealistic predictions [26]. In this chapter, the class imbalance and the temporal aspect are respected while reporting the results.

Particularly for the cyber-security incident prediction problem, the impact of adversarial interference for hackers aiming to poison and evade the machine learning models has been discussed. Hao et al. [76] proposed a prediction model to predict the web domain abuse based on features derived from the behavior of users at the time of registration. They studied different evading strategies attackers can use and demonstrated that evading attempts are expensive to attackers. Their model's reliance on different sets of features allows for limiting the decrease in false positive rate. Other researchers have also discussed the robustness of their models against adversarial attacks, such as [92, 148]. We run simulation experiments and demonstrate that the impact is very limited, as discussed in Section 6.6.

## 6.9 Conclusion

In this chapter, we proposed an approach that aggregates early signs of vulnerability exploitation from various online sources to predict *if* vulnerabilities will be exploited, a problem that is directly related to patch prioritization. Our machine learning model not only outperforms existing severity scoring standards but also outperforms approaches that combine information from social media sites like Twitter for exploit prediction. Existing scoring standards suffer high false positive rates: too many vulnerabilities are overrated, making it difficult for security teams to prioritize what to patch. Our approach, however, achieves a high true positive rate while maintaining a low false positive rate.

# 7

# Predicting Enterprise-Targeted External Cyber-attacks

## 7.1 Introduction

The majority of recent cyber-incidents are believed to have originated from threat actors sending malicious emails – emails with malicious attachments or with links to destinations that serve malicious content [68, 178]. A 2017 Verizon investigation report stated that 75% of breaches were perpetrated by outsiders exploiting known vulnerabilities [187]. Although the cyber-security research community constantly demonstrates that these incidents could have been avoided, proactively identifying and systematically understanding *when* and *why* such events are likely to occur is still challenging. We demonstrate in Chapter 6 how cyber-threat intelligence, collected from online hacker communities, is useful for predicting *if* exploits are going to be circulated in the wild. Here, we present an approach to predict *when*, in the future, certain organization-targeted cyber-attacks are likely to occur, an important prediction task for cyber-security analysts, allowing them to prioritize what defense measures to deploy first. With predictive features and enough data, statistical learning approaches often provide accurate predictions in terms of standard performance measures, such as precision and recall, which, for many prediction tasks, are most desirable. For other tasks, generating transparent and explainable predictions that allow human experts to understand the reasoning that leads to certain predictions could be more valuable than the predictions themselves [143]. This is why we equally consider here these two properties: accuracy and explainability.

In this chapter, we describe a technical approach that identifies indicators of certain enterprise-targeted cyber-attacks from online sources of cyber-threat intelligence (hacker forums and marketplaces hosted on a variety of networks) and uses them to predict attacks in the future. In doing so, we use concepts from logic programming, in particular, the concepts of point frequency function (*pfr*) from annotated probabilistic temporal logic (APT-logic) [162, 165, 172] to learn rules of the form: "if certain hacker activity is observed at a given time point, then there will be $x$ number of attacks of type $y$, targeting organization $o$ in exactly $\Delta t$ time points, with probability $p$." In addition to the online discussions obtained from our hacker data repository, we obtain more than 600 historical records of targeted real-world cyber-attack incidents. These incidents are recorded from the logs of two large enterprises participating in the IARPA Cyber-attack Automated Unconventional Sensor Environment (CAUSE)[1] program.

During the execution of the CAUSE program, our approach was integrated into a deployed system that submitted real-time warnings originated from multiple predictive models. Our approach – explained in this chapter and originally presented in [10] – produces warnings often connected to a single source. However, the ephemeral nature of many online sources leads to challenges in modeling and predicting over an extended period of time. Therefore, we extend the capabilities of the original approach using indicators that capture aggregated discussion trends across multiple and additional hacker community platforms (see Section 7.8). These platforms include online hacker sites on multiple networks as well as environments such as Chan sites and social media. The main goal that devised the design of the current approach is to generate warnings that predict *when* cyber-attacks are likely to occur. These warnings are required to be

- **Timely**, to indicate the exact point in time when a predicted attack will occur;
- **Actionable**, to provide metadata/warning details, that is, the target enterprise, type of attack, volume, software vulnerabilities, and tags identified from the hacker discussions;
- **Accurate**, to predict unseen real-world attacks with an average increase in F1 of over 45% for one enterprise and 57% for the other, compared to a baseline approach;
- **Transparent**, to allow analysts to easily trace the warnings back to the rules triggered, discussions that fired the rules, and so on.

The remainder of this chapter is organized as follows. Section 7.2, presents the preliminaries to formally detail our logic programming approach. Section 7.3 explains the data used. We describe the processing flow in Section 7.4. Section 7.5 offers an overview of the design and components of the developed approach. Empirical self-assessment results are provided in Section 7.6.3.

[1] www.iarpa.gov/index.php/research-programs/cause.

Section 7.7 introduces technical challenges that arise with predictions over an extended period of time, while Section 7.8 develops an approach to address these challenges. Section 7.9 presents the related work. Finally, Section 7.10 concludes the chapter.

## 7.2 Preliminaries

In this section, we define the syntax and semantics of annotated probabilistic temporal logic (APT-logic) applied to our domain, which is built upon the work of Shakarian et al. [165].

### 7.2.1 Syntax

**Herbrand base.** We use $B_{\mathcal{L}}$ to denote the Herbrand base (finite set of ground atoms) of a first-order logical language $\mathcal{L}$. Then, we divide $B_{\mathcal{L}}$ into two disjoint sets, $B_{\mathcal{L}\{conditions\}}$ and $B_{\mathcal{L}\{actions\}}$, so that $B_{\mathcal{L}} \equiv B_{\mathcal{L}\{conditions\}} \cup B_{\mathcal{L}\{actions\}}$. $B_{\mathcal{L}\{conditions\}}$ comprehends the atoms allowed only in the premise of APT rules, representing *conditions* or user activity performed in online hacking communities, such as $mention\_on(forum\_1, debian)$. On the other hand, $B_{\mathcal{L}\{actions\}}$ comprehends the atoms allowed only in the conclusion of APT rules, representing *actions* or malicious activities reported by the data providers in their own facilities, such as $attack(data\_provider, malicious\_email, x)$.

**Formulas.** Complex sentences (formulas) are constructed recursively from atoms, using parentheses and the logical connectives ($\neg$ negation, $\vee$ disjunction, $\wedge$ conjunction).

**Time formulas.** If $F$ is a formula and $t$ is a time point, then $F_t$ is a time formula, which states that $F$ is true at time $t$.

**Probabilistic time formulas.** If $\phi$ is a time formula and $[l,u]$ is a probability interval $\subseteq [0,1]$, then $\phi : [l,u]$ is a probabilistic time formula (*ptf*). Intuitively, $\phi : [l,u]$ says $\phi$ is true with a probability in $[l,u]$, or using the complete notation, $F_t : [l,u]$ says $F$ is true at time $t$ with a probability in $[l,u]$.

**APT rules.** Suppose condition $F$ and action $G$ are formulas, $t$ is a natural number, $[l,u]$ is a probability interval, and $fr \in \mathcal{F}$ is a frequency function symbol (we will define those functions later with the semantics of APT rules). Then $F \overset{fr}{\rightsquigarrow} G : [t,l,u]$ is an annotated probabilistic temporal (APT) rule, which, informally speaking, computes the probability that $G$ is true in exactly $\Delta t$ time units after $F$ becomes true. For instance, the APT rule below predicts that the data provider will be targeted by a single malicious email, in exactly three time units after the software product *"debian"* is discussed in a malicious hacking forum belonging to the set of forums $set\_forums\_1$, with a probability between 44% and 62%:

$$mention\_on(set\_forum\_1, debian) \overset{pfr}{\rightsquigarrow} attack(data\_provider, malicious\_email, 1) : [3, 0.44, 0.62]. \tag{7.1}$$

### 7.2.2 Semantics

**World.** A world is a set of ground atoms that belongs to $B_{\mathcal{L}}$. It describes a possible state of the (real) world being modeled by an APT-logic program. Examples of worlds follow:

- $\{spike(Amazon\_AWS)\}$,
- $\{mention\_on(set\_forum\_1, debian), attack(data\_provider, malicious\_email, 1)\}$,
- $\{attack(data\_provider, malicious\_email, 1)\}$, and
- $\{\}$.

**Thread.** A thread is a series of worlds that models the domain over time, where each world corresponds to a discrete time point in $\mathcal{T} = \{1, \ldots, t_{max}\}$. $Th(i)$ specifies that according to the thread $Th$, the world at time $i$ will be $Th(i)$. Given a thread $Th$ and a time formula $\phi$, we say $Th$ satisfies $\phi$ (denoted $Th \models \phi$)

- If $\phi \equiv F_t$ for some ground time formula $F_t$, then $Th(t)$ satisfies $F$;
- If $\phi \equiv \neg\rho$ for some ground time formula $\rho$, then $Th$ does not satisfy $\rho$;
- If $\phi \equiv \rho_1 \wedge \rho_2$ for some ground time formulas $\rho_1$ and $\rho_2$, then $Th$ satisfies $\rho_1$ and $Th$ satisfies $\rho_2$; and
- If $\phi \equiv \rho_1 \vee \rho_2$ for some ground time formulas $\rho_1$ and $\rho_2$, then $Th$ satisfies $\rho_1$ or $Th$ satisfies $\rho_2$.

**Frequency functions.** A frequency function represents temporal relationships within a thread, checking how often a world that satisfies formula $F$ is followed by a world that satisfies formula $G$. Formally, a frequency function $fr$ belonging to $\mathcal{F}$ maps quadruples of the form $(Th, F, G, t)$ to [0,1] of real numbers. Among the possible ones proposed in [162], we investigate here alternative definitions for the *point frequency function* (pfr), which specifies how frequently action $G$ follows condition $F$ in "exactly" $\Delta t$ time points. To support ongoing security operations, we need to relax the original assumption of a finite time horizon $t_{max}$ in [162, 165]. Therefore, we introduce here a different but equivalent formulation for *pfr* that does not rely on a finite time horizon. To accomplish that, we first need to define how a *ptf* can be satisfied in our model. If we consider $A$ as the set of all ptfs satisfied by a given thread $Th$, then we say that $Th$ satisfies $F_t : [l,u]$ (denoted $Th \models F_t : [l,u]$)

- If $F = a$ for some ground $a$, then $\exists a_t : [l',u'] \in A$ $s.t.$ $[l',u'] \sqsupseteq [l,u]$;
- If $F_t : [l,u] = \neg F'_t : [l,u]$ for some ground formula $F'$, then $Th \models F'_t : [1-u, 1-l]$;
- If $F_t : [l,u] = F'_t : [l,u] \wedge F''_t : [l,u]$ for some ground formulas $F'$ and $F''$, then $Th \models F'_t : [l,u]$ and $Th \models F''_t : [l,u]$; and
- If $F_t : [l,u] = F'_t : [l,u] \vee F''_t : [l,u]$ for some ground formulas $F'$ and $F''$, then $Th \models F'_t : [l,u]$ or $Th \models F''_t : [l,u]$.

The resulting formulation of pfr is shown in Equation 7.2, which is equivalent to the original one proposed in [162] when $t_{max}$ comprises the whole thread $Th$ (all time points):

$$pfr(Th, F, G, \Delta t) = \left[ \frac{\sum_{t|Th\models F_t:[l,u] \wedge Th\models G_{t+\Delta t}:[l',u']} l'}{\sum_{t|Th\models F_t:[l,u]} u}, \frac{\sum_{t|Th\models F_t:[l,u] \wedge Th\models G_{t+\Delta t}:[l',u']} u'}{\sum_{t|Th\models F_t:[l,u]} l} \right]. \tag{7.2}$$

**Satisfaction of APT rules and programs.** $Th$ satisfies an APT rule $F \overset{pfr}{\rightsquigarrow} G : [\Delta t, l, u]$ (denoted $Th \models F \overset{pfr}{\rightsquigarrow} G : [\Delta t, l, u]$) iff

$$pfr(Th, F, G, \Delta t) \subseteq [l,u]. \tag{7.3}$$

**Probability intervals.** For this application, the possible values for $l, l', u$, and $u'$ are either 0 or 1. Therefore, the rules learned using Equation 7.2 always have point probabilities. To derive a probability interval $[l,u]$ corresponding to a point probability $p$ of rule $r$, we use standard deviation (i.e., $\sigma$) computed from the binomial distribution – remember that the possible outcome of event $G$ following event $F$ is either 0 or 1. We subtract/add 1 standard deviation from/to the point probability to determine the lower/upper bounds of the probability range, that is, $[p-\sigma, p+\sigma]$. The standard deviation is computed as follows:

$$\sigma = \frac{\sqrt{support\_F * p * (1-p)}}{support\_F}. \tag{7.4}$$

where $support\_F$ is the number of times the precondition or $F$ is observed.

For example, the precondition of the rule shown in Equation 7.1 was satisfied by the thread 32 times. Of these, 17 times the postcondition of the rule was also satisfied, resulting in a point probability of approximately 0.53. The value of $\sigma$ is approximately 0.09, hence the probability range $[0.44, 0.62]$.

## 7.3 Dataset Description

This section explains the ground truth data obtained from the data providers and discusses the data collection infrastructure that supplies hacker discussion data feeds.

### 7.3.1 Online Hacker Community Infrastructure

As an extension of the data used in Chapter 6, here we collect posts from more than 300 platforms, including forums and marketplaces hosted across multiple networks.

### 7.3.2 Enterprise-Relevant External Threats

To construct rules and evaluate the performance of the learned model, we use data from historical records of attack attempts that are extracted from the logs of two enterprises participating in the IARPA CAUSE program. One of the two enterprises is a defense industrial base (referred to as "Armstrong"), while the other is a financial services organization (referred to as "Dexter"). The database is distributed to the CAUSE performers in increments, once every few months. Each data point is a record of a detected deliberate, malicious attempt to gain unauthorized access, alter or destroy data, or interrupt services or resources in the environment of the participating organizations. Those malicious attempts were detected in an uncontrolled environment and by different security defense commercial products such as anti-virus, intrusion detection systems, and hardware controls. Each ground truth (GT) record includes ID, format version, reported time, occurrence time, event type, and target industry.[2] The types of attacks included in the GT dataset are as follows:

- **Malicious email (M-E).** A malicious attempt is identified as a malicious email event if an email is received by the organization and it contains either

[2] We intentionally skip some details about other fields of the GT records due to the limitation in space and irrelevance to the scope of this chapter.

a malicious email attachment or a link (embedded URL or IP address) to a known malicious destination.

- **Malicious destination (M-D).** A visit to a URL or an IP address is identified as a malicious destination if the visited address hosts malicious content.
- **Endpoint malware (E-M).** A malware on endpoint event is identified if malware is discovered on an endpoint device. This includes, but is not limited to, ransomware, spyware, and adware.

## 7.4 Extracting Indicators of Cyber-threats

We identify the hacking community discussions where vulnerabilities are referenced using regular expressions.[3] Similar vulnerabilities, that is, affecting similar software products, are grouped together. The said grouping is determined based on a CVE mapping to groups of CPEs. Prior to conducting this study, we identified more than 100 groups of CPEs, that is, the affected software product is common within each group of CPEs (e.g., Microsoft Office, Apache Tomcat, and Intel). Moreover, CVEs are mapped to some nation-state threat actors that are known to leverage certain CVEs as part of their attack tactics. Perhaps among the most well-known of such threat groups is the North Korean group HIDDEN COBRA, which was recently identified to be responsible for an increasing number of cyber-attacks on US targets [36]. This mapping is determined based on an encoded list of threat actors along with vulnerabilities they favor. The list is compiled by manually analyzing cyber-threat reports that were published by cyber-security firms.[4] The final CPE groupings and nation-state actor mappings are used as preconditions by the *learner*.

## 7.5 A Novel Logic Programming-Based Cyber-threat Prediction System

This section provides discussions about the components of our state-of-the-art prediction system, as well as the input and output data. Figure 7.1 shows the system design, which has two main components: the *learner* and the *predictor*.

[3] For more explanation, see https://cve.mitre.org/cve/identifiers/syntaxchange.html.
[4] See the Kaspersky Lab's 2016 report as an example at https://media.kaspersky.com/en/business-security/enterprise/KL_Report_Exploits_in_2016_final.pdf.

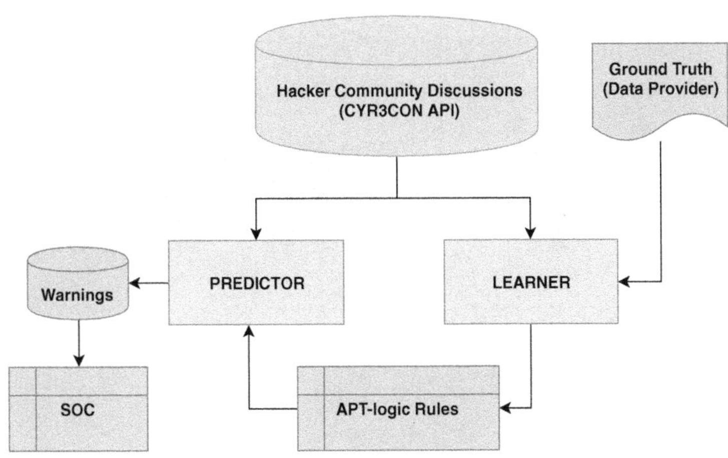


Figure 7.1 Logic programming-based cyber-threat prediction system.

### 7.5.1 Learner

The learner learns APT-logic rules that link indicators of cyber-threats and real-world attack events. The indicators of threats are annotated from a collection of hacker discussions with vulnerability mentions, following the approach discussed in Section 7.4. The attack events are cyber-attack attempts observed by the data providers. Each event, a CPE group or an attack attempt, is annotated with the date when the corresponding vulnerability was mentioned or when the incident was recorded. These dates are mapped to discrete time points to construct the *thread*, which is used in the rule learning approach discussed in Section 7.2. The output of the learner is an APT-logic program, that is, a set of APT rules and ptfs. These rules, along with indicators annotated from the hacker community discussions, are used by the predictor to produce warnings. Figure 7.2 depicts the increase in the attack likelihood.

To compute this increase, we compare the attack likelihood computed from the learned APT rules to the prior probability of attacks – the probability of attack with no knowledge of hacker activity, showing the percentage gain. The increase is significant, which is a promising observation for accurate predictions.

### 7.5.2 Predictor

The *predictor* uses the output of the *learner*, i.e., the APT-logic program and the indicators annotated from online hacker discussions. It triggers rules if any indicators are observed that match the preconditions of the rules in the

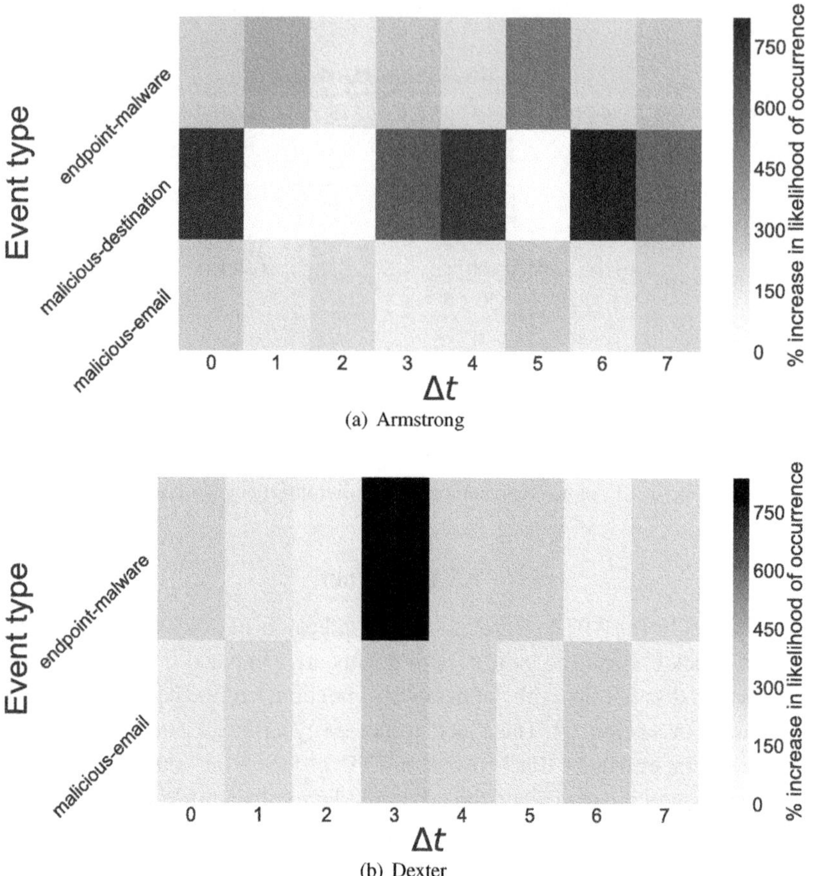

(a) Armstrong


(b) Dexter

Figure 7.2 Percentage increase in attack likelihood over attack prior probability for the learned rules, per $\Delta t$ per event type, and for the two companies (a) Armstrong and (b) Dexter.

APT-logic program [10]. If a match exists, the system generates a warning with metadata, such as the probability, event type, and target organization. This allows analysts to easily trace the warnings back to the rules that were triggered, discussions that fired the rules, and so on. Figure 7.3 shows two screenshots taken from a deployed system that uses our approach.

## 7.6 Predicting Enterprise-Targeted Attacks

During phase 2 of the IARPA CAUSE program, our approach was integrated into a deployed system that generates, fuses, and actively submits warnings

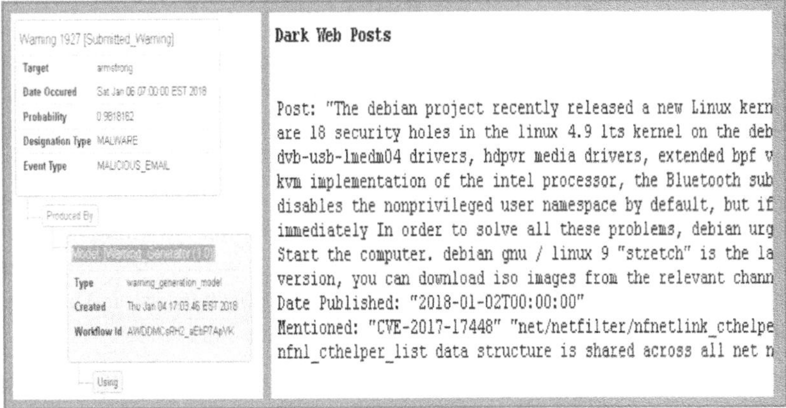


Figure 7.3 Two screenshots from a deployed system that uses our approach.

to a security operations center (SOC) for performance evaluation purposes. Details about the deployed system, provided in [10], are outside the focus of this chapter, but we follow some of the evaluation practices adopted by the CAUSE program (i.e., using the subset of the evaluation metrics that are relevant to the prediction task). Furthermore, the warnings that are submitted by each system are evaluated by the SOC on a monthly basis. However, the said evaluations are aggregated for all models belonging to a single system. To evaluate our approach, it needs to be isolated from other models used by the same system. In this section, we internally evaluate our approach before the warnings are fused with warnings from other models.

### 7.6.1 Experimental Settings

We perform evaluations on the warnings targeting Armstrong that were submitted during July, August, and September 2017, being the results aggregated by months. Dexter warnings were submitted from July 1 to 28, 2016, being the results aggregated by periods of seven days. These time windows differ because the Armstrong dataset covers a longer period than the one covered by Dexter, and there are no more Dexter data provided or evaluated by the program. The reported records of malicious destination for Dexter only cover a period that ends before the testing period starts; hence they are not evaluated. For each data provider, rules are learned from all the records preceding the testing period.

### 7.6.2 Evaluation

**Pairing ground truth events with warnings.** To receive a score, each warning needs to be paired up with a single ground truth event occurring within the same day, or one day after the attack prediction date, that is, a one-to-one relationship – this is a requirement of the CAUSE program.[5] To do so, we use the Hungarian assignment algorithm [117] to solve the warning-to-ground truth assignment problem, with the objective to maximize warning-to-attack lead time. The results of the Hungarian algorithm (i.e., warning-to-ground truth assignments) are used to evaluate the performance of the system. The same approach is used with predictions produced by the baseline model.

**Evaluation metrics.** We use the standard evaluation metrics, precision, recall, and F1, as done in Chapter 6. Here, precision is the fraction of warnings that match ground truth events, while recall is the fraction of ground truth events that are matched. F1 is just the harmonic mean of precision and recall. By using these metrics, we present a performance comparison between our approach and a baseline model. Additionally, we show that a fused model can benefit from the temporal correlations and statistical characteristics captured by the system and the baseline model, respectively.

### 7.6.3 Results

We observe that our approach outperforms a baseline system that randomly generates $x$ number of warnings each day such that each value of $x$ has a chance proportional to its frequency of occurrence in the historical data. We repeat the baseline for 100 runs and take the average of each metric. In the real-time deployment of our approach, human experts can evaluate the warnings by leveraging the other capabilities of the system, that is, *transparency* and *actionability* through a Web UI dashboard. However, in those experiments, any triggered rule is counted, which is not necessarily important given other details. That said, our approach (DARKMENTION) scores significantly higher than the baseline system, as shown in Table 7.1.

## 7.7 Technical Challenges

The desired non-functional requirements related to the generated warnings (i.e., timely, actionable, accurate, and transparent, as discussed in Section 7.1) need to be maintained over time. Given the numerous factors related to both

[5] See [10] for an elaborate explanation.

Table 7.1 *Evaluation results*

| Dataset | Type | Testing starts | No. GT events | DARKMENTION | | | | Baseline[a] (average of 100 runs) | | | | % gain in F1 |
|---|---|---|---|---|---|---|---|---|---|---|---|---|
| | | | | No. warn. | Prec. | Recall | F1 | No. warn. | Prec. | Recall | F1 | |
| Armstrong | M-E | Jul 2017 | 24 | 32 | 0.313 | **0.417** | **0.357** | 11.759 | **0.417** | 0.205 | 0.271 | 32% |
| | | Aug 2017 | 11 | 3 | **1.000** | 0.273 | **0.429** | 11.966 | **0.289** | 0.315 | 0.299 | 43% |
| | | Sep 2017 | 13 | 18 | 0.167 | 0.231 | 0.194 | 12.793 | **0.249** | **0.249** | **0.247** | –21% |
| | M-D | Jul 2017 | 4 | 12 | **0.167** | **0.500** | **0.250** | 3.534 | 0.099 | 0.091 | 0.090 | 178% |
| | | Aug 2017 | 9 | 23 | 0.174 | **0.444** | **0.250** | 3.121 | **0.232** | 0.086 | 0.120 | 108% |
| | | Sep 2017 | 3 | 10 | **0.100** | **0.333** | **0.154** | 2.948 | 0.071 | 0.075 | 0.068 | 126% |
| | E-M | Jul 2017 | 14 | 10 | 0.300 | **0.214** | **0.250** | 8.552 | **0.326** | 0.200 | 0.242 | 3% |
| | | Aug 2017 | 18 | 45 | 0.200 | **0.500** | **0.286** | 9.155 | **0.324** | 0.168 | 0.217 | 32% |
| | | Sep 2017 | 17 | 21 | **0.286** | **0.353** | **0.316** | 8.879 | 0.247 | 0.127 | 0.164 | 93% |
| Dexter | M-E | 1 Jul 2016 | 2 | 13 | 0.150 | **1.000** | **0.267** | 2.720 | **0.157** | 0.205 | 0.169 | 58% |
| | | 8 Jul 2016 | 7 | 10 | 0.500 | **0.714** | **0.588** | 2.610 | **0.655** | 0.253 | 0.348 | 69% |
| | | 15 Jul 2016 | 9 | 6 | 0.333 | **0.222** | 0.267 | 2.770 | **0.619** | 0.188 | **0.276** | –3% |
| | | 22 Jul 2016 | 4 | 2 | **0.500** | 0.250 | 0.333 | 3.050 | 0.469 | **0.355** | **0.385** | –14% |
| | E-M | 1 Jul 2016 | 1 | 2 | **0.500** | **1.000** | **0.667** | 1.790 | 0.189 | 0.330 | 0.226 | 195% |
| | | 8 Jul 2016 | 3 | 4 | **0.250** | **0.333** | **0.286** | 1.750 | 0.245 | 0.167 | 0.186 | 54% |
| | | 15 Jul 2016 | 3 | 1 | **1.000** | **0.333** | **0.500** | 1.740 | 0.281 | 0.190 | 0.217 | 130% |
| | | 22 Jul 2016 | 4 | 2 | **0.500** | **0.250** | **0.333** | 1.780 | 0.383 | 0.208 | 0.257 | 30% |

[a]A simple baseline model that generates $x$ number of warnings each day based on the prior probability of each possible value of $x$ that was seen in the training data.

intelligence data (the ephemeral nature of hacker discussion platforms) and enterprise data (data from a security information event manager, or SIEM, can be subject to schema differences due to policy changes over time), we examine further requirements for our approach.

**Changing volume of cyber-threat intelligence data.** In many applications of event prediction, the volume of signals from the monitored sensors is assumed to remain the same across the learning and predictive phases. However, this assumption does not hold for cyber-threat intelligence data. This is mainly because of the ephemeral nature of online hacker sites due to, for example, law enforcement actions, malicious hackers going "dark" (offline), operational security measures employed by cyber-criminals, and differences induced by adding newer data sources. In the approach discussed so far, changes in the volume of incoming cyber-threat intelligence data would have a direct impact on the number of warnings, affecting the system's performance.

**Concept drift.** Hacking tactics advance very rapidly to react to the latest advances in cyber-security; that is, new vulnerabilities are discovered, new exploits are integrated with malware kits, attack signatures are identified, and so on. Likewise, the attacks observed in the wild and the activities of hackers on hacker community websites, including social media, are always evolving [26]. This change in the underlying data distribution for both the hacker discussions and the predicted events is known as concept drift [190].

## 7.8 An Extension to the Current Approach

The approach presented thus far produces warnings connected to single sources. To account for the challenges presented in Section 7.7, we extend our approach to consider a variety of cyber-threat intelligence sources spanning hacker communities around the globe, including environments such as Chan sites, social media, paste sites, and Gray-hat communities,[6] in addition to hacker platforms hosted in multiple network protocols (the surface-web, the deepweb, and the darkweb). This includes more than 400 platforms with content produced in more than 18 languages. Non-English-language postings are translated to English using various commercial language translation services, such as the Google Translate API.

[6] Hackers who pivot between ethical and malicious hacking, in which they exploit software weaknesses in a computer system without the owner's permission or knowledge. The goal is often to bring the weakness to the owner's attention.

As noted, changes in the volume of the incoming cyber-threat intelligence data can impact the volume of warnings produced. In this extension, we consider indicators that are evaluated based on the volume of hacker discussions, that is, capturing discussion trends exceeding thresholds computed from a sliding time window – this approach is further discussed in this section. To account for the potential impact of concept drift, in each month, we run our learner on data from the previous six months and use the resulting rules to predict events in the examined month, as explained in Section 7.6.3.

### 7.8.1 Extracting Entity Tags

The threat intelligence sources we use supply a vast amount of textual content over time. We utilize a commercial natural language processing API, TextRazor,[7] which leverages a wide range of machine learning techniques (including recurrent neural networks) to recognize entities from the context of postings. Each extracted entity is associated with a confidence score quantifying the confidence in the annotation. We set a lower bound on the confidence score to retain only those entities that are relevant. Two steps are taken to extract the final indicators: (1) annotating spikes in the volume of individually extracted tags, and (2) for those tags, identifying sets that frequently spike together.

**Annotating spiking tags.** We seek to gain an understanding of abnormal hacker activities that could correlate with attack events. To do so, we define what abnormal activities are, and use them as preconditions of APT-logic rules. They may or may not correlate with actual attack events, but the APT-logic program will only contain the rules whose precondition is found to correlate with the attack events. To identify such abnormalities, we consider common entity tags that appear on most days, that is, on 90 days or more, as training periods span 180 days. An entity is regarded as abnormal if it is observed on a given day with a spiking volume. Spikes are determined using statistical control charts [114], that is, when the count of times an entity $f$ is observed exceeds a moving median added to a multiplier of a moving standard deviation.[8] We use the predicate $spike(f)$, which indicates whether entity $f$ is spiking on a given time point. To check whether the thread $Th$ satisfies $spike(f)$ at some time point $t$, we use three utility functions:

1. $count(f,t)$, which returns the number of times an entity $f$ is extracted on day $t$;

[7] www.textrazor.com.
[8] We use a sliding window of 20 days.

2. $median(f,t,window)$, which returns the median value of $count(f,t_i)$ observed from a series of days (denoted $window$) – the last day of this series is day $t$; and
3. $stDiv(f,t,window)$, which returns the standard deviation of $count(f,t_i)$ for that series of days.

We say the thread $Th$ satisfies $spike(f)$ at some time point $t$, denoted $Th(t) \models spike(f)$, iff

$$count(f,t) > (median(f,t,window) \\ + (multiplier \times stDiv(f,t,window))).$$

**Frequent itemset mining.** As previously explained, preconditions could be atoms or formulas (i.e., an itemset). We only consider those formulas that are frequently satisfied in the historical data. To do so, we use the Apriori algorithm [75]. The Apriori algorithm takes as input a database of transactions – the annotated spiking tags are grouped by days, where each day corresponds to a transaction. The algorithm then produces all itemsets of hacker activities that are frequently observed together. The identified itemsets are considered as preconditions and used by both the learner and the predictor.

### 7.8.2 Results

**Fusion.** Here, we use a simple combining strategy to test the performance of a fused model. We first combine the warnings from the two models, that is, our approach and the baseline. The warnings are grouped by their generation date and prediction date. Then, half of the warnings are removed from each group. The goal is to leverage the power of the individual approaches while limiting their intersection, that is, removing half of the warnings.

**Performance comparison.** Figure 7.4 shows the precision-recall curve for each of the testing months. By itself, our approach performs comparably to the baseline in terms of F1 – specifically providing higher precision in the case of lower recall. We note that when our approach is combined with the baseline, the results improve further. The combined approach can significantly outperform the baseline in terms of both precision and recall, yielding a recall increase of at least 14%, while maintaining precision. Furthermore, the baseline does not allow for a trade-off between precision and recall, while our approach produces warnings with probability values, as discussed in Section 7.2. This enables not only better trade-off between performance metrics, but also a metric approximating the importance of each warning, allowing human analysts to prioritize investigations.

Table 7.2 *Examples of preconditions of rules that would have generated warnings preceding attack incidents*

| Precondition | Probability | $\sigma$ | Warning date | Lead time (days) |
|---|---|---|---|---|
| spike(Credit card) ∧ spike(Gmail) | 0.88 | 0.07 | 26 Aug | 1 |
| spike(Email) ∧ spike(Security hacker) | 0.86 | 0.08 | 16 Aug | 1 |
| spike(Google Play) | 0.92 | 0.04 | 13 Aug | 2 |

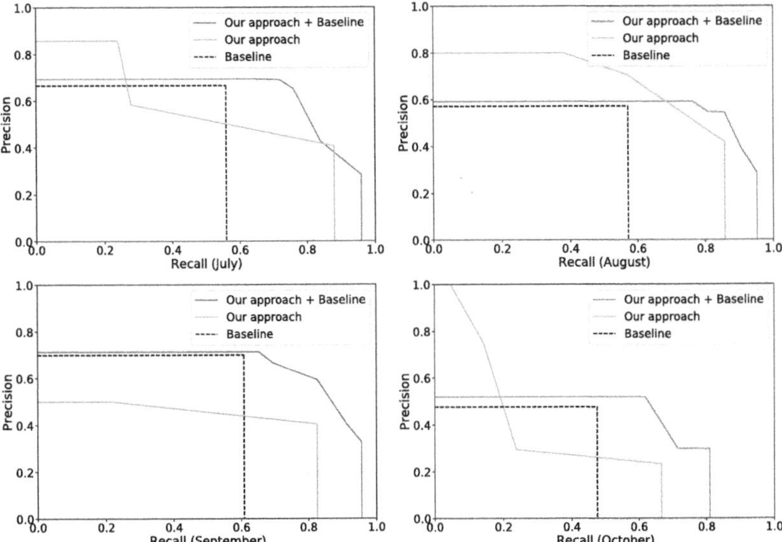


Figure 7.4 Precision-recall curves for the fused approach, our approach, and the baseline model, respectively, for four months: July, August, September, and October.

**Transparent predictions.** Our approach supports transparent predictions so that the user knows why certain warnings are generated. The user can trace back to the rule corresponding to a warning and view its precondition. Table 7.2 shows a few examples of preconditions of rules that generated warnings preceding attack incidents.

The user can further pinpoint the collection of hacker discussions that are responsible for the warning. For example, Figure 7.5 shows a word cloud generated from the collection of posts resulting in a warning submitted on August 23. The warning predicts an event on August 25, that is, $\Delta t$ of 2. An event of malicious email is then observed by Armstrong on August 26.

Figure 7.5 A word cloud generated from the text of posts that resulted in a positive warning on August 23.

## 7.9 Related Work

The task of selecting and deploying cyber-security countermeasures is generally expensive [35, 121, 147]. Therefore, the problem of predicting cyber-security-related events has gained growing interest. Yet, much of the current literature focuses on producing accurate predictions. Our work, however, considers other goals, such as producing interpretable predictions that support human-in-the-loop-driven decisions. This section reviews works that are related to both these goals.

**Predicting cyber-attack events.** Recently, predicting cyber-security events has received increasing attention [153, 170, 174]. For example, Soska and Christin [170] developed an ML-based approach that predicted whether a given website would turn malicious in the future using features derived from the web page structure as well as content and traffic statistics. Their approach was evaluated on a corpus of 444,519 websites (highly imbalanced, with only about 1% of the sites belonging to the positive class). The approach achieved a true positive rate of 66% and a false positive rate of 17%. Although they used the C4.5 decision tree classifier, the predictions were made by a single-layered ensemble approach using 100 features. The authors reported that the classification of non malicious sites was generally less trivial. Other studies focused on predicting cyber-security events of certain types, such as vulnerability exploitation [12, 12, 26, 148, 181]. These studies focused on vulnerability-targeted attacks, whereas our focus is on attacks targeting particular commercial enterprises. Similar to our prediction task, the works presented in [45, 70, 154] focused on (1) identifying and analyzing enterprise-targeted attack indicators from online cyber-security-related discussions and (2) producing predictions of possible future events. These studies mined attack indicators from (1) hacker sentiments identified in posts of hacking forums [45]; (2) word counts from hacker discussions on the deepweb and the darkweb, blogs, and Twitter [70]; or (3) social network structure generated from hacker forum discussions [154]. All these works used ML approaches solely focusing on producing accurate predictions, while we consider predictions that are accurate and transparent.

**Supporting explainable decisions.** Knowledge representation and reasoning (KRR) supports formally explainable reasoning, which is desired for many applications, including cyber-security incident prediction [167, 184]. Nunes et al. [128] developed an argumentation model for cyber-attribution using a dataset from the capture-the-flag event held at DEFCON,[9] a famous hacking conference. The model was based on a formal reasoning framework called defeasible logic programming [64]. Using a two-layered hybrid KRR-ML approach, the ML classification accuracy increased from 37% to 62%. While their approach supported automated reasoning, it was used for cyber-attribution only *after* the attacks were observed. Moreover, human-driven classification was not a desirable property. Instead, the reasoning framework was used to reduce the search space, thereby improving accuracy. Furthermore, Chapter 4 shows another example of a study that supports explainable reasoning and interpretable results. There, we investigate user adoption behavior to predict in which topic of a hacker forum users will post in the near future, given the influence produced by their peers. By formulating the problem as a sequential rule-mining task, we mine user posting rules through sequences of user posts to make adoption predictions, interpreting each rule of the form $X \Rightarrow Y$ as follows: "if $X$ (a set of hackers) engages in a given forum topic, $Y$ (a single hacker) is likely to engage in the same topic (or adopt it) with a given confidence afterward, mainly because of the influence of $X$." Note how those mined rules provide information about the reason for a given predicted post

[9] www.defcon.org.

(influence of $X$), allowing easy interpretation. Although we obtain impressive prediction results in Chapter 4, we address a prediction task that is different from the one addressed in this chapter.

## 7.10 Conclusion

In this chapter, we present a novel approach used in a system that predicts certain types of cyber-attacks targeting specific commercial enterprises. We explain the underlying logic programming framework (APT-logic) used to model the probabilistic temporal relationships between hacker activities (from hacking community online platforms) and attack incidents (recorded by the SIEM data providers). The developed approach uses APT-logic to first learn such relationships, captured in annotated rules, then use the learned rules in a deductive approach to reason about the possibility of future cyber-attacks and to generate warnings.

Moreover, this chapter addresses limitations of the original version of the approach, which used indicators of future attacks connected to single online sources – an approach no longer optimal to use because of the changing volume of intelligence data and the ephemeral nature of websites hosting cyber-criminals and malicious hackers. There are multiple reasons behind the changing landscape of hacker platforms, such as law enforcement actions, malicious hackers going "dark," operational security measures employed by cyber-criminals, and differences caused by newly added data sources. Therefore, this chapter (1) extends the sources used in [10] by using sources from other platforms, such as social media, and (2) introduces an alternative approach considering indicators that are evaluated based on volume of discussion trends exceeding a threshold computed from a sliding time window.

We demonstrate the viability of our approach by comparing it to a time series prediction baseline model. Specifically, we show that our approach performs comparably to the baseline model while supporting a favorable precision–recall trade-off and transparent predictions. Additionally, our system can benefit from the predictions produced by the baseline model. With the combined approach, recall improves by at least 14% compared to the baseline model. Finally, we look into using the system for data recorded by other data providers, and using intelligence data gathered not only from expert-hunted sources but also from sources gathered by web spiders.

# 8

# Bringing Social Network Analysis to Aid in Cyber-attack Prediction

## 8.1 Introduction

While it might be difficult to track the actual identity of users sharing information about software vulnerabilities in (malicious) hacking communities [151, 191], these threat actors leave behind footprints through their posts and interaction patterns. Thus, the information obtained from evolving reply networks of hacker discussions in online forums, in addition to the user and thread posting statistics, can be used to signal pending cyber-attacks. With this in mind, we hypothesize that the interaction dynamics focused on a set of specialized users and the attention broadcast by them to other posts in these platforms can also be leveraged to effectively generate security warnings.

In this chapter, we build a framework that makes use of the reply network structure of user interactions and a suite of social network features on top of supervised learning models to predict enterprise-related external cyber-attacks. In contrast to Chapter 7, we evaluate the dynamics of all kinds of forum discussions while filtering out noisy discussions to check whether a piece of information gains traction within important communities. We then mine patterns of anomalous behavior from these discussion dynamics and use them directly for our predictions. We quantify the correlation between the pattern of replies of a specific group of users we term *experts* – hackers who engage more frequently with popular vulnerability mentions in their posts gaining attention from other hackers[1] – and a real-world cyber-attack in the near future, checking how well those threats materialize for different organizations.

We validate our models on a binary classification problem that attempts to predict cyber-attacks on a daily basis for an organization. Using several controlled studies on features leveraging social network structure, we measure

[1] Note the difference from the general concept of key-hackers defined in Chapter 3. Here, experts are specifically linked to vulnerability mentions.

the extent to which the indicators from the hacker forums can be successfully used to predict attacks. We use information from 53 online hacker forums over a span of 17 months for the task. Our framework suggests that focusing on the reply path structure between groups of users based on random walk transitions and community structures has an advantage in terms of better performance compared to features that solely rely on either forum or user posting statistics prior to attacks. By using company agnostic unsupervised models, we overcome the lack of company-specific metadata from the attack as well as the problem of insufficient data for training the models.

We summarize the main contributions of this chapter as follows:

- We create a novel network mining technique using the directed reply network of users to extract set of *experts* over time. Following this approach, we generate several time series of features that capture the dynamics of interactions centered around these *experts* across individual online forums.
- We apply a widely used unsupervised anomaly detection technique that uses residual analysis to detect anomalies and propose an anomaly-based attack prediction technique on a daily basis. Additionally, we train a supervised learning model based on logistic regression with attack labels from an organization to predict daily attacks.
- Empirical evidence from our unsupervised anomaly detector suggests that a feature based on graph conductance – that measures the random walk[2] transition probability between groups of users – is a useful indicator for attack occurrences given by the best area under the curve (AUC) score of 0.69 for one type of attack. We obtain similar best results for the supervised model having the best F1 score of 0.53 for the same feature and attack type compared to the random (without prior probabilities) F1 score of 0.37.
- We analyze the models' performance in weeks, where attack frequency is higher, finding a superior performance when information from network community structure is used.

The remainder of this chapter is organized as follows. Section 8.2 details the dataset used in this work. Section 8.3 formally defines our problem. We then discuss the technical details of the proposed framework for attack prediction in Section 8.4, including the feature engineering and the model learning components. Section 8.5 discusses the experimental settings and results obtained, while Section 8.6 presents some discussion and case studies. Section 8.7 shows select related work. Finally, Section 8.8 concludes the chapter.

[2] Mathematical object that describes a path formed by a succession of random steps [113].

## 8.2 Dataset

The ground truth – security incidents – and hacker forum data used in this chapter are a subset of what are used in Chapter 7, as the data have been tuned to the problem here.

### 8.2.1 External Threats (GT)

We use the cyber-attacks, ground truth (GT) from the logs of two enterprises – Armstrong and Dexter – participating in the IARPA CAUSE program presented in Chapter 7. However, we collect records of attack attempts spanning from April 2016 to September 2017. We also analyze the same types of attacks or *event types* in this study: *malicious email*, *malicious destination*, and *endpoint malware* (see Chapter 7 for full definitions). The set of attack types is denoted in this chapter as $A$. We only use the categories: *event-type* and *event-occurred-date* to form our GT data for validation, avoiding the use of other dataset attributes that are not available for all security incident reports. Note that the absence of information that can accurately provide us with knowledge regarding vulnerabilities and exploits that caused the attacks makes the problem more challenging. As shown in Figure 8.1, the distribution of attacks over time is different for the events. Additionally, we observe that for the events *endpoint-malware* shown in Figure 8.1(b) and *malicious-destination* shown in Figure 8.1(c), the weekly occurrence has not been captured consistently, and there is missing information for these events in some time intervals. We take note of this while building our learning models that predict the occurrence of attacks. The total number of incidents reported for the events are as follows: 26 incidents tagged as *malicious-destination*, 119 tagged as *endpoint-malware*, and 135 tagged as *malicious-email*, resulting in a total of 280 incidents over a span of 17 months.

### 8.2.2 Online Hacker Forum Data

The focus of this work is to understand how certain groups of users respond to discussions prior to important cyber-security incidents. We want to assess whether these particular interactions can be used as indicators for external cyber-attacks *without* heavily relying on CVEs or a group of CVEs that might alleviate them. However, since our GT data have no references to any CVEs, nor is it possible to trace any CVEs given the metadata information, we use the time frame of the GT attacks for gathering the online hacker forum data and computing features based on this time frame so as to train the models

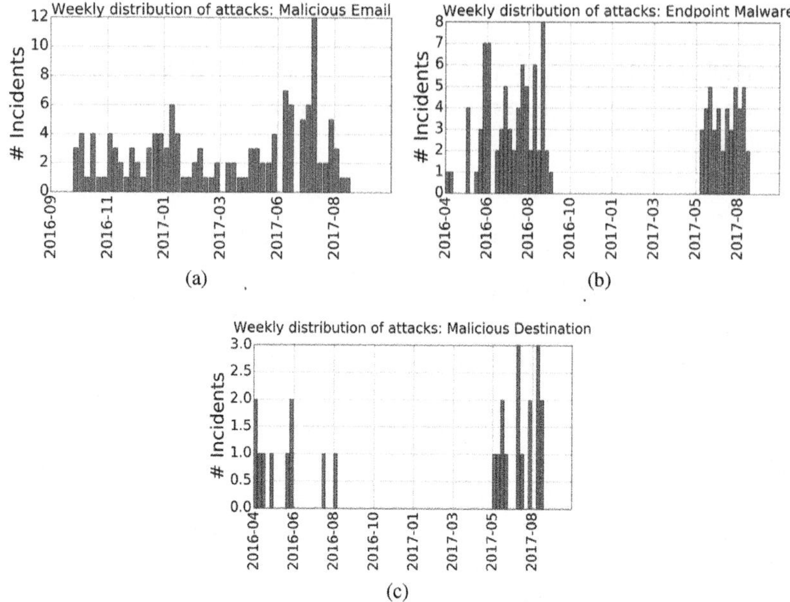


Figure 8.1 Weekly occurrence of security breach incidents of different types: (a) malicious email, (b) endpoint malware, and (c) malicious destination.

using data having close temporal associations. We provide a comprehensive discussion related to how our predictions correlate with important time events related to attacks in the real world over the past few years and which also correlate with the attack ground truth data provided.

**CVE data.** We collect all the information regarding the vulnerability mentions in online forums in the period from January 2016 to October 2017. The total number of unique CVE mentions in this period is 3,553 across all forums analyzed, and the weekly distribution of the number of vulnerability mentions posted is shown in Figure 8.2. We realize that for the months from January 2016 to May 2016, there may be a collection bias in the vulnerability mentions in forum posts. However, since we train our models over multiple months using these mentions, we overcome this collection bias error over time.

In fact, when we look at the distribution of the number of times a CVE is mentioned online (over the period considered in this study), we find 3.5 mentions on average with a median value of 1. Figure 8.3 shows that the probability of fewer mentions is very high, which makes the problem of selecting discussions surrounding vulnerabilities even more difficult since we want to prioritize vulnerabilities by looking at the content or the user-user network.

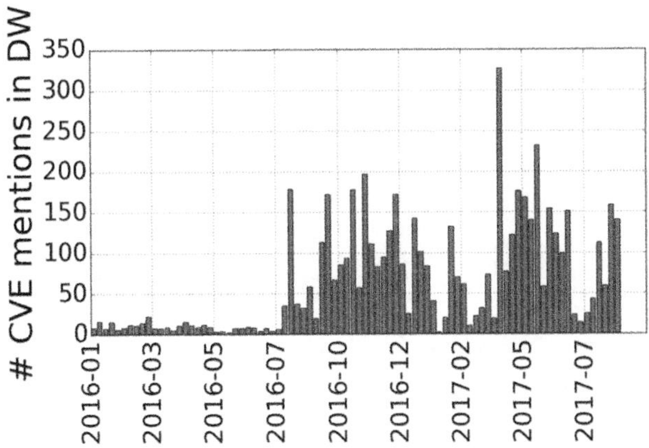


Figure 8.2 Weekly distribution of unique vulnerability mentions in posts across all online forums.

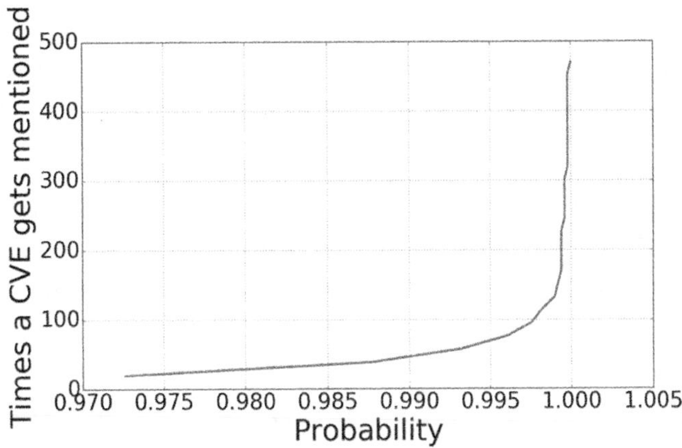


Figure 8.3 Cumulative distribution function (CDF) showing the number of times each CVE is mentioned.

**Forum data.** In this chapter, we consider the dynamics of interactions in online hacker forums, filtering out these platforms based on a threshold number of posts that were created between January 2016 and September 2017. We gather data from 179 forums where the total number of unique posts, irrespective of the thread to which they belonged, is 557,689. As shown in Figure 8.4, the number of forums with fewer than 100 posts is large, and therefore, we only consider forums that have more than 5,000 posts during that time period, resulting in 53 forums. As will be described later, we rely on a projection

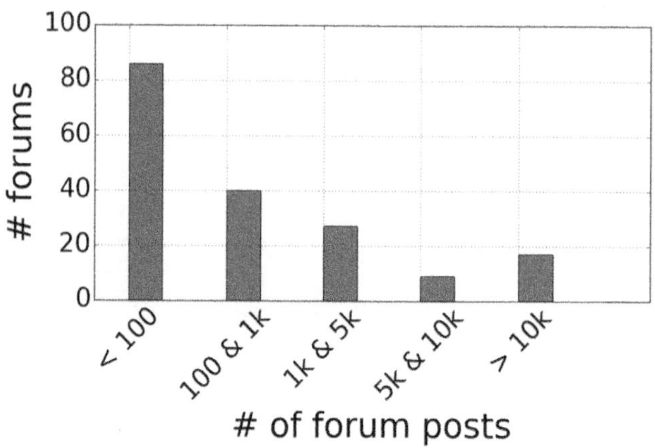


Figure 8.4 Distribution of the number of posts across all forums.

method to compute lower-dimensional features, and hence any significant patterns occurring out of these forums are captured without the requirement to manually filter and select particular forums. We note that unlike some related research that leverages the darkweb for cyber-attack prediction by using more forums for signals [70], we refrain from using forums without enough data in the time frame of this study. This is to avoid data imbalance and the issue of sparse features on days where we would need to predict attacks – an imputation measure for addressing those issues is an active area of research [129] that will be considered as a part of our future work.

As mentioned in Chapter 3, each online hacker forum or site $f$ consists of several threads $h$ initiated by a user, and several users post and reply in these threads over time. One user can appear multiple times in the sequence of posts, depending on when and how many times she or he posts in that thread. Since each thread is associated with a topic (or a title), we also use here the term topic to refer to a particular thread $h$ comprising all posts in the relevant forum. We represent the set of 53 forums filtered for this study with the symbol $F$.

### 8.2.3 CPE Groups

Similar to the CVE-CPE mapping conducted in Chapter 7, we cluster CVEs into sets of CPE groups by using the CPE tags provided by the NVD database. We only consider the operating system platform and the application environment tags for each CPE. Examples of CPEs include: *Microsoft Windows_95*, *Canonical ubuntu_linux*, *Hp elitebook_725_g3*. The first component in each of these CPEs denotes the operating system platform, and the second component denotes the application environment and its version. Some of the CPE groups might be a parent cluster of another CPE group. For example, *Microsoft Windows* is a parent cluster for CPEs like *Microsoft Windows_8* or *Microsoft Windows_10*. In this chapter, we do not consider any hierarchies in the CPEs for filtering out clusters – an example of how this hierarchy can be used is presented in Chapter 9. From April 2016 to September 2017, we observe that the top CPE groups having CVEs mentioned most widely in online forum posts are: ntp, php, adobe flash_player, microsoft windows_server_2008, linux kernel, microsoft windows_7, microsoft windows_server_2012, and canonical ubuntu_linux.

## 8.3 Prediction Problem

Before describing the framework built in this chapter for predicting external enterprise attacks, we formally describe our prediction task. Given a target organization $E$, a set of external signals from online forums as features, and a set of $A$ attack types for $E$, we solve a binary classification problem that investigates whether there would be an attack (0/1) of any type in $A$ for $E$ on a daily basis. Note the difference between the problem addressed in Chapter 7, where the magnitude of attacks is also predicted.

The mechanism for attack predictions, as shown in Figure 8.5, can be described in three steps : (1) given a time point $t$ on which we need to predict an enterprise attack of a particular *event-type*, (2) we use features from online forums $\delta$ days prior to $t$, and (3) we use these features as input to a machine learning model to predict an attack on $t$. Thus, one of the main tasks involves learning the attack prediction model, one for each *event-type*. We describe the attack prediction framework in the following section.

## 8.4 Framework for Attack Prediction

We segregate the designed framework, proposed in this chapter for predicting organization-specific attacks, into the three steps of any classic machine learning approach. Note how this approach differs from the logic programming approach designed in Chapter 7:

1. **Feature engineering:** In this first step, we leverage the reply network formed from the thread replies in online forums to build several features as input to the model:

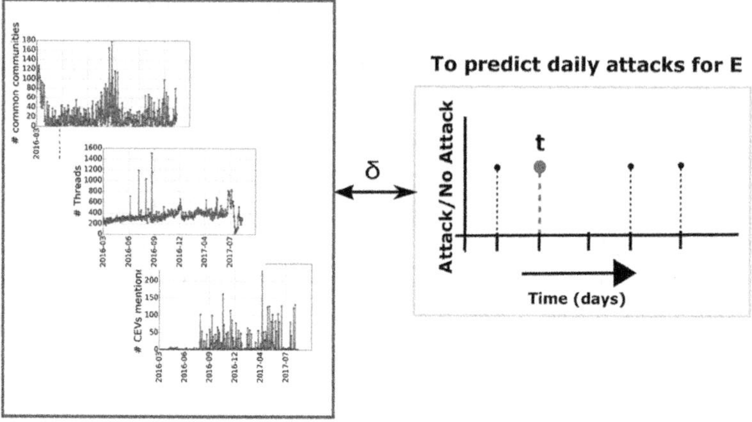


Figure 8.5 The prediction task. We use external time series signals from online forum discussions to predict attack on a daily basis for enterprise $E$.

- *Graph-based features*: Features pertaining to the dynamics of replies from users with credible knowledge to regular posts – the intuition here is to see whether a post gaining attention from active and reputed users can be a predictive signal.
- *Forum metadata*: Features formed with forum metadata used as baselines for our graph-based features.

As a first task toward feature engineering, we devise an algorithm to create the reply network structure from the replies in the threads.

2. **Training (learning) models for prediction:** In this second step, we first split the time frame of our attack study into two segments: one corresponding to the training span and the other being the test span. As done in previous chapters, we avoid temporal intermixing. Therefore, the training–test split respects the forecasting aspect of our prediction, using features $\delta$ days prior to the day for which the attack is predicted. Thus, instead of using cross-validation, we fix our training time span as the first few time points in our ground truth dataset (chronologically ordered) while the test span succeeds the training span. We build several time series of individual features from step 1 using only forum discussions in the training span and use them as input along with the attack ground truth to a supervised model for learning the parameters (we build separate models for different attack types and organizations). This step, along with the first step, is shown in Figure 8.6 on the left side, under the training span stage.

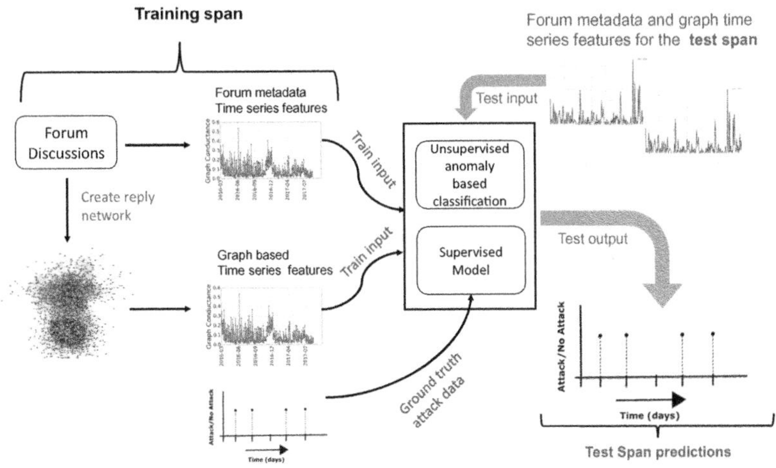


Figure 8.6 Overview of the framework used for attack prediction.

3. **Attack prediction:** In the third and final step, we first compute the time series of the same set of features in the training span. However, we now use the forum discussions in the test span ($\delta$ days prior to the prediction time point). We then input these time series into the supervised model as well as an additional unsupervised model – that does not require any training using ground truth – to output attacks on a daily basis in the test span. This step is displayed in the right component of Figure 8.6.

In the following sections, we explain the steps in detail that also describe the intuition behind the approach used for the attack prediction in this chapter.

### 8.4.1 Step 1: Feature Engineering

For the purposes of network analysis, we assume the absence of global user IDs across forums.[3] Therefore, we analyze the social interactions using networks induced on specific forums instead of considering the global network of users across all forums. We denote the directed and unweighted reply graph of a forum $f \in F$ by $G^f = (V^f, E^f)$, where $V^f$ denotes the set of users who posted or replied in some thread in forum $f$ and $E^f$ denotes the set of 3-tuple

[3] Even in the presence of global user IDs across all forums analyzed in this chapter, a lot of anonymous or malicious users would create multiple profiles in those forums and also multiple posts with different profiles, generating a challenge for researchers to identify and merge them. This problem is actually an active area of research addressed in social media mining and cyber-security.

$(u_1, u_2, rt)$ directed edges – here, $u_1, u_2 \in V^f$ and $rt$ is the time at which $u_1$ replied to a post of $u_2$ in some thread in $f$ ($u_1 \rightarrow u_2$ denotes the edge direction). We emphasize that this notation of the network discards links between users of two different forums, as we do not connect or merge threads posted in two separate forums. We denote by $G_\tau^f = (V_\tau^f, E_\tau^f)$ a temporal subgraph of $G^f$, with $\tau$ being a time window such that $V_\tau^f$ denotes the set of individuals who posted in $f$ in that window and $E_\tau^f$ denotes the set of tuples $(v_1, v_2, rt)$ such that $rt \in \tau$, $v_1, v_2 \in V_\tau^f$.

**Constructing the reply network.** We adopt an incremental analysis approach by splitting the set of time points in our frame of study (both for the training and test span) into a sequence of time windows $\Gamma = \{\tau_1, \tau_2, \ldots, \tau_Q\}$, where each subsequence $\tau_i$, $i \in [1, Q]$ is equal in time span and the subsequences are ordered by their starting time points for their respective span. This streaming aspect of the reply networks and the feature computation are based on our observation that the significance of users (in terms of *important* posts in the forums) change very rapidly. To this end, computing features on a monthly basis is not expedient for a one-year span. From that perspective, we create evolving networks (which incorporate historical knowledge) and compute features on a daily basis.

Next, we describe the operations: *create*, which takes a set of posts in $f$ within a time window $\tau$ as input and creates a temporal subgraph $G_\tau^f$, and *merge*, which takes two temporal graphs as input and merges them to form an auxiliary graph that incorporates historical information. To keep the notations simple, we will drop the symbol $f$ when we describe those operations for a specific forum since they apply to all $f \in F$. Those two operations describe how we map the features extracted from the network structure $G^f$ to a time series:

1. *Create*: This operation creates the reply network based on individual threads within a forum $f$ on a daily basis. Let $h$ be a particular thread or topic within a forum $f$ containing users' posts $V_h^f = \{u_1, \ldots, u_k\}$ created at corresponding times $T_h^f = \{t_1, \ldots, t_k\}$, where $k$ denotes the number of posts in that thread and $t_i \geq t_j$ for any $i > j$ – posts are chronologically ordered. Since we are considering a reply network on the forum posts and information is lacking as to who replied to whom, we use some heuristics to connect the users based on temporal and spatial information. We note that in situations where the data comes with the hierarchical reply structure of who-replies-to-whom, this procedure can be avoided, and we can move to the next stage. Two simple approaches would be to consider (1) a *temporal constraint* – for each user $u_i$ of a post in a thread $h$, in forum $f$,

at time $t_i$, we would create an edge $(u_i, u_k, t)$ such that $t_i - t_k < thresh_{temp}$, where $u_k$ denotes the user for the respective posts at time $t_k \in \tau$ and $thresh_{spat}$ denotes a time threshold – and (2) a *spatial constraint*, for all edges $(u_i, u_k, t_i)$, where $u_k$ denotes the user of the $k$th post in the time-ordered sequence of posts and $k - i \leq thresh$ – here, $thresh$ denotes a count threshold. The disadvantage of considering only the temporal constraint would be that for posts that receive less participation, we would have a sparse network. On the other hand, the disadvantage of considering only the spatial constraint is that the networks would not be time normalized and would be biased toward threads with larger number of posts. This would consequently lead to over dense networks irrespective of the time differences.

We decide to use both constraints in the following way: for the $i$th post $p_{h,i}$ in the thread $h$ created at time $t_i$, the objective is to create links from the author of this post to the posts created prior to it as reply links – a similar strategy was used in Chapter 3 to generate directed social networks of users. However, here we consider a maximum of $thresh_{spat}$ count of posts prior to $p_{h,i}$ (note that the posts in the thread are considered chronologically ordered), that is, all posts $p_{h,k}$ such that $k - i \leq thresh_{spat}$. The users for those respective posts would be the potential users to whom $u_{h,i}$ replied (unidirectional links), which we denote by $\{u_{h,i\to k}\}$ and the corresponding set of posts $\{p_{h,i\to k}\}$. The next layer of constraints considering temporal boundaries prunes out candidates from $\{u_{h,k}\}$ by using the following two procedures:

- If $t_i - t_k < thresh_{temp}$, we form edges linking $u_{h,i}$ to all user in $\{u_{h,i\to k}\}$ (note the direction of reply). This takes care of the first few posts in $h$ where there might not be enough time to create a sensation, but the users might be replying as a general discussion in the thread. So we consider user of $i$th post replies potentially to all these users of $\{u_{h,i\to k}\}$ at one go, whether it is at the beginning or in the middle of an ongoing thread discussion.
- If $t_i - t_k >= thresh_{temp}$, we first compute the mean of the time differences between two successive posts in $\{p_{h,i\to k}\}$. We also denote the time difference between $t_i$ and the time of the last post in $\{p_{h,i\to k}\}$, considering that the chronological ordering is maintained, as $\Delta t_i$. If the computed mean is less than $\Delta t_i$, we form edges linking $u_{h,i}$ to all users in $\{u_{h,i\to k}\}$ (this is similar to the first constraint). Else, as long as the mean is greater than $\Delta t_i$, we start removing the posts in $\{p_{h,i\to k}\}$ furthest in time to $t_i$ in order and recalculate the mean after removal of

every single post. We repeat this procedure until at some iteration either the recomputed mean is less than $\Delta t_i$ or $t_i - t_k < thresh_{temp}$. This heuristic considers the case when posts receive a lot of replies at a certain time of the thread life cycle, although it is not reasonable to consider posts that have been created a while ago as being replied to by the current post in consideration.

Following these two procedures, we make $V^f = \cup_h V_h^f$ and $E^f = \cup_h E_h^f$, which correspond to removing multiple interactions between the same set of users in multiple threads and without weighting these edges. As mentioned before in this section, a temporal subgraph of $G^f$ is denoted by $G_\tau^f$, where $(u, v, rt) \in E_\tau$ informs that $u$ replied to $v$ at a particular time $rt \in \tau$. Our objective after creating the reply network $G_\tau^f$ is to compute features from this network that can be used as input to a machine learning model for predicting future cyber-attacks. Those features act as unconventional signals that we leverage in this chapter for signaling external attacks that are about to occur against specific organizations. In order to successfully achieve this feature engineering goal, we need to form time series of a feature $x$ (among a set of network features) denoted by $\mathcal{T}_{x,f}$, for every forum $f \in F$ separately. Formally, $\mathcal{T}_{x,f}$ is a stochastic process that maps each time point $t$ to a real number.

2. *Merge*: In order to create a time series feature $\mathcal{T}_{x,f}$ for feature $x$, considering the existing threads in forum $f$, we use the two following reply networks: (1) a historical network $G_{H_\tau}$ that spans over time $H_\tau$ such that $\forall t' \in H_\tau$, and for any $t \in \tau$, we have $t' < t$, and (2) the network $G_t^f$ induced by interactions between users in $E_t$, which varies temporally for each $t \in \tau$. We note that the historical network $G_{H_\tau}$ is different for each subsequence $\tau$. As the subsequences $\tau \in \Gamma$ progress with time, the historical network $G_{H_\tau}$ also changes. We discuss the choice of spans $\tau \in \Gamma$ and $H_\tau$ later in Section 8.5. Finally, for computing feature values for each time point $t \in \tau$, we merge the two networks $G_{H_\tau}$ and $G_t$ to form the auxiliary network $G_{H_\tau,t} = (V_{H_\tau,t}, E_{H_\tau,t})$, where $V_{H_\tau,t} = V_{H_\tau} \cup V_t$ and $E_{H_\tau,t} = E_{H_\tau} \cup E_t$. A visual illustration of this *merge* operation is presented in Figure 8.7. At the end of this process, we consider several network features over each $G_{H_\tau,t}^f$, computing the feature values at time point $t$ to form $\mathcal{T}_{x,f}$ for feature $x$ and forum $f$.

**Network-based features.** We leverage the network $G_{H_\tau}^f$ to compute features on a regular basis – the advantage is that $G_{H_\tau}^f$ contains historical information, although this information does not update on a regular basis. For extracting network-based features, we focus on the interactions convened by users in

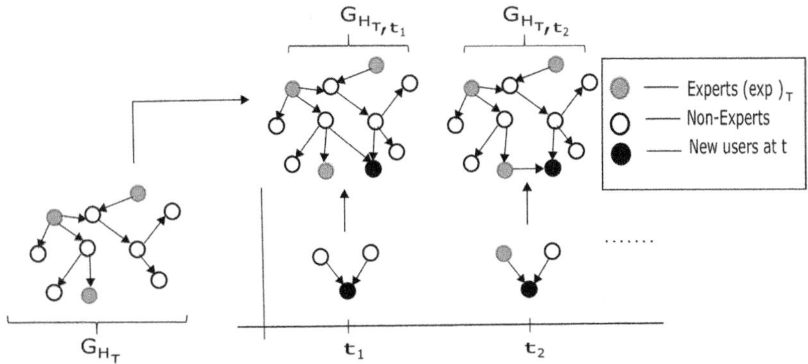


Figure 8.7 An illustration to show the *merge* operation: $G_{H_\tau}$ denotes the historical network in which the experts (shown in gray) are computed. $\{G_{t_1}, G_{t_2}, \ldots\}$ denote the networks at time $t_1, t_2, \ldots \in \tau, \tau \in \Gamma$. Note that the experts are extracted only from $G_{H_\tau}$ and not on a regular basis.

forums with a knack toward posting credible information. The objective is to investigate whether any spike in attention toward posts on a day created by users with some *credible reputation* translates to predictive signals for cyber-attacks on an organization. This also helps filter out noisy discussions or replies from unwanted or naive users who post information irrelevant to vulnerabilities or without any malicious intent. We hypothesize that predictive signals would exhibit users in these daily reply networks whose posts have received attention (in the form of direct or indirect replies) from some "expert" users – whether a faster reply would translate to an important signal for an attack is one of the questions we addressed in this context. In order to be able to extract posts that receive attention on a daily basis, we first need to extract "expert" users whose activity we seek to gather.

**Expert users.** For each forum $f$, we use the historical network $G^f_{H_\tau}$ to extract the set of $experts$ relevant to the time frame $\tau$, that is, $exp^f_\tau \in V^f_{H_\tau}$. First, we extract the top CPE groups $CP^{top}_\tau$ in the time frame $H_\tau$ based on the number of historical mentions of CVEs. These would be used as top CPEs for $\tau$. To do so, we sort the CPE groups based on the sum of the CVE mentions that correspondingly belong to each group and take the top five CPE groups in each $H_\tau$. Using these notations, the experts $exp^f_\tau$ from history $H_\tau$, considered for time span $\tau$, are defined as users in $f$ with the following three constraints:

1. Users who have mentioned a CVE in their post in $H_\tau$. This ensures that the user engages in the forums with content that is relevant to vulnerabilities.
2. Let $\theta(u)$ denotes the set of CPE tags of the CVEs mentioned by user $u$ in his or her posts in $H_\tau$, such that it follows the constraint either

$\theta(u) \in CP_\tau^{top}$, where the user's CVEs are grouped in less than five CPEs, or $CP_\tau^{top} \in \theta(u)$, in cases where a user has posts with CVEs in $H_\tau$, grouped in more than five CPEs. This constraint filters out users who discuss vulnerabilities that are not among the top CPE groups in $H_\tau$.
3. The in-degree of the user $u$ in $G_{H_\tau}$ should cross a threshold. This constraint ensures that there is a significant number of users who potentially responded to this user, establishing $u$'s central position in the reply network. These techniques to filter out relevant candidates based on network topology have been widely used in the bot detection communities [119].

We avoid using other centrality metrics instead of using the in-degree in the third constraint since our focus here is not to judge the position of the user from the centrality perspective – for example, a high degree of betweenness does not denote that the user receives multiple replies on his or her posts. Instead, we want to filter out users who receive multiple replies on their posts or, in other words, whose posts receive attention. Essentially, this set of experts $exp_\tau$ from $H_\tau$ is used for all the time points in $\tau$, as shown in Figure 8.7.

**Why focus on experts?** To show the significance of these properties in comparison to other users, we perform the following hypothesis test. We collect the time periods of three widely known security events: the WannaCry ransomware attack that happened on May 12, 2017, exploited through the vulnerability MS-17-010; the Petya cyber-attack on June 27, 2017, through associated vulnerabilities CVE-2017-0144, CVE-2017-0145, and MS-17-010; and the Equifax breach, primarily occurring on March 9, 2017, via vulnerability CVE-2017-5638. We consider two sets of users across all forums: (1) $exp_\tau$, with $G_{H_\tau}$ denoting the corresponding historical network prior to $\tau$ in which these three events occurred, and (2) all $U_{alt}$ users who are not experts and who fail to satisfy either one of the following two constraints – they have mentioned CVEs in their posts that do not belong to $CP^{top}$ or their in-degree in $G_{H_\tau}$ lies below the threshold. We consider $G_{H_\tau}$ being induced by users in the last three weeks prior to the occurrence week of each event for both cases. We also consider the total number of interactions, ignoring the direction of reply of these users with other users. Let $\mathbf{deg_{exp}}$ denote the vector of the count of interactions in which the *experts* are involved and $\mathbf{deg_{alt}}$ denote the vector of counts of interactions in which the users in $U_{alt}$ are involved. We randomly pick a number of users from $U_{alt}$ equal to the number of experts and sort the vectors by count. We conduct a two-sample $t$-test on the vectors $\mathbf{deg_{exp}}$ and $\mathbf{deg_{alt}}$. The null hypothesis $H_0$ and the alternate hypothesis $H_1$ are defined as follows:

$$H_0 : \mathbf{deg_{exp}} \leq \mathbf{deg_{alt}}, \quad H_1 : \mathbf{deg_{exp}} > \mathbf{deg_{alt}}. \tag{8.1}$$

The null hypothesis is rejected at significance level $\alpha = 0.01$ with a $p$-value of 0.0007. This suggests that with high probability, experts tend to interact more prior to important, impactful cyber-security breaches than other users who randomly post CVEs.

Now, we conduct a second $t$-test where we randomly pick four weeks not in the weeks considered for the data breaches, getting users $U_{alt}$ with the same constraints. We use the same hypotheses as above, and when we perform statistical tests for significance, we find that the null hypothesis is not rejected at $\alpha = 0.01$ with a $p$-value close to 0.05. This empirical evidence from the $t$-test also suggests that the interactions with $exp_\tau$ are more correlated with an important cyber-security incident than the other users who post CVEs not in top CPE groups, and therefore, it is better to focus on users exhibiting our desired properties as experts for cyber-attack prediction. Note that the $t$-test evidence also incorporates a special temporal association since we collect events from three interwoven time frames – which correspond to the event dates – and we do not select any time frame to show the evidence.

Next, we describe the following graph-based features that we use to compute $\mathcal{T}_{x,f}[t]$ at time $t$, for which we also take as input the relevant experts $exp_\tau$. We describe four network features that capture this intuition behind the attention broadcasted by these users. The idea is that a cyber-adversary looking to thwart the prediction models, from working by curating similar reply networks using bots, would need not only to introduce such random networks but also to get the desired attention from these experts. The latter could be challenging to achieve, given that human attention is known to be different compared to bots. [54].

**Graph conductance.** As studied in [43, 118, 141], social networks are fast mixing: this means that a random walk on the social graph converges quickly to a node following the stationary distribution of the graph. Applied to social interactions in a reply network, the intuition behind computing the graph conductance is to understand the following: can we compute bounds of steps within which any attention on a post would be successfully broadcast from the non experts to the *experts* when a post closely associated with an attack is discussed [34]? One way of formalizing the notion of **graph conductance** $\phi$ is as follows:

$$\phi = \min_{X \subset V : \pi(X) < \frac{1}{2}} \phi_X. \tag{8.2}$$

where $X$ is the set of experts, defined as

$$\phi_{Experts} = \frac{\sum_{x \in exp_\tau} \sum_{y \in V_t \setminus exp_\tau} \pi(exp_\tau) P_{xy}}{\pi(exp_\tau)}, \tag{8.3}$$

and $\pi(.)$ is the stationary distribution of the network $G_{H_\tau,t}$.

For subset of vertices $exp_\tau$, its conductance $\phi_{Experts}$ represents the probability of taking a random walk from any of the *experts* to one of the users in $V_t \setminus exp_\tau$, normalized by the probability weight of being an expert. Applied to the reply network comprising both experts and regular users, the key intuition behind conductance is that the mixing between expert nodes and the users of important posts is fast, while the mixing between expert nodes and lay nodes without important posts is slow – considering our view of importance as seeking attention. Hence, the higher the value of conductance is, the higher is the probability that the experts are paying attention to the posts, reflecting a good chance that the conversations on those days could be reflective of a future cyber-attack.

**Shortest paths.** To understand the dynamics among the non experts and the experts prior to an attack, we compute the shortest distance between them as follows:

$$SP(exp_\tau, V_t \setminus exp_\tau) = \frac{1}{|exp_\tau|} \sum_{e \in exp_\tau} \min_{u \in V_t \setminus exp_\tau} s_{e,u}. \tag{8.4}$$

where $s_{e,u}$ denotes the shortest path in the graph $G_{H_\tau,d}$ from the expert $e$ to a user $u$ in the direction of the edges.

Since the edges are formed in the direction of the replies based on time constraints, it also denotes how fast an expert replies in a thread that leads back in time to a post created by $u$. Such distance metrics have been widely studied to understand patterns of interactions [180].

**Expert replies.** To analyze whether *experts* reply to users more actively when there is an important discussion going on surrounding any vulnerabilities or exploits, we compute the number of replies by an *expert* to users in $V_t \setminus exp_\tau$. We calculate the number of out-neighbors of $exp_\tau$ considering $G_{H_\tau,t}$.

**Common communities.** To evaluate the role of communities in the reply network and to assess whether experts engage with select other users when information related to vulnerability exploitation gains attention, we extract the communities on the networks $G_{H_\tau}$ by leveraging the Louvain community detection method [21]. Since it is not computationally feasible to compute communities in $G_{H_\tau,t}$ for all the time points $t \in \tau$, we first compute all the communities for the users in the historical network $G_{H_\tau}$. Following this, we use an approximation based on heuristics to compute the communities of new users $V_{new} = V_{H_\tau,t} \setminus V_{H_\tau}$ in Algorithm 8.1. Let $c_{experts}$ denote the set of communities that users in $exp_\tau$ belong to – note the call to the Louvain method in line 1 of Algorithm 8.1. Let $c(u)$ denote the community index of a user $u$. We define the common communities measure as follows:

$$CC(exp_{\tau}, V_t \setminus exp_{\tau}) = \{\mathcal{N}(c(u)) \mid c(u) \in c_{experts} \wedge u \in V_t \setminus exp_{\tau}\}. \quad (8.5)$$

$CC(.)$ measures the number of non experts at time $t \in \tau$ that share the same communities with $exp_{\tau}$. We use two approximation constraints, demonstrated in lines 16-25 of Algorithm 8.1, to assign a new user $u \in V_{new}$ to an expert community as follows:

1. *Condition 1*: If an expert has an incoming edge to $u$, we increase the count of common communities by 1.
2. *Condition 2*: If $u$ has an incoming neighbor who shares a community in the set of communities of experts, we increase the count of common communities by 1. This is shown in line 19 of Algorithm 8.1 with the $InNeighbors()$ method call.

**User/forum metadata features.** In addition to the network features, we compute the following forum-based statistics for a forum $f$ at time point $t$: (1) the number of unique vulnerabilities mentioned in $f$ at time $t$, (2) the number of users who posted in $f$, (3) the number of unique threads in $f$ at time $t$, and (4) the number of threads in which there is at least one $expert$'s post among all the posts in $f$ at $t$. A brief summary of all the features used in this chapter is given in Table 8.1.

### 8.4.2 Step 2: Training Models for Prediction

In this section, we explain how we use the time series features $\mathcal{T}_{x,f}$ across forums to predict an attack at any given time point $t$. We consider two machine learning models for our framework: (1) a supervised learning model in which the time series $\mathcal{T}_x$ is formed by averaging $\mathcal{T}_{x,f}$ across all forums in $f \in F$ at each time point $t$ and (2) an unsupervised learning model in which we take the time series $\mathcal{T}_{x,f}$ for each feature and each forum $f \in F$ separately, applying dimensionality reduction techniques across the forums dimension. For the unsupervised approach, we use anomaly detection methods for the prediction task – this model does not use the training span ground truth attack data and directly works on features in the training and test span to predict attacks. However, in the supervised learning scenario, we build separate prediction models for each attack type in $A$ and for each organization. We do not use the two learning models in conjunction, nor do we combine data from different

**Algorithm 8.1** Algorithm for Computing Common Communities (CC)

```
Input: exp_τ, G_{H_τ}, (V_t, E_t)
Output: CC(exp_τ, V_t ∖ exp_τ) – the number of communities shared by
        V_t ∖ exp_τ with exp_τ at t
communities = Louvain_community(G_{H_τ}) ;           // dictionary
  storing node to community index mapping
c_expSet ← () ;
foreach user u ∈ exp_τ do
|   c_expSet.add(communities[u]) ;
end
V_{H_τ,t} ← V_{H_τ} ∪ V_t ;
E_{H_τ,t} ← E_{H_τ} ∪ E_t ;
CC(exp_τ, V_t ∖ exp_τ) ← 0 ;                        // stores count
/* Iterate over the users in V_t who have not been
   assigned communities from H_τ                             */
foreach user u ∈ V_t do
    if u ∈ V_{H_τ} and communities(u) ∈ c_expSet then
    |   CC(exp_τ, V_t ∖ exp_τ) += 1;
    end
    else
        foreach user v ∈ exp_τ do
            /* Condition 1                                   */
            if (v, u) ∈ E_{H_τ,t} then
                CC(exp_τ, V_t ∖ exp_τ) += 1;
                break ;
            end
            /* Condition 2                                   */
            foreach user n ∈ inNeighbors(E_{H_τ,t}, u) do
                if communities(n) ∈ c_expSet then
                    CC(exp_τ, V_t ∖ exp_τ) += 1;
                    break ;
                end
            end
        end
    end
end
return CC(exp_τ, V_t ∖ exp_τ)
```

types of attacks.[4] We treat attack prediction here as a binary classification problem in which the objective is to predict whether there would be an attack

[4] We leave this approach to a future work project to see how models built on one attack type could generalize to other types and whether we can use different attack types together as a multilabel classification problem, although such models of synthesis have been previously used for attack prediction [185].

Table 8.1 *List of features used for learning*

| Group | Features | Description |
|---|---|---|
| Expert-centric | Graph conductance | $\tau_x[t] = \frac{\sum_{x \in exp_\tau} \sum_{y \in V_t \setminus exp_\tau} \pi(exp_\tau) P_{xy}}{\pi(exp_\tau)}$, where $\pi(.)$ is the stationary distribution of the network $G_{H_\tau,t}$ and $P_{xy}$ denotes the probability of random walk from vertices $x$ to $y$. The conductance represents the probability of taking a random walk from any of the $experts$ to one of the users in $V_t \setminus exp_\tau$, normalized by the probability weight of being on an expert. |
| | Shortest path | $\tau_x[t] = \frac{1}{\lvert exp_\tau \rvert} \sum_{e \in exp_\tau} \min_{u \in V_t \setminus exp_\tau} s_{e,u}$, where $s_{e,u}$ denotes the shortest path from an expert $e$ to user $u$ following the direction of edges. |
| | Expert replies | $\tau_x[t] = \frac{1}{\lvert exp_\tau \rvert} \sum_{e \in exp_\tau} \lvert OutNeighbors(e) \rvert$, where $OutNeighbors(.)$ denotes the out neighbors of user in the network $G_{H_\tau,t}$. |
| | Common communities | $\tau_x[t] = \{\mathcal{N}(c(u) \mid c(u) \in c_{experts} \wedge u \in V_t \setminus exp_\tau\}$, where $c(u)$ denotes the community index of user $u$, $c_{experts}$ that of the experts, and $\mathcal{N}(.)$ denotes a function that counts the number of users who share communities with experts. |
| Forum/user metadata | No. threads | $\tau_x[t] = \lvert\{h \mid \text{thread h was posted on t}\}\rvert$ |
| | No. users | $\tau_x[t] = \lvert\{u \mid \text{user u posted on t}\}\rvert$ |
| | No. expert-threads | $\tau_x[t] = \lvert\{h \mid \text{thread h was posted on t by users u} \in \text{experts}\}\rvert$ |
| | No. CVE mentions | $\tau_x[t] = \lvert\{CVE \mid \text{CVE was mentioned in some post on t}\}\rvert$ |

Note. Each feature $\tau_x$ is computed separately across forums.

at a given time point $t$ (refer to Figure 8.5). Since the incident data contain the number of incidents that occurred at time point $t$, we assign a label of 1 for $t$ if there was at least one attack at $t$ and 0 otherwise.

**Supervised learning.** We first discuss the technical details of the machine learning model that (1) learns parameters based on the training labels of different attack types in $A$ during the training span and (2) uses these parameters to predict whether an organization $E$ would be vulnerable to an attack at $t$. We note again that we build different models for each attack type in $A$ for $E$, such that predicting for each type means that we have to learn different models. However, the set of time series features gathered in the previous step as input is consistent across all models. In [182, 192], the authors studied the effect of longitudinal sparsity in high-dimensional time series data,

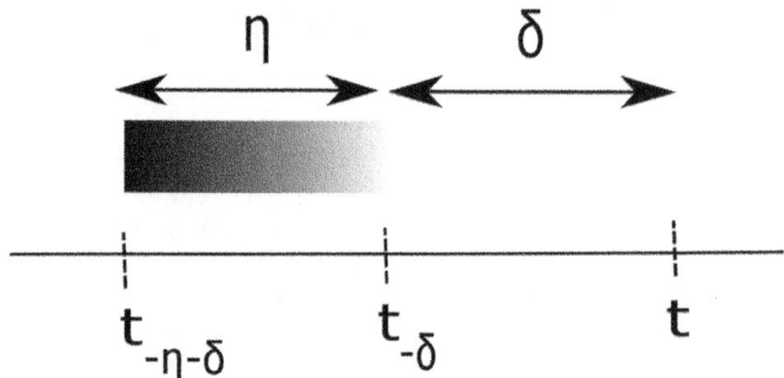


Figure 8.8 Temporal feature selection window for predicting an attack at time $t$.

where they proposed to assign weights to the same features at different time spans for capturing the temporal redundancy. We use two parameters here: $\delta$, which denotes the start time prior to $t$ from where we consider the features for prediction, and $\eta$, which is the time span (window) for the features to be considered. We illustrate this process in Figure 8.8, where to predict an attack at time $t$, we use the features for each time $t \in [t_{-\eta-\delta}, t_{-\delta}]$.

We use logistic regression with longitudinal ridge sparsity that models the probability of an attack as follows:

$$P(attack(t) = 1|\,\mathbf{X}) = \frac{1}{1 + e^{-(\beta_0 + \sum_{k=\eta+\delta}^{\delta} \beta_k\, x_{t-k})}}. \tag{8.6}$$

The final objective function, which minimizes over $N$ instances where $N$ here is the number of time points spanning the attack time frame, is

$$l(\beta) = -\sum_{i=1}^{N}(y_i(\beta_0 + \mathbf{x_i}^T\beta) - \log(1 + \exp^{\beta_0 + \mathbf{x_i}^T\beta}) + \lambda\beta^T\beta. \tag{8.7}$$

To obtain the aggregate series $\mathcal{T}_x$ from individual forum features $\mathcal{T}_{x,f}$, we just average the values across all forums for each time point. Here, we use each feature separately, although we will discuss the combinations of features together with sparsity constraints later.

**Unsupervised learning.** Now, we discuss the unsupervised learning model that takes as input the time series features in the training span and predicts the attack types in $A$ on an organization $E$ in the test span. However, unlike the supervised model, this model's prediction output does not depend on the type of attack or the organization $E$. It produces the same output for any attack. Informally, anomalies are patterns in data that do not conform to a well-defined notion of normal behavior. The problem of finding these patterns is referred to as anomaly detection [29, 77]. Considering our cyber-security context, the importance of anomaly detection comes from the idea that anomalies in data translate to information that can explain actionable deviations from normal behavior, thus leading to a cyber-attack. We use subspace-based anomaly detection methods that take as input $\mathcal{T}_{x,f}$ and aggregates them across all forums to find anomalies in the cumulative time series for feature $x$. We derive motivation for this technique from the widely used projection-based anomaly detection methods [87, 157] that detect volume anomalies from the time series of network link traffic. Additionally, there have been techniques in graph-based anomaly detection that find graph objects that are rare and considered outliers [4]. However, our motivation behind using anomaly detection does not arise from a feature analysis perspective or finding anomalous users but from a time series perspective – we observe that there could be spikes in time series of the same feature, in different forums, on different days. The question is, how do we aggregate those spikes together instead of averaging them to an extent that the spikes die out in the aggregate? From that perspective, we find that the method used in [87] suits our framework – we want to be able to filter out the spikes from the same feature computed in different forums while projecting the dimension space of several forums to a one-dimensional subspace. The overall procedure for detecting anomalies from the time series data on each feature has been described through the following steps – we will again drop the subscript $x$ to generalize the operations for all features.

**Aggregating time series.** We create a matrix $\mathbf{Y}$ with dimensions (# time points) × (F), where the rows denote values at a single time step $t$ for forums $f \in F$. While $\mathbf{Y}$ denotes the set of measurements for all forums $F$, we will also frequently work with $\mathbf{y}$, a vector of measurements from a single time step $t$.

**Subspace separation.** Principal component analysis (PCA) [166] is a method to transform the coordinates of the data points by projecting them to a set of new axes termed as the principal components. We apply PCA on matrix $\mathbf{Y}$, treating each row of $\mathbf{Y}$ as a point in $\mathbb{R}^F$. Applying PCA to $\mathbf{Y}$ yields a set of $F$ principal components, $\{\mathbf{v}\}_{i=1}^{F}$. In general, the $kth$ principal component $\mathbf{v}_k$ is:

$$\mathbf{v}_k = \underset{\|\mathbf{v}\|=1}{\arg\max} \left\| \left( \mathbf{Y} - \sum_{i=1}^{k-1} \mathbf{Y}\, \mathbf{v_i} \mathbf{v_i^T} \right) v \right\|. \tag{8.8}$$

We determine the *principal axes* (*components*) by choosing the first few components that capture the maximum variance along their direction. Then, the matrix $\mathbf{Y}$ can be mapped onto the new axes leading to *residual* or *anomalous subspace*. For detecting anomalies, we need to separate the vectors $\mathbf{y} \in \mathbb{R}^F$ at any time step into normal and anomalous components. We will refer to these as the *state* and *residual* vectors of $\mathbf{y}$. The key idea in the subspace-based detection step is that, once $S$ and $\widetilde{S}$ have been constructed, the separation can be done by projecting $\mathbf{y}$ onto these subspaces. We tend to decompose this $\mathbf{y}$ as $\mathbf{y} = \widehat{\mathbf{y}}+\widetilde{\mathbf{y}}$. To do so, we arrange the set of principal components corresponding to the normal subspace $(\mathbf{v}_1, \mathbf{v}_2, \ldots, \mathbf{v}_r)$ as columns of a matrix $\mathbf{P}$ of size $f \times r$, where $r$ denotes the number of *normal principal axes* determined from the previous step. We can then form $\widehat{\mathbf{y}}$ and $\widetilde{\mathbf{y}}$ as

$$\widehat{\mathbf{y}} = \mathbf{P}\mathbf{P}^T\mathbf{y} = \mathbf{C}\mathbf{y} \quad \text{and} \quad \widetilde{\mathbf{y}} = (\mathbf{I} - \mathbf{P}\mathbf{P}^T)\mathbf{y} = \widetilde{\mathbf{C}}\mathbf{y}. \tag{8.9}$$

where the matrix $\mathbf{C} = \mathbf{P}\mathbf{P}^T$ represents the linear operator that performs projection onto the normal subspace, and $\widetilde{\mathbf{C}}$ likewise projects onto the residual subspace. Here, $\widehat{\mathbf{y}}$ is referred to as the state vector and $\widetilde{\mathbf{y}}$ as the residual vector.

**Detection of anomalies.** The idea of anomaly detection is to monitor the residual vector that captures abnormal changes in $\mathbf{y}$. As mentioned in [87, 171], there has been substantial research into designing statistical metrics for detecting abnormal changes in $\widetilde{\mathbf{y}}$ using thresholding. We leverage here one of the widely used metrics, the squared prediction error (SPE) on the residual vector: $SPE \equiv \|\widetilde{\mathbf{y}}\| \equiv \|\widetilde{\mathbf{C}}\mathbf{y}\|^2$. This produces the SPE residual vector, and when combined over all time points, it produces the residual vector time series denoted by $\mathcal{R}$. The SPE residual vector at any time point is considered normal if $SPE \leq \delta_\alpha^2$, where $\delta_\alpha^2$ denotes the threshold for the SPE at the $1-\alpha$ confidence level. We keep this threshold dynamic and use it as a parameter for evaluating the anomaly-based prediction models described in Section 8.5. Figure 8.9 demonstrates the decomposition of the time series into the SPE state and residual vectors. While Figure 8.9 (b) captures most of the normal behavior, the SPE residual time series in Figure 8.9 (c) captures all the anomalies across all the forums. The key point of this anomaly detection procedure is that instead of monitoring the time series feature $\mathcal{T}_{x,f}$ separately across all forums in $F$, we reduce it to monitoring the SPE residual time series vector $\mathcal{R}_x$ for predicting cyber-attacks.

### 8.4.3 Step 3: Attack Prediction

**Anomaly detection to attack prediction.** Following the subspace projection method to obtain $\mathcal{R}_x$ from the input time series feature $\mathcal{T}_{x,f}$ for all forums $f \in F$, we use threshold mechanisms on $\mathcal{R}_x$ to flag the time point $t$ as an anomaly if $\mathcal{R}_x[t]$ is greater than a threshold value. Given a time point $t$ as a test instance, we project the time series vector $\mathcal{T}_x[t_{-(\eta+\delta)} : t_{(-\delta)}]$ – which contains the information of feature $x$ across all forums in $F$ – on the anomalous subspace $\widetilde{\mathbf{C}} = \mathbf{I}-\mathbf{P}\mathbf{P}^T$ shown in Equation 8.9, if that time window is not already

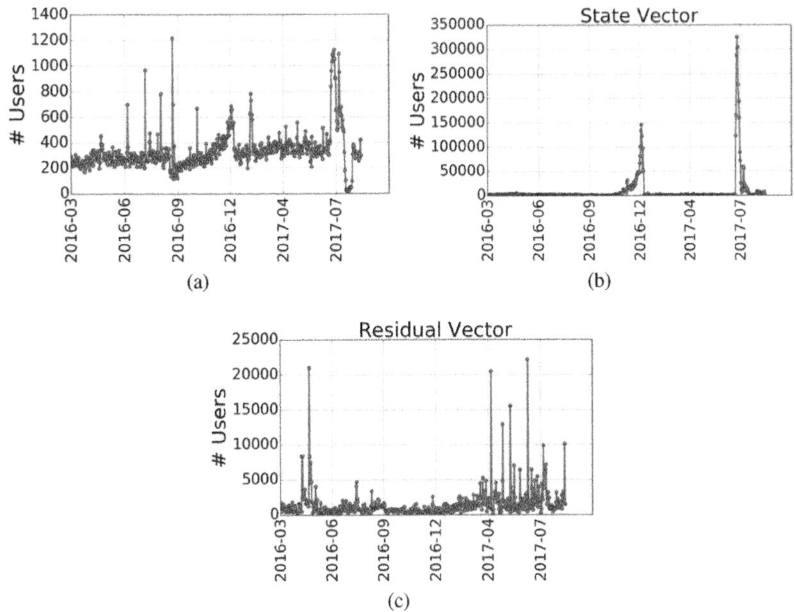


Figure 8.9 (a) The time series $\mathcal{T}$ for the number of users feature computed on a daily basis and averaged across all forums $F$. (b) The SPE *state* time series vector after subspace separation (not averaged). (c) The SPE residual time series vector $\mathcal{R}$ after subspace separation (not averaged).

part of the training data. Following this, we calculate the squared prediction error (SPE) that produces a one-dimensional vector $\mathbf{y}_{test}$ of dimension $\mathbb{R}^{\eta \times 1}$. We count the number of anomalous time points $t_a$ – denoted by $\mathcal{N}(t_a)$, with $t_a \in [t_{-(\eta+\delta)}, t_{(-\delta)}]$ – that cross a chosen threshold. Finally, we flag an attack at $t$ if $\mathcal{N}(t_a) >= max(1, \frac{\zeta}{7})$. This metric gives a normalized count threshold over a week for any $\zeta$ (window parameter), and for this $\zeta$ being less than a week, we just count whether there is at least one anomaly in that time gap.

The fact that we avoid the attack ground truth data to learn event-based parameters has pros and cons. While in the absence of sufficient data for training supervised models, anomaly detectors can investigate various markers or features for abnormal behavior leading to attacks. However, such methods cannot be tailored to specific attack types in organizations.

**Supervised model prediction.** For the logistic regression model, we first create the feature time series $\mathcal{T}_x$ for the test span and use it to calculate the probability of attack in Equation 8.6. When the probability is greater than 0.5, we output a positive attack case; otherwise, we predict a non attack case.

## 8.5 Experiments and Results

### 8.5.1 Parameter Settings

In this chapter, the granularity for each time index in the $\mathcal{T}$ function is one day, which means that we compute feature values over all days of our data. For incrementally computing the values of the time series, we consider the time span of each subsequence $\tau \in \Gamma$ as 1 month, and for each $\tau$, we consider $H_\tau = 3$ months immediately preceding $\tau$. Thus, for every additional month of training or test data that is provided to the model, we use the preceding three months to create the historical network and compute the corresponding features on all days in $\tau$. As mentioned earlier, this streaming nature of feature generation ensures we engineer the features relevant to the time frame of attack prediction. For choosing the experts, we remove users with in-degree less than 10 in $G_{H_\tau}$ from $exp_\tau$, after trying other values. We accomplish that by investigating the post content of a few experts, finding that beyond this threshold of 10, many users whose posts are not relevant to attack signals are included.

For the reply network construction, we have two parameters, $thresh_{spat}$ and $thresh_{temp}$, which correspond to the spatial and temporal constraints, respectively. For setting these constraints, we apply a 2D grid search over them by constructing the reply network using their pairwise combinations. Then, for each combination, we fit the in-degree distribution to a power law with an exponent of 1.35. We fix the power law exponent based on a study done in [142]. The authors there found that a reply network, created when the thread reply hierarchy was known in two forums, was best fit to a power law (in-degree distribution) when the exponents were in the range $[1.35, 1.75]$. We take the pair combination that gives us the minimum difference when we calculate the error arising from our degree distribution and $p(k) \sim k^{-1.35}$. Using this procedure, we find that $thresh_{spat} = 10$ (posts) and $thresh_{temp} = 15$ (minutes) have the best fit in terms of the reply network created.

The hyper parameters $\eta$ and $\delta$ of the logistic regression model have been selected using a cross-validation approach that we briefly discuss in section 8.5.2. Similarly for the detection of anomalies, we test the threshold parameter for the residual vector $\delta_\alpha^2$ (mentioned in Section 8.4.3) on different values and plot the ROC curve to test the performance. We set to 1 the anomaly count threshold parameter $\zeta$, such that we tag a cyber-attack on $t$ when the count of anomalies in the selected window $[t_{-\eta-\delta}, t_{-delta}]$ crosses $\zeta$. The reason behind this is simple: as we observe many days with spikes, we just attribute an attack to a day if there is at least one anomaly in the time window prior to it. We do realize that this parameter needs to be cross-validated, but our observations suggest that there would be very low precision in the performance when $\zeta$ is set to a high value.

### 8.5.2 Results

To demonstrate the effectiveness of the features on real-world cyber-attacks, we perform separate experiments with the learning models described in Section 8.4.2. Although for the anomaly detection-based prediction, we use the same set of features as input for attack prediction across different attack types, for the supervised model, we build different learning models using the ground truth available from separate attack types in $A$. Additionally, we only perform supervised classification for the *malicious-email* and the *endpoint-malware* attack types, leaving out *malicious-destination* due to lack of sufficient training data.

As mentioned in Section 8.4.2, we consider a binary prediction problem in this chapter, assigning an attack flag of 1 for at least one attack on each day, and 0 otherwise. For *malicious-email*, out of 335 days considered in the dataset, there have been reported attacks on 97 days, which constitutes a positive class ratio of around 29%. For *endpoint-malware*, the total number of attack days is 31 out of 306 days of the considered span in the training dataset, which constitutes a positive class ratio of around 10%. Finally, for *endpoint-malware*, we have a total of 26 days of attacks out of a total of 276 days considered in the training set, constituting a positive class ratio of 9.4%. Table 8.2 shows the statistics of the training and test data for the three cyber-attack types from Armstrong. Although we do not use remedial diagnostics in our learning models to account for this class imbalance, the absence of a large training dataset and the missing attack data information accounting for irregularities make a strong case for using sampling techniques to address these issues. One of the challenges in remedial diagnostics for class imbalance here is that we need to take into account the temporal dependencies while incorporating any sampling techniques as remedies. However, we run a complementary experiment using SMOTE sampling as a simple measure for introducing synthetic samples into the training dataset. We discuss the details of this strategy later.

For evaluating the performance of the models, we split the time frame of each event into 70%–30% averaged to the nearest month separately for each

Table 8.2 *Statistics of the training and test samples from Armstrong*

| | **Train positive samples** | **Train negative samples** | **Test positive samples** | **Test negative samples** |
|---|---|---|---|---|
| **Malicious email** | 65 | 178 | 32 | 60 |
| **Endpoint malware** | 49 | 134 | 31 | 92 |
| **Malware destination** | 7 | 115 | 8 | 84 |

*event-type*. To do so, we take the first 70% of time in months as the training dataset and the remaining 30% in sequence for the test dataset. As done in the previous chapters, we avoid shuffle split as often done in cross-validation techniques, being consistent when using sequential information for computing features. As shown in Figures 8.1, we use different time frames for the training model and the test sets, as the period of attack information varies for each event. For *malicious-email*, which remains our primary testbed evaluation event, we consider the time period from October 2016 to May 2017 (eight months) in the online hacker forums as our training data and the period from June 2017 to August 2017 (three months) as our test data. For *endpoint-malware*, we use the time period from April 2016 to September 2016 (six months) as our training data and June 2017 to August 2017 (three months) as our test data for evaluation.

**Unsupervised model prediction performance.** The subspace projection method described before is used to filter out anomalies from the SPE residual time series vector $\mathcal{R}_x$. We then leverage those anomalies to predict the attacks, trying to see the trade-offs between the number of true alerts and the number of false alerts obtained. We consider the first eight principal components among the 53 forums studied, using the first three as the *normal axes* and the remaining five as the *residual axes*.[5]

For evaluating the prediction performance, we examine the receiver operating characteristic (ROC) curves for the features over different spans of $\delta$ and $\eta$. However, Figure 8.10 presents our keys findings when we set $\eta = 8$ days and $\delta = 7$ days, although we could not come to general conclusions over the choices of the parameters $\eta$ and $\delta$ from these results. Each point in these ROC curves denotes a threshold among the vector values obtained from the squared prediction error of the projected test input $\mathbf{y}$ – those points cross the threshold as anomalies. We present the results in each plot grouped by the *event-type* and the features, considering forum and graph-based statistics. Figures 8.10 (a) and (b) show that, for *malicious-email*, we obtain the best AUC results of 0.67 for the vulnerability mention feature among the forum statistics groups and an AUC of 0.69 for graph conductance among the set of graph-based features. For *malicious-destination*, we obtain a best AUC of 0.69 for the common community count feature among the set of graph-based features and a best AUC of 0.66 on the number of users at $t_d$ among the forum statistics. For *endpoint-malware*, we obtain a best AUC of 0.69 on the number of users stats and 0.63 on the common communities *CC* feature. Empirically, we find that

[5] Empirical evidence shows that the first three principal components capture the maximum variance.

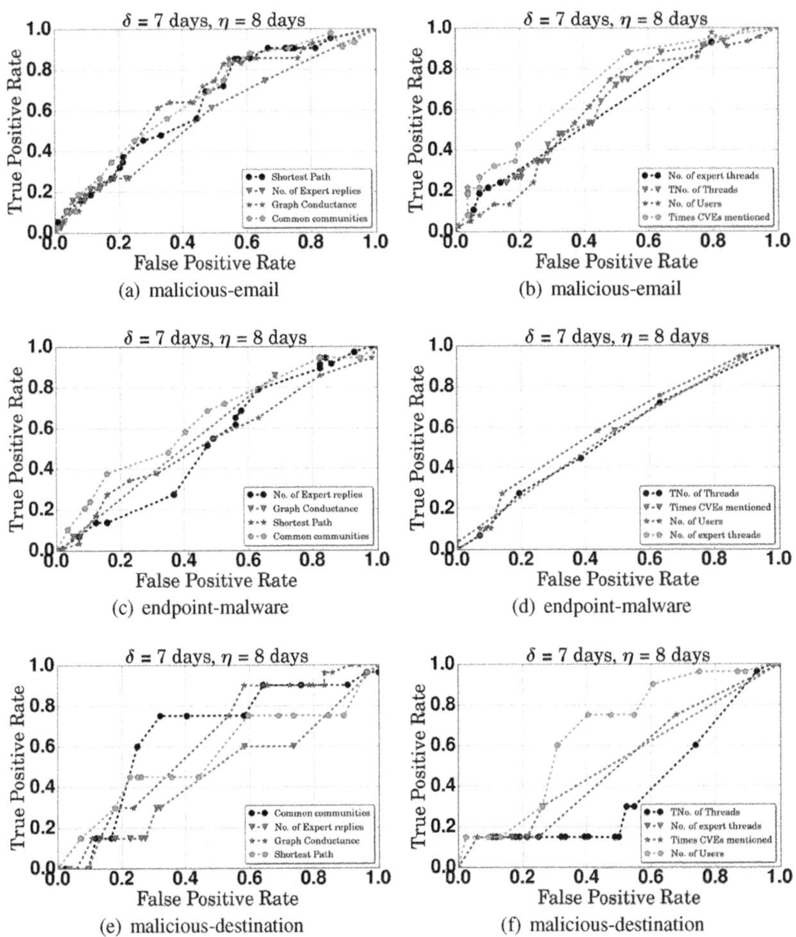


(a) malicious-email (b) malicious-email

(c) endpoint-malware (d) endpoint-malware

(e) malicious-destination (f) malicious-destination

Figure 8.10 ROC curves for prediction using unsupervised anomaly detection methods: $\delta$ = 7 days, $\eta$ = 8 days.

among the network features that rely on the set of *experts*, it is not sufficient to look at how these experts reply to other users in terms of frequency – they exhibit the least AUC in the unsupervised setting. The fact that common communities and graph conductance turn out to be better predictors than just the shortest path distance or the number of replies by experts suggests that *experts* tend to focus on posts of a few individuals when any significant post arises. Thus, focusing on individuals who are close to *experts* in terms of random walks and communities is favorable.

One of the reasons behind the poor performance of the detector on the *malicious-destination* type of attacks compared to *malicious-email* is that the weekly average number of incidents for the three attack types are *malicious-email* = 2.9, *endpoint-malware* = 3.6, and *malicious-destination* = 1.52. Hence, although the total number of incidents are similar for both attack types, the number of days on which the attacks occur is lesser for *malicious-destination*, which affects the binary classification conducted here.

**Supervised model prediction performance.** For the logistic regression model, we consider a one-week time window $\eta$ while keeping $\delta$ = 8 days, similar to the unsupervised setting. Due to the absence of sufficient positive examples, we avoid using this model for predicting attacks of type *malicious-destination*. From among the set of statistics features used for predicting the *malicious-email* attacks shown in Figure 8.11(b), we observe the best results using the number of threads as the signal, obtaining precision of 0.43, recall of 0.59, and F1 score of 0.5 against the random F1 of 0.34. From among the set of graph-based features, we obtain the best results from graph conductance with precision of 0.44, recall of 0.65, and F1 score of 0.53, which shows

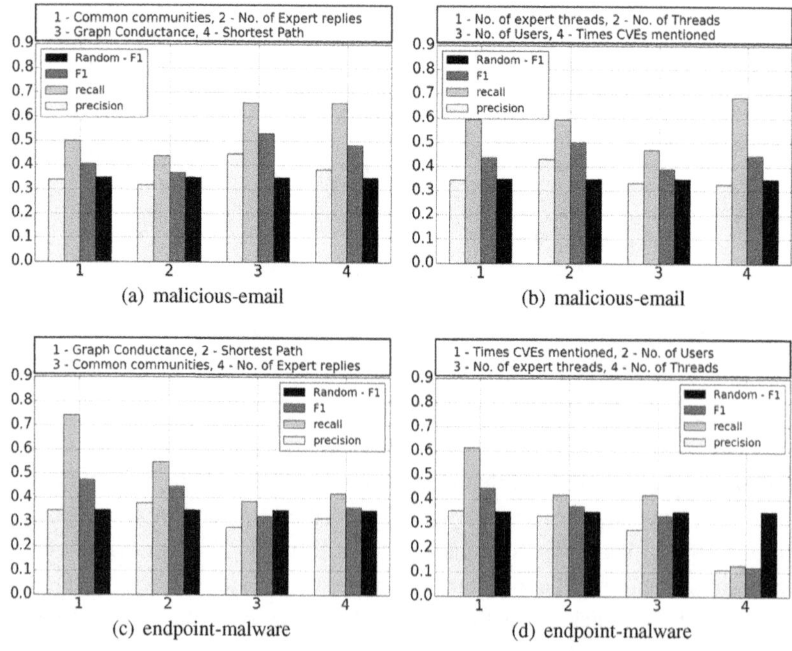


(a) malicious-email

(b) malicious-email

(c) endpoint-malware

(d) endpoint-malware

Figure 8.11 Classification results for the features considering the supervised model: $\delta$ = 7 days, $\eta$ = 8 days.

an increase in recall over the number of threads measure. Additionally, we observe that in the case of supervised prediction, the best features in terms of F1 score are graph conductance and shortest paths, whereas number of threads and vulnerability mentions turn out to be the best among the statistics. For the attacks belonging to the type *endpoint-malware*, we observe similar characteristics for the graph features, obtaining a best precision of 0.34, recall of 0.74, and F1 score of 0.47 against a random F1 of 0.35 – followed by the shortest paths measure. However, for the statistics measures, we obtain precision of 0.35, recall 0.61, and F1 score of 0.45 for the vulnerability mentions, followed by the number of threads, which gives us an F1 score of 0.43. Although the common communities features does not help much in the overall prediction results, in the following section, we describe a special case that demonstrates the predictive power of the community structure in networks.

The challenging nature of the supervised prediction problem is due to not only the issue of class imbalance but also the lack of large samples of attacks in the dataset which, if present, could have been used for sampling purposes. As an experiment, we also use random forests as the classification model, not observing any significant improvements in the results over the random case. This suggests that the LR model with temporal regularization helps in these cases of time series predictions. Additionally, we use SMOTE to address the class imbalance, plotting the results for the malicious email attacks in Figure 8.12. Comparing those results with those of Figure 8.11, we find that while for all features, the recall increases, the precision drops substantially. We find that among the graph features, both graph conductance and the number of expert replies perform equally well with F1 score of 0.52, while the number of threads with CVE mentions achieves the best results with F1 score of 0.49.

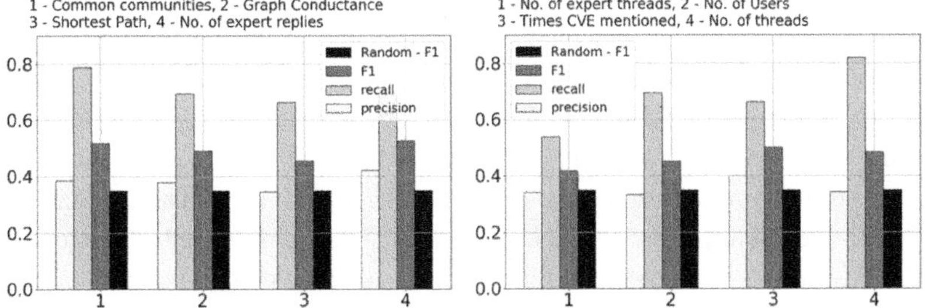


Figure 8.12 Classification results for malicious-emails using SMOTE sampling on top of the supervised model.

**Model with feature combinations.** One of the major problems with the dataset is the imbalance in the training and test data. The added complexities arise from the fact that if we consider all features over the time window of feature selection, the total number of features $z$ (variables) for the learning models is $z = \#\text{ features} \times (\eta)$. In our scenario, this is almost equal to the number of data points we have for training depending on $\eta$ and also depending on whether we consider different variations of the features in Table 8.1, exposing us to the risk of overfitting. Thus, in order to use all features in each group together for prediction, we apply three additional regularization terms in the longitudinal regression model: the L1 penalty, the L2 penalty, and the *group lasso* regularization [109]. The final objective function can be written as

$$l(\boldsymbol{\beta}) = -\sum_{i=1}^{N} \log(1 + e^{-y_i(\beta^T \mathbf{x_i})}) + \frac{m}{2}\|\beta\|_2^2 + l\|\beta\|_1 + g.GL(\beta), \tag{8.10}$$

where $m$, $l$, and $g$ are the hyper parameters for the regularization terms and the $GL(\beta)$ term is $\sum_{g=1}^{G}\|\beta_{\mathcal{I}_g}\|_2$, with $\mathcal{I}_g$ denoting the index set belonging to the $g$th group of variables, $g = 1 \ldots G$.

Each $g$ is the time index $t_h \in [t_{-\eta-\delta}, t_{-\delta}]$, so this group variable selects all features belonging to a time point in history while reducing other time points to 0. It has the desired property of conducting variable selection at the temporal group level and is invariant under (group-wise) orthogonal transformations like ridge regression. While there are other models that could be used for prediction that incorporates the temporal and sequential nature of the data – like hidden Markov models (HMM) and recurrent neural networks (RNN) – the logit model allows us to transparently adjust to the sparsity of data, especially in the absence of a large dataset. For the model with the group lasso regularization in Equation 8.10, we set the parameters $m, l$, and $g$ to 0.3, 0.3, and 0.1, respectively, based on a grid search on $m$ and $l$, keeping $g$ low so that most time points within a single feature are set to 0 to avoid overfitting.

We cross-validated this model on the two hyper parameters $\eta$ and $\delta$. While the recall increases for all combinations of hyper parameters for all features compared to results shown in Figure 8.13, the precision remains the same across different values of the hyper-parameters. We test on different $\eta$, keeping $\delta$ fixed at eight days, and also test on different $\delta$, keeping $\eta$ fixed at seven days. The best results were obtained for *malicious-email* prediction using $n = 7$ and $\delta = 8$ days. We get the best F1 value of 0.56 (using $\eta = 7$ days and keeping $\delta$ fixed at 8) using this feature combination model against the best F1 score of 0.53 obtained from using single features without regularization.

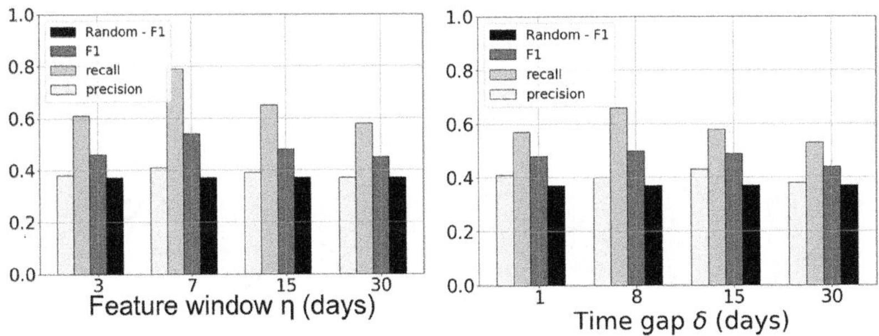


Figure 8.13 Classification results for malicious email with feature combination and considering group lasso regularization: $m = 0.3, l = 0.3, g = 0.1$. Refer to Equation 8.10 for the model used for this prediction.

## 8.6 Discussion

As with most machine learning models that attempt binary and multiclass classification, including neural networks, the features attributed to the predictions can in most situations explain correlation. The causation needs more controlled studies, such as visualization by projecting features onto a lower-dimensional space, ablation studies or understanding feature importance, and using regularization techniques for ensuring sparsity for some features or eliminating redundancy [143]. To this end, we investigate whether our framework correlates signals from hacker discussions with real-world events or other types of attacks. We present three controlled studies that show the extent to which our results are interpretable.

### 8.6.1 Prediction in High-Activity Weeks

One of the main challenges in predicting external threats without any method to correlate them with external data sources like the online discussion threads or any other database is that it is difficult to validate which kinds of attacks are most correlated with these data sources. To accomplish this goal, we examine a controlled experiment setup for the *malicious-email* attacks where we only consider the weeks that exhibited high frequency of attacks compared to the overall time frame – in our case, we consider weeks having more than five attacks (in each) during the test time frame. These high numbers may be due to multiple attacks in one day or few attacks on all days. The main idea is to see how well the supervised model performs in these weeks of interest, compared to the random predictions with and without prior distribution of

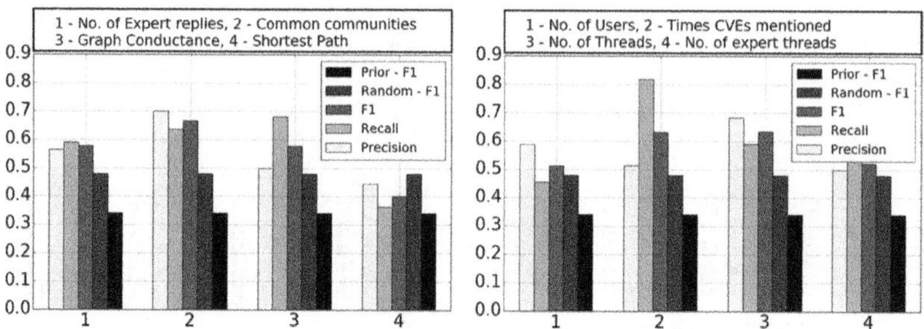


Figure 8.14 Classification results for *malicious-email* attacks in high frequency weeks, considering $\delta$ = 7 days and $\eta$ = 8 days.

attack information. We run the same supervised prediction method but evaluate them only on those specific weeks.

From the results presented in Figure 8.14, we find that the best results are obtained by the common communities feature, with precision of 0.7, recall of 0.63, and F1 score of 0.67, compared to the random (no priors) F1 score of 0.48 and the random (with priors) F1 score of 0.34 for the same time parameters. Among the statistics measures, we obtain a highest F1 score of 0.63 for the vulnerability mentions feature. Additionally, unlike the results over all the days, for these specific weeks, the model achieves high precision while maintaining comparable recall, emphasizing the fact that the number of false positives is also reduced during these periods. This empirically suggests that for weeks that exhibit a higher number of attacks, looking at online sources for vulnerability mentions and the network structure, analytics can definitely help predict cyber-attacks.

### 8.6.2 Experiments with Another Security Breach Dataset

One of the reasons behind the use of the Armstrong dataset as our ground truth data is the length of the time frame over which the attack data were available – not just the number of attack cases reported (one could have a lot of attack cases reported for only a few days). Since we are conducting a binary classification problem, the more spread the attacks are, the more training points we have for our models and test points for evaluation. However, as a complementary experiment on the learnability of the model parameters specific to companies, we test the prediction problem on a dataset of security incidents from Dexter. As shown in Figure 8.1, the distribution of attacks over time is different for the events.

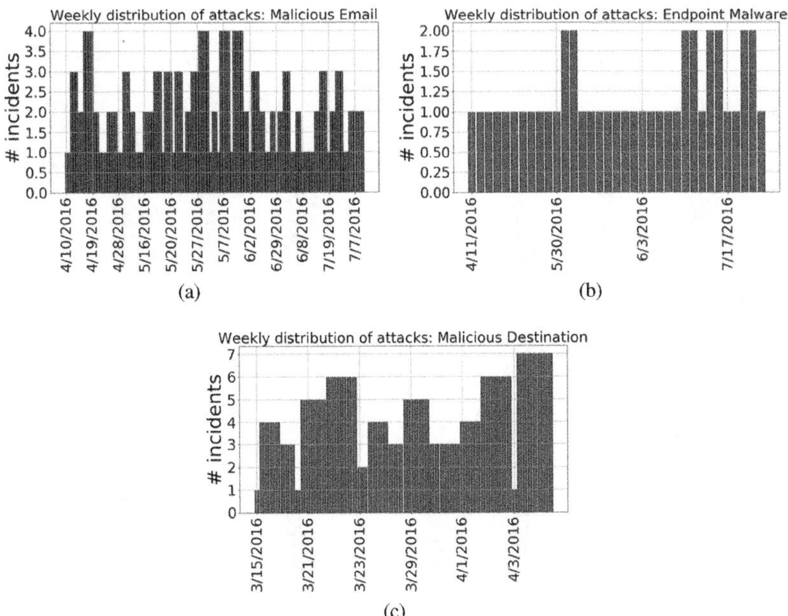


Figure 8.15 Weekly occurrence of security breach incidents for Dexter of different types: (a) malicious email, (b) endpoint malware, and (c) malicious destination.

We observe that compared to the Armstrong dataset, the time span for which the attack ground truth data are available is much shorter – we obtain around five months of attack data for the three events shown in Figure 8.15, from April to August 2016. We have 58 distinct days with at least one incident tagged as *malicious-destination*, 35 distinct days tagged as *endpoint-malware*, and 114 distinct days for *malicious-email*. A total of 565 incidents (not distinct days) over a span of five months are considered for Dexter, which is twice the number reported for Armstrong. However, compared to the Armstrong data, which is spread over 17 months, we have only 4 months to train and test using Dexter data. We use the same framework for predicting attacks on Dexter, presenting the results in Figure 8.16. We obtain the best F1 score of 0.6 on the malicious email attacks using the graph conductance measure and the best F1 score of 0.59 using the expert threads statistics forum metadata feature (refer to Table 8.1), against a random F1 score of 0.37.

The results in Figure 8.16 suggest that the network features focused on experts – where we consider how fast these individuals reply to posts that can be connected to regular posts – improve the results over other features that do not consider the reply path structure.

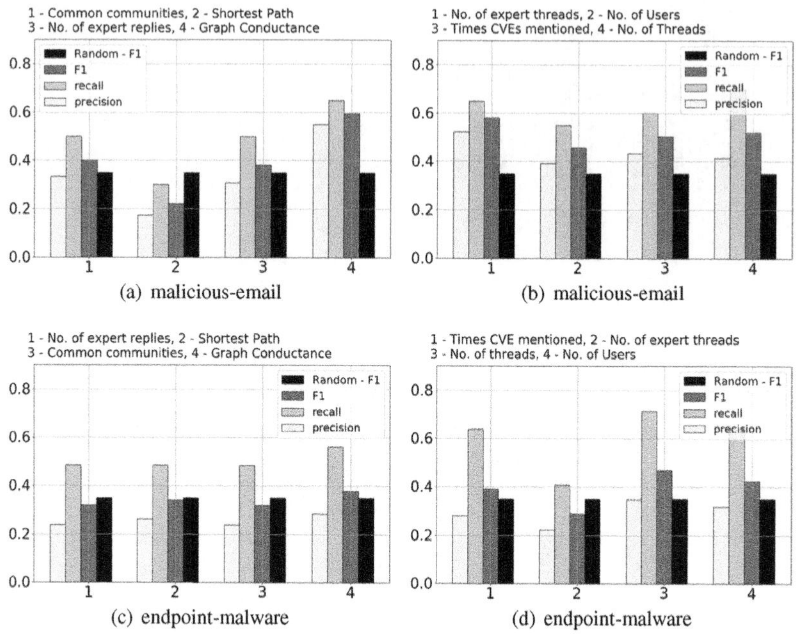

(a) malicious-email (b) malicious-email

(c) endpoint-malware (d) endpoint-malware

Figure 8.16 Classification results on Dexter events for the supervised model: $\delta$ = 7 days, $\eta$ = 8 days.

## 8.7 Related Work

In this chapter, we discuss some of the past and ongoing research in the cybersecurity domain that also caters to the general area of predicting future cyberbreach incidents. Most of the work on vulnerability exploitation that leverages discussions in the underground forums [5, 52, 110] and in social media platforms like Twitter [83, 148, 153] has focused on two aspects: (1) analyzing the dynamics of underground forums and markets that drive it, giving rise to the belief that the "life cycle of vulnerabilities" in these platforms has significant impact on "real-world" cyber-attacks [19, 85], and (2) prioritizing vulnerabilities using social media platforms or binary file appearance logs of machines to predict risk of attack through vulnerability exploitation [20]. The two components of the majority of those studies are analysis of vulnerabilities and their likelihood of exploitation in these forums or platforms – like our research work conducted in Chapter 6 – and vulnerability severity based prediction to associate them to cyber-attack incidents [148].

We note that few studies have focused on filtering the markets and forums that most contribute to the cyber-threat scenario [160, 169, 195]. One way to understand the attack indicators surrounding online hacker platforms, that could lead to malicious attempts to breach systems at scale, is to monitor the interactions that receive attention within those websites. In the following, we discuss two areas within which our work conducted in this chapter falls when addressing cyber-attack prediction based on signals derived from online hacker discussions, including on social media. However, we point out the main differences that bring out the significance and novelty of our approach and the problem addressed.

1. **Cyber-attack prediction using social media data:** There have been several attempts to use external social media data to predict cyber-attacks [39, 83, 92, 93]. However, the problem these studies focus on is to build predictive models that correlate social media signals to attacks on proprietary systems that are not observed for a given organization. In contrast to this, our attack prediction problem proposes to build models specific to an organization using external sensors not obtained from the internal system data of this organization. The closest work in this area is conducted in [129], where the authors used signals from GDELT, Twitter, and OTX, based on keywords related to the organization for forecasting cyber-attacks. One of the challenges regarding our dataset is that we could not find any keywords related to the name of our target organization in online forums – similar issues are reported in [70], where the authors relied on some curated keyword search from Twitter, blogs, and the darkweb for attack prediction. Our work has a slight advantage in that since our selection of forums and features including vulnerability information does not depend on human engineered knowledge – rather, it focuses on the trends in time, making our streaming nature of prediction scalable and cross-network.
2. **Social network analysis for cyber-security.** Network analysis to understand the topology of darkweb forums has been studied at breadth in [135], where the authors analyzed the reply networks of forums to identify members of Islamic community. Similarly in [91], the authors used topic modeling and the network structure of darkweb forums to understand the interactions between extremist groups. However, such analysis of reply networks has been conducted on static networks [9], where the authors measured network features of users for prediction. A recent study done in [154] shows how to leverage the network structure of forum reply networks for cyber-attack prediction. Those studies suggest the nature of interactions can unveil important actors in the darkweb and their discussions can provide signals for cyber-attacks. One of our contributions

here is that we use evolving networks of the users with certain constraints that can now be leveraged for streaming prediction on a daily basis and in an automated manner. Our hypothesis lies on the premise that the attention broadcast by these users toward other posts are in fact sensors for impending cyber-attacks.

## 8.8 Conclusions

In this chapter, we empirically demonstrate that the reply network structure from online, cross-network hacker discussions can be leveraged to predict external enterprise threats. We leverage the network and interaction patterns in the forums to understand the extent to which they can be used as useful indicators. Against class-imbalanced attack data, our method achieves a best F1 score of 0.53 for one type of attack using logistic regression models, while being able to maintain high recall. Using an unsupervised anomaly detector, we are able to achieve a maximum AUC of 0.69 by leveraging the network structure. Similar to the work conducted in Chapter 7, this work leverages two different datasets to correlate attacks and user interactions – the limitations clearly lie in being precisely able to infer the path to the attack through discussions. This would require some additional mechanisms on leveraging the content to check whether the discussions catered to a particular exploit that caused the attack. However, we believe the proposed framework contributes to the understanding of how user interaction patterns can be mined using attributes related to vulnerabilities and how they can be leveraged to create a framework for attack prediction.

# 9
# Finding At-Risk Systems without Software Vulnerability Identifiers (CVEs)

## 9.1 Introduction

Chapter 6 shows that many organizations currently rely on the vulnerability rating system (CVSS-score) provided by NIST to identify whether their systems are at risk from disclosed vulnerabilities. However, we show and confirm through experiments poor correlation between the CVSS score and the likelihood that a vulnerability will be targeted by hackers. Thus, we propose, in Chapter 6, an alternative approach for organizations to proactively identify if their vulnerable systems are of interest to hackers, leveraging for that information from online hacker sites. Note that the approaches proposed in Chapters 6, 7, and 8 to predict cyber-threats only consider hacker discussions (directly or indirectly) that have explicit CVE mentions, which is actually a very small portion of the discussions analyzed. Thus, a limitation of those approaches is that hacker discussions with no vulnerability identifiers (CVEs) are not taken into account.

In this chapter, we propose a framework to identify systems that might be of interest to hackers using the first three components of the common platform enumeration (CPE) naming scheme (Table 9.1 illustrates examples of them), not relying on explicit CVE mentions to accomplish this identification task. There is a hierarchical structure in the CPE components (from platform to vendor to product) that we leverage. For instance, if we are considering operating systems, then a limited number of vendors might be affected by a given vulnerability, for example, Microsoft, Apple, or Google. If we identify which vendor might be affected (say, Microsoft), then the products are related to the Windows operating system. This hierarchy helps us to narrow the search space as we go down the hierarchy.

We design a system that leverages cyber-threat intelligence (hacker discussions from online marketplaces and forums) and makes a decision regarding

Table 9.1 *System components and examples*

| **Components** | **Explanation and examples** |
|---|---|
| Platform | Can be either hardware (h), operating system (o), or application (a) based on what the vulnerability exploits |
| Vendor | The owner of the vulnerable product; examples include Google, Microsoft, The Mozilla Foundation, and the University of Oxford |
| Product | The product that is vulnerable; examples include Internet Explorer, Java Runtime Environment, Adobe Reader, and Windows 2000 |

at-risk systems, at the same time providing arguments as to *why* a particular decision was made. It explores multiple competing hypotheses (in this case, multiple platforms, vendors, products) based on the discussions for and against a particular at-risk component. The resulting system is a hybrid that combines DeLP[1] with machine learning classifiers. Previously, a similar reasoning system was employed for attributing cyber-attacks to responsible threat actors evaluated on a capture-the-flag dataset [128]. This chapter makes the following main contributions:

- We frame identifying at-risk systems as a multilabel classification problem and apply several machine learning approaches to compare their performance. We find that a large number of possible label choices for vendors and products with less representation in training account for the majority of the misclassified samples.
- To address misclassification, we propose a hybrid reasoning framework that combines machine learning techniques with defeasible argumentation to reduce the set of possible labels for each system component. The reasoning framework can provide arguments supporting the decisions, indicating *why* a particular system was identified over others; this aspect is important for a security analyst to better understand the decision.
- We report on experiments showing that the reduced set of labels used in conjunction with the classifiers leads to significant improvement in precision (15%–57%) while maintaining comparable recall.

The remainder of this chapter is organized as follows. Section 9.2 presents an overview of the proposed system. In Section 9.3, we discuss the dataset and provide an analysis. This is followed by the argumentation model based on [64] in Section 9.4. After that, the experimental setup and results

[1] Formalism that combines results of logic programming and defeasible argumentation [64].

(along with the DeLP programs for each system component) are discussed in Section 9.5. This is followed by a discussion of the results and related work in Section 9.6 and Section 9.7, respectively. Finally, Section 9.8 concludes the chapter.

## 9.2 System Overview

Figure 9.1 gives an overview of the reasoning system formed by the three main modules:

- **Knowledge base:** Our knowledge base consists of online hacker discussions from forums and marketplaces obtained from our data repository (see Chapter 1 for details). For this study, we collect data from 302 websites. We use the hacker discussions in terms of posted content (from forums) and item[2] descriptions (from markets), the website it is posted on, and the user posting the discussion as inputs to both the argumentation and machine learning models. We also input the CPE hierarchy from the NVD to the argumentation model. We discuss and provide further analysis of the data in Section 9.3. For the experiment, we sort the dataset by time (depending on when the discussion was posted); the first 80% is reserved for training (knowledge base) and the remaining 20% for testing. We follow a similar time split to compute the CPE hierarchy as well.

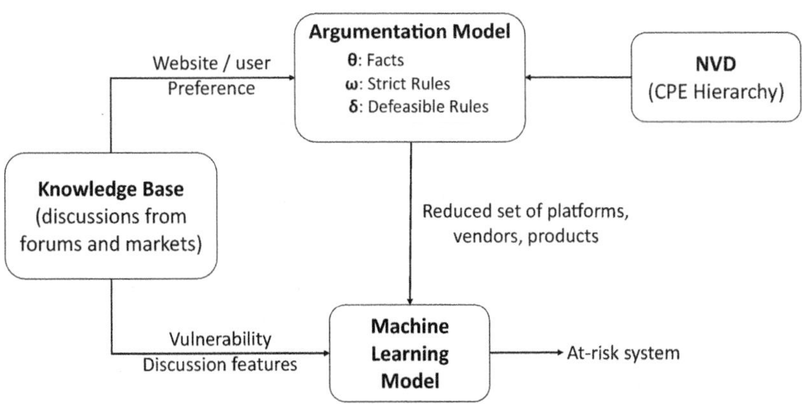


Figure 9.1 Reasoning system.

[2] We use "item" here since "product" is being used to identify a vulnerable product in the CPE hierarchy.

- **Argumentation model:** This component constructs arguments for a given query (at-risk system component) using elements in the knowledge base. We use a formalism called DeLP that combines logic programming with defeasible argumentation. It is made up of three constructs: *facts*, or observations from the knowledge base that cannot be contradicted; *strict rules*, or logical combinations of facts that are always true; and *defeasible rules*, which can be thought of as strict rules but are only true if no contradictory evidence is present. We discuss the argumentation framework with examples for each of the constructs in Section 9.4. Arguments help reduce the set of possible choices for platforms, vendors, and products; this reduced set of possible system components acts as one of the inputs to the machine learning model. The argumentation model thus constrains the machine learning model to identify the system from the reduced set of possible platforms, vendors, and products.
- **Machine learning model:** The machine learning model takes the knowledge base and query as input, along with the reduced set of possible system components from the argumentation model, and provides a result identifying the system. It is constrained by the argumentation model to select the components from the reduced platform, vendor, and product set, which aids the machine learning model (improving precision) as demonstrated in the results section of this chapter. We use text-based features extracted from the discussions (TF-IDF/Doc2Vec) for the machine learning model. As any standard machine learning model can be used in this module, we provide a comparison of different machine learning models to select the best one.

## 9.3 Dataset

### 9.3.1 Online Hacker Data

As mentioned before, we use data comprising forum discussions and marketplace items offered for sale in online sites hosted across multiple network protocols. Table 9.2 shows the characteristics for the websites, posts/items, and users. The data comprises websites with different languages, and a single website might have discussions in multiple languages.

Figure 9.2 shows the percentage of total websites in our hacker collection for the top 10 languages used to post discussions. The majority of the websites have discussions in English (73%), with other languages having an even distribution. Non-English text is translated into English using the Google Translate API.

Table 9.2 *Characteristics of online hacker data*

| | |
|---|---|
| Number of hacker websites | 302 |
| Number of unique users | 635,163 |
| Number of unique posts / items | 6,277,638 |
| Number of hacker websites (CVE mentions) | 135 |
| Number of unique users (CVE mentions) | 3,361 |
| Number of unique posts / items (CVE mentions) | 25,145 |

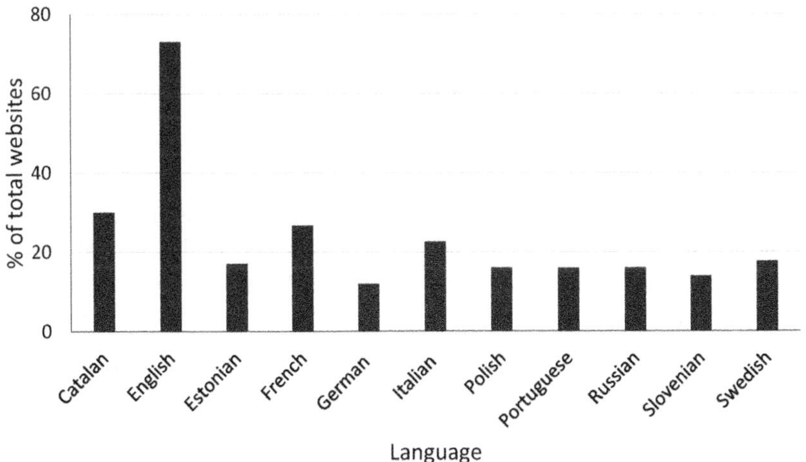


Figure 9.2 Percentage of total websites belonging to the top 10 languages in the hacker collection.

**Ground truth.** In order to evaluate the performance of the reasoning framework, we need ground truth associated with the hacker discussions. To obtain ground truth, we consider discussions from forums and marketplaces that mention a CVE number. From the CVE number we can look up the vulnerable systems using the NVD; we note that for both training and testing we remove the CVE number while computing features. Table 9.2 also shows the characteristics for the websites, posts/items, and users that mention a CVE number. The hacker discussion, with CVE mentions belong to 135 websites posted by 3,361 users. On analyzing the CVE mentions, most of the older vulnerabilities target products that are no longer in use. For that reason, we only consider CVE discussions posted after 2013 (starting January 1, 2014). These discussions make up around 70% of the total CVE discussions.

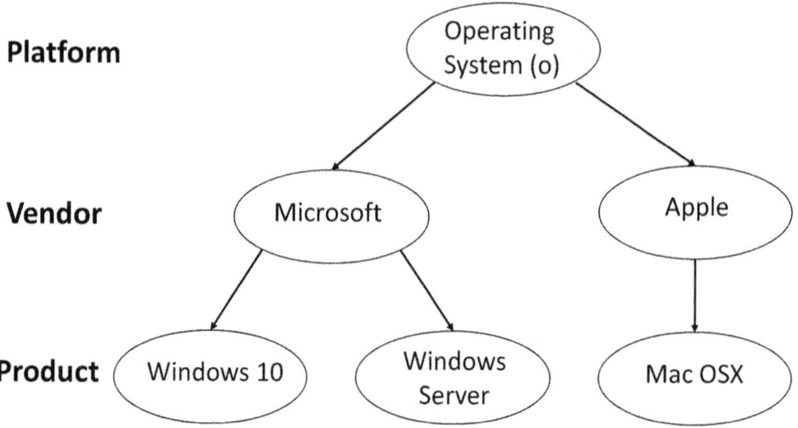


Figure 9.3 Subset of CPE hierarchy.

**CPE hierarchy.** We extract the hierarchy for the systems impacted by all vulnerabilities disclosed in the NVD [124], maintaining this hierarchy as a dictionary to build arguments on top of it. Figure 9.3 shows a subset of the built hierarchy with the three system components (platform, vendor, and product).

**Website/user preference.** We compute and maintain a list of system components discussed for each website and user. This lets us know if a particular website is preferred by hackers to discuss specific at-risk systems. The user list gives us the preference of the user regarding what at-risk systems are of interest to him or her. For platforms, most discussions pose a threat to operating systems (57%), followed by applications (43%), and hardware makes up a small fraction of the discussions (3%). There are discussions that pose a risk to multiple platforms. For vendors, the top five at-risk systems based on CVE mentions in the hacker discussions are Microsoft (24%), Linux (9%), Apple (6%), Oracle (5%), and Adobe (5%). Similar to platforms, discussions can pose a risk to multiple vendors. For products, the distribution is more even, since a single vendor can have multiple products. Even though Microsoft dominates the vendor discussion, it also has the most number of products that are at risk. The top five at-risk products based on CVE mentions in the hacker discussions are Windows server (5%), Windows 8.1 (4%), Linux kernel (3.8%), Mac OSX (2.3%), Flash player (1.9%).

## 9.4 Argumentation Model

Our approach relies on a model of the world where we can analyze competing hypotheses. Such a model allows for contradictory information so it can handle inconsistency in the data similar to the model employed for attributing cyber-attacks to threat actors [128, 164]. Before describing the argumentation model in detail, we introduce some necessary notation. Variables and constant symbols represent items such as the platform/vendor/product at risk by the discussion. Post/webID/userID represent the hacker discussion, where it was posted, and who posted it, respectively (we note that for privacy concerns the webID/userID are represented as integers in the data provided by the APIs – the names are not disclosed). We denote the set of all variable symbols with $\mathbf{V}$ and the set of all constants with $\mathbf{C}$. For our model, we require six subsets of $\mathbf{C}$:

- $\mathbf{C}_{post}$, denoting the hacker discussion,
- $\mathbf{C}_{web}$, denoting the websites where the hacker discussion was posted,
- $\mathbf{C}_{user}$, denoting the users who posts hacker discussions, and
- $\mathbf{C}_{platform}$, $\mathbf{C}_{vendor}$, $\mathbf{C}_{product}$ denoting the three components at risk by the discussion.

We use symbols in all capital letters to denote variables. In the running example, we use a subset of the collected hacker discussions.

**Example 1** *The following system and post/web/user information will be used in the running example:*
$\mathbf{C}_{post} = \{post_1, post_2, \ldots, post_n\}$
$\mathbf{C}_{web} = \{webID_1, webID_2, \ldots, webID_n\}$
$\mathbf{C}_{user} = \{userID_1, userID_2, \ldots, userID_n\}$
$\mathbf{C}_{platform} = \{h,\ o,\ a\}$
$\mathbf{C}_{vendor} = \{microsoft,\ google,\ the\_mozilla\_foundation\}$
$\mathbf{C}_{product} = \{internet\_explorer,\ windows\_10,\ adobe\_reader\}$ ■

The language also contains a set of predicate symbols that have constants or variables as arguments and denote events that can be either *true* or *false*. We denote the set of predicates with $\mathbf{P}$; examples of predicates are shown in Table 9.3. For instance, $user\_preference(userID_1, microsoft)$ will either be true or false and denotes the event where $userID_1$ prefers to post discussions regarding *microsoft* systems at risk.

A *ground atom* is composed of a predicate symbol and a tuple of constants, one for each argument; hence, ground atoms have no variables. The set of all ground atoms is denoted with $\mathbf{G}$. A *ground literal* $L$ is either a ground atom or a negated ground atom. An example of a ground atom for our running example is $posted(post_1,\ webID_1)$. In the following, we will use $\mathbf{G}'$ to denote a subset of $\mathbf{G}$.

In order to be able to deal with conflicting information and offer explainable results, we choose a structured argumentation framework [140] for our model;

Table 9.3 *Example predicates and explanation*

| Predicate | Explanation |
|---|---|
| posted($post_1$, $webID_1$) | $post_1$ was posted on the website $webID_1$ |
| at_risk($\mathcal{D}$, $V$) | Post $\mathcal{D}$ discussed vendor $V$ being at risk |
| user_preference ($userID_1$, $microsoft$) | $userID_1$ prefers to post discussions regarding Microsoft systems at risk |
| previously_seen ($webID_1$, $adobe\_flash$) | At-risk discussions regarding Adobe Flash are discussed in $webID_1$ |
| parent($microsoft$, $safari$) | Vendor Microsoft is a parent of product Safari |

our approach works by creating *arguments* (in the form of a set of rules and facts) that compete with each other to identify at-risk systems, given a hacker discussion. In this case, arguments are *defeated* based on the evaluation of contradicting information in other arguments. This procedure is commonly known as a *dialectical process* since it follows the same structure as dialogues between humans – as such, arguments that are *undefeated* (or *warranted*, in DeLP) prevail. Structuring the analysis in this manner also allows us to leverage the resulting structure, since the set of all prevailing arguments gives a clear map of how the conclusion is supported by the available data.

The clear benefit of the transparency afforded by such a process is that it lets a (human) security analyst not only add new arguments based on new evidence but also eliminate information identified as incorrect (perhaps because it is out of date or because it comes from a source newly identified as untrustworthy) and fine-tune the model for better performance. Since the argumentation model can deal with inconsistent information, it draws a natural analogy to the way humans settle disputes when there is disagreement. Having a clear explanation of why one argument is chosen over others is a desirable characteristic for both the analyst and for organizations to make decisions and policy changes. We now briefly discuss some preliminaries on DeLP.

**Defeasible logic programming.** DeLP is a formalism that combines logic programming with defeasible argumentation; we refer the interested reader to [64] for a fully detailed presentation of the system. In summary, the formalism is made up of several constructs, namely, *facts*, *strict rules*, and *defeasible rules*. Facts represent statements obtained from evidence and are therefore always considered to be true; similarly, strict rules are logical combinations of elements (facts or other inferences) that can always be performed. On the contrary, defeasible rules can be thought of as strict rules that *may* be true in some situations, but *could* be false if certain contradictory evidence

$\Theta : \theta_1 = \text{posted}(post_1, webID_1)$
$\theta_2 = \text{posted}(post_1, userID_1)$
$\theta_3 = \text{parent}(o, microsoft)$
$\theta_4 = \text{parent}(apple, safari)$
$\theta_5 = \text{user\_preference}(userID_1, apple)$
$\theta_6 = \text{previously\_seen}(webID_1, o)$

$\Omega : \omega_1 = \neg\, \text{at\_risk}(post_1, sandisk) \leftarrow \text{at\_risk}(post_1, o),\ \neg\text{parent}(o, sandisk)$
$\omega_2 = \neg\, \text{at\_risk}(post_1, internet\_explorer) \leftarrow \text{at\_risk}(post_1, apple),\ \neg\text{parent}(apple, internet\_explorer)$

$\Delta : \delta_1 = \text{at\_risk}(post_1, microsoft) \prec \text{at\_risk}(post_1, o),\ \text{parent}(o, microsoft)$
$\delta_2 = \text{at\_risk}(post_1, safari) \prec \text{at\_risk}(post_1, apple),\ \text{parent}(apple, safari)$
$\delta_3 = \text{at\_risk}(post_1, apple) \prec \text{user\_preference}(userID_1, apple)$
$\delta_4 = \text{at\_risk}(post_1, o) \prec \text{previously\_seen}(webID_1, o)$

Figure 9.4 A ground argumentation framework.

is presented. These three constructs are used to build *arguments*, and DeLP programs are simply sets of facts, strict rules, and defeasible rules. We adopt the usual notation for DeLP programs, denoting the program (or knowledge base) with $\Pi = (\Theta, \Omega, \Delta)$, where $\Theta$ is the set of facts, $\Omega$ is the set of strict rules, and $\Delta$ is the set of defeasible rules. Examples of the three constructs are provided with respect to the dataset in Figure 9.4. We now describe the notation used to formally denote these constructs.

**Facts** ($\Theta$) are ground literals that represent atomic information or its (strong) negation ($\neg$).

**Strict rules** ($\Omega$) represent cause and effect information; they are of the form $L_0 \leftarrow L_1, \ldots L_n$, where $L_0$ is a literal and $\{L_i\}_{i>0}$ is a set of literals.

**Defeasible rules** ($\Delta$) are weaker versions of strict rules and are of the form $L_0 \prec L_1, \ldots, L_n$, where $L_0$ is the literal and $\{L_i\}_{i>0}$ is a set of literals.

When a hacker discussion happens online, the model can be used to derive arguments to determine the at-risk system (in terms of platform, vendor, and product). Derivation follows the same mechanism as classical logic programming [94]; the main difference is that DeLP incorporates defeasible argumentation, which decides which arguments are warranted, which arguments are defeated, and which arguments should be considered to be *blocked* – the latter are arguments that are involved in a conflict for which a winner cannot be determined.

Figure 9.4 shows a ground argumentation framework demonstrating constructs derived from our online hacker data. For instance, $\theta_1$ indicates the fact that a hacker discussion $post_1$ was posted on the website $webID_1$, and $\theta_5$ indicates that user $userID_1$ prefers to post discussions regarding *apple* products.

| | |
|---|---|
| $\langle \mathcal{A}_1$, at_risk$(post_1, microsoft)\rangle$ | $\mathcal{A}_1 = \{\delta_1, \delta_4, \theta_3\}$ |
| $\langle \mathcal{A}_2$,at_risk$(post_1, safari)\rangle$ | $\mathcal{A}_2 = \{\delta_2, \delta_3, \theta_4\}$ |
| $\langle \mathcal{A}_3$, at_risk$(post_1, apple)\rangle$ | $\mathcal{A}_3 = \{\delta_3, \theta_5\}$ |
| $\langle \mathcal{A}_4$, at_risk$(post_1, o)\rangle$ | $\mathcal{A}_4 = \{\delta_4, \theta_6\}$ |

Figure 9.5 Example ground arguments from Figure 9.4.

For the strict rules, $\omega_1$ says that for a given post $post_1$ posing a threat to operating system (o), the vendor *sandisk* cannot be at risk if the parent of *sandisk* is not operating system (o)[3]. Defeasible rules can be read similarly; $\delta_2$ indicates that if $post_1$ poses a threat to the vendor *apple*, the product *safari* can be at risk if *apple* is the parent of *safari*. By replacing the constants with variables in the predicates, we can derive a non-ground argumentation framework that can be applied in general.

**Definition 1** *(**Argument**) An argument for a literal L is a pair $\langle \mathcal{A}, L\rangle$, where $\mathcal{A} \subseteq \Pi$ provides a minimal proof for L meeting the requirements: (1) L is defeasibly derived from $\mathcal{A}$[4], (2) $\Theta \cup \Omega \cup \Delta$ is not contradictory, and (3) $\mathcal{A}$ is a minimal subset of $\Delta$ satisfying 1 and 2, denoted $\langle \mathcal{A}, L\rangle$.*

Literal $L$ is called the *conclusion* supported by the argument, and $\mathcal{A}$ is the *support*. An argument $\langle \mathcal{B}, L\rangle$ is a *subargument* of $\langle \mathcal{A}, L'\rangle$ iff $\mathcal{B} \subseteq \mathcal{A}$. The following examples discuss arguments for our scenario.

**Example 2** *Figure 9.5 shows example arguments based on the KB from Figure 9.4; here, $\langle \mathcal{A}_3$, at_risk$(post_1, apple)\rangle$ is a subargument of $\langle \mathcal{A}_2$, at_risk$(post_1, safari)\rangle$.* ∎

A *proper defeater* of an argument $\langle A, L\rangle$ is a counter-argument that, by some criterion, is considered to be better than $\langle \mathcal{A}, L\rangle$; if the two are incomparable according to this criterion, the counter-argument is said to be a *blocking* defeater. The default criterion used in DeLP for argument comparison is *generalized specificity* [173], but any domain-specific criterion (or set of criteria) can be deployed. A sequence of arguments is called an *argumentation line*. There can be more than one defeater argument, which leads to a tree structure that is built from the set of all argumentation lines rooted in the initial argument. In this *dialectical tree*, every child can defeat its parent (except for the root), and the leaves represent unchallenged arguments; this creates a map of all possible argumentation lines that can be used to decide whether or not

[3] This encodes the CPE hierarchical structure.
[4] This means that there exists a derivation consisting of a sequence of rules that ends in $L$ – that possibly includes defeasible rules.

an argument is defeated. Arguments that have no attackers or arguments for which all attackers have been defeated are said to be *warranted*.

Given a literal $L$ and an argument $\langle \mathcal{A}, L \rangle$, in order to decide whether or not a literal $L$ is warranted, every node in the dialectical tree $\mathcal{T}(\langle \mathcal{A}, L \rangle)$ is recursively marked as "D" (*defeated*) or "U" (*undefeated*), obtaining a marked *dialectical tree* $\mathcal{T}^*(\langle \mathcal{A}, L \rangle)$ where

- All leaves in $\mathcal{T}^*(\langle \mathcal{A}, L \rangle)$ are marked as "U", and
- Let $\langle \mathcal{B}, q \rangle$ be an inner node of $\mathcal{T}^*(\langle \mathcal{A}, L \rangle)$. Then, $\langle \mathcal{B}, q \rangle$ will be marked as "U" iff every child of $\langle \mathcal{B}, q \rangle$ is marked as "D". Node $\langle \mathcal{B}, q \rangle$ will be marked as "D" iff it has at least one child marked as "U."

Given argument $\langle \mathcal{A}, L \rangle$ over $\Pi$, if the root of $\mathcal{T}^*(\langle \mathcal{A}, L \rangle)$ is marked "U," then $\mathcal{T}^*(\langle \mathcal{A}, h \rangle)$ *warrants* $L$ and that $L$ is *warranted* from $\Pi$. It is interesting to note that warranted arguments correspond to those in the grounded extension of a Dung abstract argumentation system [49].

An implemented DeLP system therefore takes as inputs a set of facts, strict rules, and defeasible rules, as well as a *query literal*. While the set of facts and strict rules must be consistent (non contradictory), the set of defeasible rules can be inconsistent – the presence of such inconsistency is the root of "interesting" cases. We engineer our at-risk system framework as a set of defeasible and strict rules whose structure was created manually, but are dependent on values learned from a historical corpus of online hacker data. Then, for a given post discussing a vulnerability, we instantiate a set of facts for that situation; this information is then provided as input into the DeLP system, which uses heuristics to generate all arguments for and against every possible component of the system (platforms, vendors, products) for the post discussion. Dialectical trees based on these arguments are analyzed, and a decision is made regarding which components are *warranted*. This results in a *reduced set* of potential choices, which we use as input into a classifier to obtain the at-risk system.

## 9.5 Experiments

We frame the identification of at-risk systems as a multilabel classification problem for each of the system components (platform, vendor, and product) – the basic step involves extracting textual features from the discussions to be used as input to the machine learning models. We now describe the data preprocessing steps and the standard machine learning approaches, along with the metrics used for evaluating the models.

### 9.5.1 Data Representation

As mentioned above, we use text-based features to represent the online hacker discussions, which are then used as input to the machine learning models. Some of the discussions are in foreign languages (see Figure 9.2), which are automatically translated to English using the Google Translate API. The following preprocessing steps are taken to address different challenges. We employ two feature engineering techniques, namely, TF-IDF and Doc2Vec.

**Text cleaning.** We remove all non-alphanumeric characters from hacker discussions. This removes any *special characters* that do not contribute toward making the decision.

**Misspellings and word variations.** Misspellings and word variations are frequently observed in online hacker discussions, leading to separate features in the feature vector if a standard bag-of-words (BOW) approach is used. In BOW, we create a dictionary of all the word occurrences in the training set; then, for a particular discussion, the feature vector is created by looking up which words have occurred and their count in the discussion. Misspellings and word variations will thus be represented as different words; to address this, we use character $n$-gram features. As an example, consider the word "execute" – if we were using tri-gram character features, the word "execute" would yield the set of features:

$$\{\text{“}exe\text{”}, \text{“}xec\text{”}, \text{“}ecu\text{”}, \text{“}cut\text{”}, \text{“}ute\text{”}\}$$

The benefit of this technique is that the variations or misspellings of the word, such as "execution," "executable," or "exxecute," will all have common features. We found that using character $n$-grams in the range 3–7 worked best in our experiments.

**TF-IDF features.** We vectorize the $n$-gram features using the term frequency-inverse document frequency (TF-IDF) model (technique used and explained in Chapter 6), which creates a vocabulary of all the $n$-grams in the discussion. As also done in Chapter 6, we consider only the top 1,000 most frequent features of this vectorization process.

**Doc2Vec features.** Doc2Vec is a feature engineering technique to generate document vector (in our case "document" refers to a discussion), which acts as input to the classifier to identify at-risk systems. In Doc2Vec, first, a vector representation of each word in the document is computed by taking into account the words around it (to maintain context), and then these word vectors are averaged to get a representation of the document. We implement Doc2Vec using the *gensim* library in Python.[5] It was been previously used to classify tweets [183] as well as product descriptions [90].

### 9.5.2 Supervised Learning Approaches

We conducted experiments using five standard machine learning approaches to build our classifiers, including support vector machines (SVMs), random forests (RFs), naïve Bayes (NB), decision tree (DT), and logistic regression (LOG-REG). Those classifiers were implemented using the scikit-learn Python library and aim to identify the class(es) (platforms, vendors, and products) of each test sample (hacker discussion analyzed).

### 9.5.3 Evaluation Metrics

In our experiments, we evaluate performance based on three metrics, *precision*, *recall*, and *F1 score*, as done in previous chapters. Here, precision is the fraction of labels (platforms, vendors, or products) that the model associates with the discussion that are *actual labels* in the ground truth. Recall, on the other hand, is the fraction of ground truth labels *identified* by the model. As mentioned before, F1 score is the harmonic mean of precision and recall. In our results, we report the average precision, recall, and F1 for all the test discussions.

### 9.5.4 Baseline Model (BM)

For the baseline model, we only leverage the machine learning technique to identify the at-risk systems. We create training and testing sets by sorting the discussions by posted time on the website (to avoid temporal intermixing). We reserve the first 80% of the samples for training and the rest (20%) for testing. We employed both TF-IDF and Doc2Vec as feature engineering techniques. As we observe that TF-IDF performs better than Doc2Vec in all our experiments, we only report the results using TF-IDF features.

**Results.** Table 9.4 shows the average performance of the machine learning technique for each component of the at-risk system.

For *platform* identification, SVM performs the best with averages *precision*, 0.72; *recall*, 0.78; and *F1 score*, 0.76. LOG-REG has similar precision, but lower recall. Similarly, for vendor identification, SVM performs the best with

[5] https://radimrehurek.com/gensim/models/doc2vec.html.

Table 9.4 *Precision, recall, and F1 score for NB, LOG-REG, DT, RF, and SVM to identify at-risk systems*

| **Component** | **Model** | **Precision (avg)** | **Recall (avg)** | **F1 score (avg)** |
|---|---|---|---|---|
| Platform | NB | 0.68 | 0.65 | 0.66 |
| | LOG-REG | **0.72** | 0.76 | 0.74 |
| | DT | 0.66 | 0.70 | 0.68 |
| | RF | 0.70 | 0.75 | 0.72 |
| | SVM | **0.72** | **0.78** | **0.76** |
| Vendor | NB | 0.37 | 0.34 | 0.36 |
| | LOG-REG | 0.28 | 0.25 | 0.27 |
| | DT | 0.39 | 0.43 | 0.41 |
| | RF | **0.40** | 0.43 | 0.41 |
| | SVM | **0.40** | **0.48** | **0.44** |
| Product | NB | 0.19 | 0.14 | 0.16 |
| | LOG-REG | 0.20 | 0.13 | 0.16 |
| | DT | 0.22 | 0.15 | 0.18 |
| | RF | 0.22 | **0.25** | 0.24 |
| | SVM | **0.26** | 0.24 | **0.25** |

averages *precision*, 0.40; *recall*, 0.48; and *F1 score*, 0.44, with RF having similar precision. For *platform* identification, SVM has the best performance: *precision*, 0.28; *recall*, 0.24 (comparable to RF); and *F1 score*, 0.25. Since SVM performs consistently better for all three classification problems, we use SVM as our machine learning component in the reasoning framework (see Figure 9.1).

### 9.5.5 Reasoning Framework (RFrame)

As we go down the CPE hierarchy, the number of possible labels for vendors and products increases largely as the number of discussions representing each label decreases, thus making learning difficult and decreasing performance. We address this issue by proposing a set of strict and defeasible rules for platform, vendor, and product identification. These rules arise from the discussion evaluated and do not require parameter learning. We use the notation described in Table 9.5 for defining our constructs (facts, strict rules, and defeasible rules).

We note that facts cannot have variables, only constants (however, to compress the program for presentation purposes, we use *meta-variables* in facts). To begin, we define the facts (see Figure 9.6): $\theta_1$ states that a hacker discussion $\mathcal{D}$ was posted on the website $\mathcal{W}$ (can be either forum or marketplace), and $\theta_2$ states that the user $\mathcal{U}$ posted the discussion. For each level in the CPE hierarchy, we define additional rules, as follows.

Table 9.5 *Notation and explanations*

| Notation | Explanation |
|---|---|
| $\mathcal{D}$ | The hacker discussion (posted on the website) under consideration |
| $\mathcal{W}$ | Website (marketplace or forum) where the hacker discussion was posted |
| $\mathcal{S}_w$, $\mathcal{V}_w$, and $\mathcal{P}_w$ | The set of platforms, vendors, and products at risk by the hacker discussions previously seen in $\mathcal{W}$ under consideration, respectively |
| $\mathcal{U}$ | User posting the hacker discussion |
| $\mathcal{S}_u$, $\mathcal{V}_u$, and $\mathcal{P}_u$ | The set of platforms, vendors, and products at risk by the hacker discussions previously posted by user $\mathcal{U}$ under consideration, respectively |
| $\mathcal{S}_p$, $\mathcal{V}_p$, and $\mathcal{P}_p$ | The set of platforms, vendors, and products identified by the machine learning model at each level in the hierarchy for hacker discussions under consideration, respectively |
| $\mathsf{s}_i$, $\mathsf{v}_i$, and $\mathsf{p}_i$ | Each element of the set $\mathcal{S}_p$, $\mathcal{V}_p$, and $\mathcal{P}_p$ representing a single platform, vendor or product, respectively |

$$\Theta: \quad \theta_1 = \mathsf{posted}(\mathcal{D}, \mathcal{W}) \qquad \theta_2 = \mathsf{posted}(\mathcal{D}, \mathcal{U})$$

Figure 9.6 Facts defined for each test discussion.

For $s \in \mathcal{S}_w$:

$$\Delta: \quad \delta_1 = \mathsf{at\_risk}(\mathcal{D}, s) \prec \mathsf{previously\_seen}(\mathcal{W}, s)$$

For $s \in \mathcal{S}_u$:

$$\delta_2 = \mathsf{at\_risk}(\mathcal{D}, s) \prec \mathsf{user\_preference}(\mathcal{U}, s)$$

Figure 9.7 Defeasible rules for platform identification.

**Platform model.** The first level of system identification is determining the platforms. We compute previously discussed platforms on hacker websites under consideration. Similarly, which platform the user under consideration prefers (based on their previous postings) is also computed. This shows preferred platform discussions on websites and by users, which can aid the machine learning model in reducing the number of platforms from which it can identify. The DeLP components that model platform identification are shown in Figure 9.7. For the defeasible rules, $\delta_1$ indicates that all the platforms $\mathcal{S}_w$ previously seen in the website $\mathcal{W}$ where the current discussion $\mathcal{D}$ is observed are likely at risk, and $\delta_2$ indicates that all the platforms $\mathcal{S}_u$ from user $\mathcal{U}$'s previous postings are also likely at risk.

| | |
|---|---|
| | For $s \in \mathcal{S}_p$: |
| $\Theta$ : | $\theta_1 = \mathsf{at\_risk}(\mathcal{D}, s)$ |
| | For $s \in \mathcal{S}_p$: |
| $\Omega$ : | $\omega_1 = \neg\, \mathsf{at\_risk}(\mathcal{D}, \mathsf{v}_i) \leftarrow \mathsf{at\_risk}(\mathcal{D}, s), \neg \mathsf{parent}(s, \mathsf{v}_i)$ |
| | For $v \in V_w$: |
| $\Delta$ : | $\delta_1 = \mathsf{at\_risk}(\mathcal{D}, v) \prec \mathsf{previously\_seen}(\mathcal{W}, v)$ |
| | For $v \in V_u$: |
| | $\delta_2 = \mathsf{at\_risk}(\mathcal{D}, v) \prec \mathsf{user\_preference}(\mathcal{U}, v)$ |
| | For $s \in \mathcal{S}_p$: |
| | $\delta_3 = \mathsf{at\_risk}(\mathcal{D}, \mathsf{v}_i) \leftarrow \mathsf{at\_risk}(\mathcal{D}, s), \mathsf{parent}(s, \mathsf{v}_i)$ |

Figure 9.8 Defeasible rules for vendor identification.

**Vendor model.** The second level is identifying the at-risk vendor. For this case, we use the platform result from the previous model, taking that as a DeLP *fact*. The DeLP components that model vendor identification are shown in Figure 9.8.

In Figure 9.8, the fact $\theta_1$ indicates the platform identified for the discussion – note that multiple platforms may be identified. The strict rule $\omega_1$ states that for a given post $\mathcal{D}$ posing a threat to platform $s$, the vendor $\mathsf{v}_i$ cannot be at risk if the parent of $\mathsf{v}_i$ is not the identified platform $s$. This rule is based on the CPE hierarchy obtained from NVD. For the defeasible rules, $\delta_1$ indicates that all the vendors $V_w$ previously seen in the website $\mathcal{W}$ where the current hacker discussion $\mathcal{D}$ is observed are likely at risk, $\delta_2$ indicates that all the vendors $V_u$ from user $\mathcal{U}$'s previous postings are also likely at risk, and $\delta_3$ states that for a given post $\mathcal{D}$ posing a threat to platform $s$, all the vendors whose parent is the identified platform are likely at risk. This rule is also based on the CPE hierarchy from NVD.

**Product model.** The third level is identifying the at-risk product. For this case, we use the vendor result from the previous model; as before, we use that as a DeLP *fact*. The DeLP components that model product identification are shown in Figure 9.9. Here, the fact $\theta_1$ indicates the vendor identified for the discussion – again, multiple vendors may be identified. The strict rule $\omega_1$ states that for a given post $\mathcal{D}$ posing a threat to vendor $v$, the product $\mathsf{p}_i$ cannot be at risk if the parent of $\mathsf{p}_i$ is not the identified vendor $v$ (again, based on the CPE hierarchy). For the defeasible rules, $\delta_1$ indicates that all the products $\mathcal{P}_w$ previously seen in the website $\mathcal{W}$ where the current hacker discussion $\mathcal{D}$ is observed are likely at risk, $\delta_2$ indicates that all the products $\mathcal{P}_u$ from user $\mathcal{U}$'s previous postings are also likely at risk, and $\delta_3$ states that for a given post $\mathcal{D}$ posing a threat to vendor $v$, all the products whose parent (in the CPE hierarchy) is the identified vendor are likely at risk.

Table 9.6 *Performance comparison between the baseline model (BM) and reasoning framework (RFrame)*

| Component | Model | Precision (avg) | Recall (avg) | F1 score (avg) |
|---|---|---|---|---|
| Platform | BM | 0.72 | **0.78** | 0.76 |
| | RFrame | **0.83** | **0.78** | **0.80** |
| Vendor | BM | 0.40 | **0.48** | 0.44 |
| | RFrame | **0.56** | 0.44 | **0.50** |
| Product | BM | 0.26 | **0.24** | 0.25 |
| | RFrame | **0.41** | 0.21 | **0.30** |

For $v \in V_p$:
$$\Theta : \theta_1 = \text{at\_risk}(\mathcal{D}, v)$$

For $v \in V_p$:
$$\Omega : \omega_1 = \neg\, \text{at\_risk}(\mathcal{D}, \text{p}_i) \leftarrow \text{at\_risk}(\mathcal{D}, v), \neg\text{parent}(v, \text{p}_i)$$

For $p \in \mathcal{P}_w$:
$$\Delta : \delta_1 = \text{at\_risk}(\mathcal{D}, p) \prec \text{previously\_seen}(\mathcal{W}, p).$$

For $p \in \mathcal{P}_u$:
$$\delta_2 = \text{at\_risk}(\mathcal{D}, p) \prec \text{user\_preference}(\mathcal{U}, p).$$

For $v \in V_p$:
$$\delta_3 = \text{at\_risk}(\mathcal{D}, \text{p}_i) \leftarrow \text{at\_risk}(\mathcal{D}, v), \text{parent}(v, \text{p}_i)$$

Figure 9.9 Defeasible rules for product identification.

**Results.** We evaluate the reasoning framework using an experimental setup similar to the one discussed in the baseline model. We report the precision, recall, and F1 score for each of the system components and compare them with the best performing baseline model (BM). Table 9.6 shows the comparison between the two models.

For *platform* identification, RFrame outperforms BM in terms of precision, 0.83 versus 0.72 (a 15.27% improvement), while maintaining the same recall. Similarly, for *vendor* and *product* identification, there was significant improvement in precision: 0.56 versus 0.40 (a 40% improvement) and 0.41 versus 0.26 (a 57.69% improvement), respectively, with comparable recall with respect to the baseline model. The major reason for the jump in precision is the reduction of possible labels based on the arguments introduced.

## 9.6 Discussion

The performance of the reasoning system highlights that our hybrid framework identifies at-risk systems with higher precision with respect to the approach using only machine learning classifiers. In our application, we desire a high precision – while maintaining at least comparable recall – in order to provide high-value risk assessment of systems; low precision is often equated to a less reliable framework. The majority of misclassifications are a result of less data representing those systems in the training set; for some system components, the instances can be as low as having only one discussion in the training set. This issue becomes more relevant as we go down the hierarchy with large numbers of vendors and products. In some test instances, for the same platform and vendor, a new product not previously known to be at risk becomes vulnerable due to a newly disclosed vulnerability. In this case, the reasoning framework is not able to identify the product since it was not previously observed.

From a security analyst's perspective, the reasoning framework not only provides a list of possible at-risk systems but also provides arguments indicating *why* a particular system was identified as being at risk. This allows the security analyst to evaluate the decisions made by the framework and fine-tune them if necessary. For cases where a new product (not previously discussed in training) is at risk, even a partial identification of the system (in terms of platform and vendor) is of value to the analyst. Based on the alert provided by the framework, the analyst can manually evaluate the arguments and the discussions to identify possible products, depending on the platform and vendor identified by the framework.

## 9.7 Related Work

This section reviews works that used two distinct approaches for carrying out threat assessment of systems by using (1) open source intelligence and (2) software analysis.

**Identifying targeted systems through open source intelligence.** Open source intelligence has been used to identify vulnerabilities that are likely to be exploited, determining which systems are at risk. In [198], the authors predicted the likelihood that a software had a vulnerability not yet discovered using the National Vulnerability Database (NVD). They showed that the NVD has a poor prediction capability in doing so due to limited amount of information available. On the other hand, [148] predicted if a real-world exploit was available based on vulnerabilities disclosed from Twitter data. The authors reported high accuracies of 90% using a resampled, balanced, and temporal mixed dataset, not reflective of real-world scenarios [26]. Identifying threats to critical infrastructure by analyzing interactions on hacker forums was studied in [95]. Here the authors relied on keyword based queries to identify such threats from hacker interactions. Tools to automatically identify products offered in cyber-criminal markets were proposed in [160]. This technique extracted products mentioned in the description of the item that was being offered.

More recently, researchers have shown increased interest in gathering threat intelligence from online hacker sources to proactively identify digital threats and study hacker communities to gather insights. Researchers have focused on building infrastructure to gather threat information from markets (regarding goods and services sold) and forums (discussions regarding exploits) [126, 145], studying the different product categories offered in hacker markets – creating a labeled dataset [103], analyzing hacker forums and carding shops to identify potential threats [16], and identifying expert hackers to determine their specialties [1]. For vulnerability research, we cover in Chapter 6 a study that leverages vulnerability mentions on hacker websites to predict vulnerability exploitation. However, this technique relies on CVE mentions to identify the targeted systems, not taking into account discussions where a CVE number is not mentioned. Here, we look to identify the at-risk systems *without having a CVE number*, which is a different problem from the one addressed in Chapter 6.

**Identifying targeted systems through software analysis.** Another way of identifying targeted software with vulnerabilities deals with analyzing the *software itself* to determine which software component is most likely to contain a vulnerability. Mapping past vulnerabilities to vulnerable software components was proposed in [122], where the authors found that components with function calls and import statements are more likely to have a vulnerability. A similar method was employed by [156, 188], where text mining was used to forecast whether a particular software component contains vulnerabilities. Similar text mining techniques for vulnerability discovery are listed in [65]. The text mining methods create a count dictionary of terms used as features to identify vulnerabilities. These methods suffer from not knowing which vulnerabilities might be of interest to hackers. On the other hand, we work with discussions posing a threat to systems that are clearly of interest to malicious hackers since they are discussing them on online platforms.

## 9.8 Conclusion

In this chapter, we demonstrate how a reasoning framework based on the DeLP structured argumentation system can be leveraged to identify at-risk systems based on online hacker discussions that do not include a CVE number. DeLP programs built on discussions found on forums and marketplaces identify threatened systems in terms of their hierarchical components, affording a reduction in the set of possible platforms, vendors, and products that are likely to be at risk. This reduction in potential labels leads to better precision while almost maintaining comparable recall, as compared to the baseline model, which only leverages machine learning techniques. By using the proposed approach, organizations can achieve a better threat assessment for their systems, even if software vulnerability identifiers (CVEs) are not explicitly mentioned in the hacker discussions.

# 10

# Final Considerations

Today's widespread of cyber-attack incidents makes them one of the primary threats faced by organizations worldwide. This threatening scenario is organically caused by the democratization of access to malicious code generated by the emergence of malicious hacker communities on the World Wide Web. The current methods that attempt to counter hacking offensives have been failing to demonstrate effectiveness, probably by focusing only on the defender's environment and neglecting the other side of the spectrum: the attacker. Being aware of the problem, the cyber-security industry has been moving toward a more intelligence-driven security perspective known as proactive cyber-threat intelligence. This emerging field aims to inform, among other things, which exploits adversaries are likely to use and which software vulnerabilities they are likely to exploit, providing security teams mechanisms to predict and stop an attack before the infection occurs.

As malicious hackers increasingly rely on online communities to share knowledge and achieve their cyber-criminal goals – from the discussion and identification of software vulnerabilities to the preparation and execution of cyber-attacks, it is possible now to leverage artificial intelligence, especially machine learning and social network analysis techniques, for exploring these communities and to gather intelligence for an effective deployment of security measures. This is where this book comes into play. We demonstrate throughout the chapters how an intimate understanding of the malicious hacker communities greatly adds power to proactive cyber-threat intelligence, allowing defenders to be more effective while anticipating cyber-threats. As the hacker market is in clear expansion in terms of players and traded exploits, and the threat – the malicious hacker communities – is continually making adjustments to the current defense posture, we design a series of studies that address important challenges still largely unexplored in this emerging security field: Who are the skilled and influential individuals forming those hacker groups?

How ideas propagate among the threat actors? How do hacker communities organize along the lines of technical expertise? Is it possible to find exploits-in-the-wild before someone reports to having been compromised? Can we even predict cyber-attacks by analyzing patterns of online hacking activity? Which platforms are popular among malevolent hackers and therefore at a higher risk of vulnerability exploitation?

## 10.1 Contributions

The studies presented in this book are divided into two parts. After motivating the use of proactive cyber-threat intelligence and introducing online hacker communities – focusing on forums and marketplaces – we analyze in the first part of the book (Chapters 3, 4, and 5) the structure of these communities and the behavior of their members. We scrutinize the threat actors creating and distributing malicious code online, getting knowledge about dynamic reputation systems, hacker engagement, and highly specialized groups of hackers that can aid in the identification of credible threats. After that, in the second part of the book (Chapters 6, 7, 8, and 9), we leverage multiple learning techniques to predict cyber-threats, by identifying exploits-in-the-wild, predicting enterprise-targeted external cyber-attacks, or finding at-risk systems. We analyze hacker discussions to find confident patterns of attack behavior that can be used for our predictions. We give a brief overview of those studies now.

In Chapter 3, we mine "key-hackers" on popular hacker forums, identifying individuals who are likely to succeed in their cyber-criminal goals. We develop a profile for each forum member using features derived from content, social network, and seniority analysis, aiming to differentiate standard from key cyber-actors. Then, after defining a metric for collecting ground-truth data based on user reputation, we train our model on a given forum using optimization and machine learning algorithms fed with those features to later test its performance on a different forum. Our results show that we are able to identify a considerable fraction of existing key-hackers, demonstrating that our model generalizes relatively well.

In Chapter 4, we investigate how social influence contributes to online hacker engagement by analyzing user adoption behavior on hacker forums. We investigate where and when hackers will post a message in the near future considering their recurrent interactions with other hackers. We formulate this problem as a sequential rule mining task, designing experiments using multiple posting time granularities and time windows. We observe considerable precision results and two-digit precision gains when compared to the prior probabilities of hackers' posts, indicating how user adoption behavior can be used by security specialists to dynamically map the ever-evolving networks of malicious hackers.

In Chapter 5, we search for communities of vendors on online marketplaces with similar expertise in specific subfields of hacking, a feature typically owned by reputable hackers that can be used for surveillance purposes. We develop a method based on social network analysis techniques that identifies communities of hacking-related vendors using the similarity of their product offerings, validating our method by cross-checking the community assignments of these individuals on two mutually exclusive sets of marketplaces. Our model achieves reasonable consistency between more than 30 communities of vendors revealed in each subset of markets, evidencing a clear clustering property of those hacker groups.

In Chapter 6, we consider the problem of predicting exploits-in-the-wild for known software vulnerabilities. We present machine learning models that leverage cyber-threat intelligence collected from four data sources: vulnerability databases, proof-of-concept exploit archives (White-hat community), vulnerability disclosures on enterprise websites (commercial firms), and more than 150 malicious hacking forums and marketplaces across multiple networks. We view the problem as a binary classification problem (i.e., the positive class will be exploited), developing models that outperform the standard vulnerability severity scoring system (CVSS base score) with a more than doubled F1 score.

In Chapter 7, we develop a novel approach used in a system that predicts certain types of cyber-attacks targeting specific commercial enterprises. We explain the underlying logic programming framework (APT-logic) used to model the probabilistic temporal relationships between hacker activities (from online hacker communities) and attack incidents (recorded by the SIEM of the data providers). Our approach outperforms a statistical forecasting baseline for the majority of the attack types analyzed.

In Chapter 8, we study user interaction patterns on hacker forums and empirically argue whether the reply network structure created from the hacker discussions can be leveraged to predict external enterprise threats. We find that a feature based on graph conductance that measures the random walk transition probability between groups of hackers is a useful indicator for attack occurrences, given that it achieves the best predictive results for one of the attack types analyzed. The results confirm our hypothesis that the pattern of replies represented by the path structure in those forums centered around a few credible hackers can uncover important signals for future cyber-attacks.

In Chapter 9, we consider the problem of identifying systems likely to be at risk by hacker discussions on marketplaces and forums without relying on explicit CVE mentions. We propose a reasoning system that combines defeasible logic programming (DeLP) and machine learning classifiers and that takes into account the hierarchical structure of systems in terms of platform, vendor, and product to make this identification task. The proposed system considerably improves precision while maintaining recall over baseline approaches.

## 10.2 Future Directions

The work conducted in this book can be extended in many ways to enhance proactive cyber-threat intelligence, either by addressing current limitations or by proposing new models, methods, frameworks, and algorithms. We discuss some potential future research ideas in this section.

**Identification of zero-day exploits**. An important challenge in the security field is the identification of zero-day exploits, as defenders are hard-pressed to protect against "invisible" threats. Although zero-day exploits target undisclosed vulnerabilities, they usually exist "in the wild" for more than 300 days before official identification and publication [19]. Thus, researchers can gather cyber-threat intelligence to discover what kind of zero-day exploit is being developed and offered online.

**Social network extraction of malicious hackers**. Many research works conducted on hacker forums [101, 102, 106, 155] explore social network features to accomplish their goals. However, due to the fragmented and interactionally disjointed nature of those environments, extracting social network structure by using only hacker interaction data is inaccurate. For example, we use a heuristic that is based on an assumption that is adopted in much of the existing literature: a post under a given hacker discussion is a reply to all posts preceding it. We adopt this assumption because the forums we use do not provide information about which post a given reply is directed to. Thus, natural language processing (NLP) methods can be used to derive more accurate reply-to information on hacker forums, leading to a better approximation of the real hacker network topology.

**Forum spidering**. In order to automate data collection from hacking platforms, spiders need to automatically find and download relevant HTML pages. Some hacking sites, especially those existing in encrypted networks like Tor, are able to detect and block those robots [126]. Thus, one contribution to the threat intelligence area could be the design of human-like spiders. Those robots should be able to bypass detection methods by mimicking human browsing behavior, while also learning which information should be collected.

**Adversarial reasoning**. Malicious hackers are continually evolving and adjusting their strategies to defeat defense postures. Defenders should also employ adaptive strategies to assess hackers' capabilities, perceptions, intents, actions, and behaviors [146]. Thus, the development of models combining game theory, control theory, and cognitive modeling to reason about how and why cyber-attacks will occur is crucial to successfully defeat attackers.

**Cascade prediction**. Predicting when a hacking message will go "viral" is relevant for cyber-security since information cascades can signal hacktivism campaigns or mass adoption of cyber-threats [161]. Then, defenders will benefit from modeling information diffusion on malicious hacker communities to investigate which influential and topological patterns can be leveraged for the early extraction of meaningful popular threads.

**Improvement of ground truth data**. In general, attack signatures of exploits supplied by security companies, such as Symantec, underrepresented vulnerabilities that do not affect products from vendors other than Microsoft and Adobe. To address such limitations, researchers can develop crowdsourcing mechanisms, possibly supporting human-in-the loop capabilities, that are able to reason about the correctness of reported exploits.

**Checking the user acceptance of proposed systems**. Across all the pieces of work in this book, the focus has been on developing approaches that (1) offer specific capabilities to the human analysts (e.g., understand the reasoning that led to certain predictions) and (2) outperform the existing baseline methods and the benchmark approaches, if there are any. We accomplish that by: (1) formally explaining the techniques and providing examples of predictions, and (2) empirically demonstrating the improvement in performance compared to existing standard baseline methods. However, the usability of the developed approaches to human analysts has not been tested. Thus, we do not know whether some performance achieved by the systems proposed is enough for human analysts to trust these models and use them in production settings. Unlike most cyber-security AI applications, which are designed to support automated actions, such as spam filtering and intrusion detection, the proposed systems are designed to ultimately support human decisions, and their acceptance by users could be an interesting research direction to pursue in the future.

**Analysis of website metadata as features**. Metadata about the website in which vulnerabilities are discussed, such as age and size of community (or number of users), and metadata related to users, such as the number communities to which they are connected, the programming languages they use, and the type of weaknesses on which they focus, could also be incorporated into the learning models to improve their performance.

# References


[1] Abbasi, A., Li, W., Benjamin, V., Hu, S., and Chen, H. (2014). Descriptive analytics: Examining expert hackers in web forums. In *Proceeding of ISI 2014*, (pp. 56–63). IEEE.

[2] Abbosh, O., and Bissell, K. (2019). Securing the digital economy: Reinventing the internet for trust. Tech. rep., Accenture.

[3] Ajzen, I., and Fishbein, M. (1980). *Understanding Attitudes and Predicting Social Behavior*. Prentice Hall.

[4] Akoglu, L., Tong, H., and Koutra, D. (2015). Graph based anomaly detection and description: A survey. *Data Min. Knowl. Discov.*, *29*(3), 626–688. https://doi.org/10.1007/s10618-014-0365-y.

[5] Allodi, L. (2017). Economic factors of vulnerability trade and exploitation. In *Proceedings of the 2017 ACM SIGSAC Conference on Computer and Communications Security*, CCS '17, (pp. 1483–1499). ACM.

[6] Allodi, L., and Massacci, F. (2012). A preliminary analysis of vulnerability scores for attacks in wild: The ekits and sym datasets. In *Proceedings of the 2012 ACM Workshop on Building Analysis Datasets and Gathering Experience Returns for Security*, (pp. 17–24). ACM.

[7] Allodi, L., and Massacci, F. (2014). Comparing vulnerability severity and exploits using case-control studies. *ACM Tran. Inform. Syst. Security*, *17*(1), 1.

[8] Allodi, L., Massacci, F., and Williams, J. M. (2017). The work-averse cyber attacker model: Theory and evidence from two million attack signatures. *Social Science Research Network (SSRN)*.

[9] Almukaynizi, M., Grimm, A., Nunes, E., Shakarian, J., and Shakarian, P. (2017). Predicting cyber threats through hacker social networks in darkweb and deepweb forums. In *Proceedings of the 2017 International Conference of the Computational Social Science Society of the Americas*, (pp. 1–7). ACM.

[10] Almukaynizi, M., Marin, E., Nunes, E., Shakarian, P., Simari, G. I., Kapoor, D., and Siedlecki, T. (2018). Darkmention: A deployed system to predict enterprise-targeted external cyberattacks. In *2018 IEEE International Conference on Intelligence and Security Informatics (ISI)*, (pp. 31–36). https://doi.org/10.1109/ISI.2018.8587334.

[11] Almukaynizi, M., Nunes, E., Dharaiya, K., Senguttuvan, M., Shakarian, J., and Shakarian, P. (2017). Proactive identification of exploits in the wild through

vulnerability mentions online. In *2017 International Conference on Cyber Conflict (CyCon US)*, (pp. 82–88). IEEE.

[12] Almukaynizi, M., Nunes, E., Dharaiya, K., Senguttuvan, M., Shakarian, J., and Shakarian, P. (2019). Patch before exploited: An approach to identify targeted software vulnerabilities. In *AI in Cybersecurity*, (pp. 81–113). Springer.

[13] Anwar, T., and Abulaish, M. (2012). Identifying cliques in dark web forums–an agglomerative clustering approach. In *2012 IEEE International Conference on Intelligence and Security Informatics*, (pp. 171–173). IEEE.

[14] Barreno, M., Bartlett, P. L., Chi, F. J., Joseph, A. D., Nelson, B., Rubinstein, B. I., Saini, U., and Tygar, J. D. (2008). Open problems in the security of learning. In *Proceedings of the 1st ACM Workshop on AISec*, (pp. 19–26). ACM.

[15] Barreno, M., Nelson, B., Joseph, A. D., and Tygar, J. (2010). The security of machine learning. *Machine Learn.*, *81*(2), 121–148.

[16] Benjamin, V., Li, W., Holt, T., and Chen, H. (2015). Exploring threats and vulnerabilities in hacker web: Forums, IRC and carding shops. In *2015 IEEE International Conference on Intelligence and Security Informatics (ISI)*, (pp. 85–90). IEEE.

[17] Benjamin, V., Zhang, B., Jr. Nunamaker, J., and Chen, H. (2016). Examining hacker participation length in cybercriminal internet-relay-chat communities. *J. Manage. Inform. Syst.*, *33*(2), 482–510.

[18] Biggio, B., Nelson, B., and Laskov, P. (2011). Support vector machines under adversarial label noise. *ACML*, *20*, 97–112.

[19] Bilge, L., and Dumitraş, T. (2012). Before we knew it: An empirical study of zero-day attacks in the real world. In *Proceedings of the 2012 ACM Conference on Computer and Communications Security*, CCS '12, (pp. 833–844). ACM. http://doi.acm.org/10.1145/2382196.2382284.

[20] Bilge, L., Han, Y., and Dell'Amico, M. (2017). Riskteller: Predicting the risk of cyber incidents. In *Proceedings of the 2017 ACM SIGSAC Conference on Computer and Communications Security*, CCS '17, (pp. 1299–1311). ACM. http://doi.acm.org/10.1145/3133956.3134022.

[21] Blondel, V. D., Guillaume, J.-L., Lambiotte, R., and Lefebvre, E. (2008). Fast unfolding of communities in large networks. *J. Stat. Mech. Theory Experiment*, *2008*(10), P10008.

[22] Borgatti, S. P., Carley, K. M., and Krackhardt, D. (2006). On the robustness of centrality measures under conditions of imperfect data. *Social Networks*, *28*(2), 124–136.

[23] Bozorgi, M., Saul, L. K., Savage, S., and Voelker, G. M. (2010). Beyond heuristics: Learning to classify vulnerabilities and predict exploits. In *Proceedings of the 16th ACM SIGKDD International Conference on Knowledge Discovery and Data Mining*, (pp. 105–114). ACM.

[24] Breiman, L. (1996). Bagging predictors. *Machine Learn.*, *24*(2), 123–140.

[25] Breiman, L. (2001). Random forests. *Machine Learn.*, *45*(1), 5–32.

[26] Bullough, B. L., Yanchenko, A. K., Smith, C. L., and Zipkin, J. R. (2017). Predicting exploitation of disclosed software vulnerabilities using open-source data. In *Proceedings of the 2017 ACM International Workshop on Security and Privacy Analytics*, (pp. 45–53). ACM.

[27] Burt, R. S. (1987). Social contagion and innovation: Cohesion versus structural equivalence. *Am. J. Sociol.*, *92*(6), 1287–1335.

[28] Carr, D. (2008). How Obama tapped into social networks' power. www.nytimes.com/2008/11/10/business/media/10carr.html.

[29] Chandola, V., Banerjee, A., and Kumar, V. (2009). Anomaly detection: A survey. *ACM Comput. Surv.*, *41*(3), 15:1–15:58. http://doi.acm.org/10.1145/1541880.1541882.

[30] Chawla, N. V., Bowyer, K. W., Hall, L. O., and Kegelmeyer, W. P. (2002). Smote: Synthetic minority over-sampling technique. *J. Artif. Int. Res.*, *16*(1), 321–357. http://dl.acm.org/citation.cfm?id=1622407.1622416.

[31] Chen, H. (2011). Dark web: Exploring and mining the dark side of the web. In *2011 European Intelligence and Security Informatics Conference (EISIC)*, (pp. 1–2). Springer.

[32] Chen, H., Liu, R., Park, N., and Subrahmanian, V. (2019). Using Twitter to predict when vulnerabilities will be exploited. In *Proceedings of the 25th ACM SIGKDD International Conference on Knowledge Discovery & Data Mining*, (pp. 3143–3152). ACM.

[33] Chen, Y.-D., Brown, S., Hu, P. J., King, C.-C., and Chen, H. (2011). Managing emerging infectious diseases with information systems: Reconceptualizing outbreak management through the lens of loose coupling. *Inform. Syst. Res.*, *22*(3), 447–468.

[34] Chierichetti, F., Lattanzi, S., and Panconesi, A. (2010). Rumour spreading and graph conductance. In *Proceedings of the Twenty-First Annual ACM-SIAM Symposium on Discrete Algorithms*, SODA '10, (pp. 1657–1663). Society for Industrial and Applied Mathematics. http://dl.acm.org/citation.cfm?id=1873601.1873736.

[35] Chung, C., Khatkar, P., Xing, T., Lee, J., and Huang, D. (2013). Nice: Network intrusion detection and countermeasure selection in virtual network systems. *IEEE Trans. Dependable Secure Comput.*, *10*(4), 198–211. https://doi.org/10.1109/TDSC.2013.8.

[36] CISA. (2017). HIDDEN COBRA–North Korea's DDoS botnet infrastructure. www.us-cert.gov/ncas/alerts/TA17-164A.

[37] CISCO. (2016). Cisco 2016 midyear cybersecurity report. www.cisco.com/c/dam/m/en_ca/never-better/assets/files/midyear-security-report-2016.pdf.

[38] Clauset, A., Newman, M. E. J., and Moore, C. (2004). Finding community structure in very large networks. *Phys. Rev. E*, *70*, 066111.

[39] Colbaugh, R., and Glass, K. (2011). Proactive defense for evolving cyber threats. In *Proceedings of 2011 IEEE International Conference on Intelligence and Security Informatics*, (pp. 125–130). IEEE.

[40] Coleman, G. (2014). *Hacker, Hoaxer, Whistleblower, Spy: The Many Faces of Anonymous*. Verso Books.

[41] Coleman, J. S., Katz, E., and Menzel, H. (1967). Medical innovation: A diffusion study. *Social Forces*, *46*(2), 291.

[42] Cyber Reconnaissance, I. (2020). CYR3CON. www.cyr3con.ai/.

[43] Danezis, G., and Mittal, P. (2009). Sybilinfer: Detecting sybil nodes using social networks. In *Proceedings of the Network and Distributed System Security Symposium (NDSS' 2009)*, (pp. 1–15). Internet Society.

[44] Das, G., Lin, K.-I., Mannila, H., Renganathan, G., and Smyth, P. (1998). Rule discovery from time series. In *Proceedings of the Fourth International Conference on Knowledge Discovery and Data Mining*, KDD'98, (pp. 16–22). AAAI.

[45] Deb, A., Lerman, K., and Ferrara, E. (2018). Predicting cyber-events by leveraging hacker sentiment. *Information*, *9*(11), 280. https://doi.org/10.3390/info9110280.

[46] Décary-Hétu, D., and Dupont, B. (2013). Reputation in a dark network of online criminals. *Global Crime*, *14*(2–3), 175–196.

[47] Deogun, J., and Jiang, L. (2005). Prediction mining – an approach to mining association rules for prediction. In D. Ślezak, J. Yao, J. F. Peters, W. Ziarko, and X. Hu (Eds.) *Rough Sets, Fuzzy Sets, Data Mining, and Granular Computing*, (pp. 98–108). Springer Berlin Heidelberg.

[48] Domingos, P., and Richardson, M. (2001). Mining the network value of customers. In *Proceedings of the Seventh ACM SIGKDD International Conference on Knowledge Discovery and Data Mining*, KDD '01, (pp. 57–66). ACM.

[49] Dung, P. M. (1995). On the acceptability of arguments and its fundamental role in nonmonotonic reasoning, logic programming and n-person games. *Artificial Intelligence*, *77*(2), 321–357.

[50] Durumeric, Z., Kasten, J., Adrian, D., et al. (2014). The matter of heartbleed. In *Proceedings of the 2014 Conference on Internet Measurement Conference*, (pp. 475–488). ACM.

[51] Edkrantz, M., and Said, A. (2015). Predicting cyber vulnerability exploits with machine learning. In *Proceedings of the 13th Scandinavian Conference on Artificial Intelligence*, vol. 278, (pp. 48–57). IOS press.

[52] Edkrantz, M., Truvé, S., and Said, A. (2015). Predicting vulnerability exploits in the wild. In *2015 IEEE 2nd International Conference on Cyber Security and Cloud Computing*, (pp. 513–514). IEEE.

[53] Fang, Z., Zhao, X., Wei, Q., Chen, G., Zhang, Y., Xing, C., Li, W., and Chen, H. (2016). Exploring key hackers and cybersecurity threats in chinese hacker communities. In *2016 IEEE Conference on Intelligence and Security Informatics (ISI)*, (pp. 13–18). IEEE.

[54] Ferrara, E., Varol, O., Davis, C., Menczer, F., and Flammini, A. (2016). The rise of social bots. *Commun. ACM*, *59*(7), 96–104. http://doi.acm.org/10.1145/2818717.

[55] Fink, C., Schmidt, A., Barash, V., Kelly, J., Cameron, C., and Macy, M. (2016). Investigating the observability of complex contagion in empirical social networks. In *Proceedings of 10th International AAAI Conference on Web and Social Media (ICWSM '16)*, (pp. 121–130).

[56] Fisk, N. (2006). *Social learning theory as a model for illegitimate peer-to-peer use and the effects of implementing a legal music downloading service on peer-to-peer music piracy*. PhD thesis, Rochester Institute of Technology.

[57] Fortunato, S. (2010). Community detection in graphs. *Phys. Rep.*, *486*(3), 75–174.

[58] Fournier-Viger, P., Faghihi, U., Nkambou, R., and Nguifo, E. M. (2012). Cmrules: Mining sequential rules common to several sequences. *Knowledge-Based Systems*, *25*(1), 63–76.

[59] Fournier-Viger, P., Gueniche, T., and Tseng, V. S. (2012). Using partially-ordered sequential rules to generate more accurate sequence prediction. In *Advanced Data Mining and Applications*, (pp. 431–442). Springer.

[60] Fournier-Viger, P., Wu, C., Tseng, V. S., Cao, L., and Nkambou, R. (2015). Mining partially-ordered sequential rules common to multiple sequences. *IEEE Trans. Know. Data Eng.*, *27*(8), 2203–2216.

[61] Fournier-Viger, P., Wu, C.-W., Tseng, V. S., and Nkambou, R. (2012). Mining sequential rules common to several sequences with the window size constraint. In *Advances in Artificial Intelligence*, (pp. 299–304). Springer.

[62] Frei, S., Schatzmann, D., Plattner, B., and Trammell, B. (2010). Modeling the security ecosystem-the dynamics of (in) security. In *Economics of Information Security and Privacy*, (pp. 79–106). Springer.

[63] Galar, M., Fernandez, A., Barrenechea, E., Bustince, H., and Herrera, F. (2012). A review on ensembles for the class imbalance problem: Bagging-, boosting-, and hybrid-based approaches. *IEEE Trans. Syst., Man Cybernetics, Part C*, *42*(4), 463–484.

[64] García, A. J., and Simari, G. R. (2004). Defeasible logic programming: An argumentative approach. *Theory Pract. Log. Program.*, *4*(1+2), 95–138. https://doi.org/10.1017/S1471068403001674.

[65] Ghaffarian, S. M., and Shahriari, H. R. (2017). Software vulnerability analysis and discovery using machine-learning and data-mining techniques: A survey. *ACM Comput. Surv.*, *50*(4), 56.

[66] Girvan, M., and Newman, M. E. J. (2002). Community structure in social and biological networks. *Proc. Nat. Acad. Sci.*, *99*(12), 7821–7826.

[67] Glenski, M., and Weninger, T. (2017). Predicting user-interactions on Reddit. In *Proceedings of the 2017 IEEE/ACM International Conference on Advances in Social Networks Analysis and Mining 2017*, ASONAM '17, (pp. 609–612). ACM.

[68] GOV.UK. (2019). 2019 cyber security breaches survey. www.gov.uk/government/statistics/cyber-security-breaches-survey-2019.

[69] Goyal, A., Bonchi, F., and Lakshmanan, L. V. (2010). Learning influence probabilities in social networks. In *Proceedings of the Third ACM International Conference on Web Search and Data Mining*, WSDM '10, (pp. 241–250). ACM.

[70] Goyal, P., Hossain, K., Deb, A., Tavabi, N., Bartley, N., Abeliuk, A., Ferrara, E., and Lerman, K. (2018). Discovering signals from web sources to predict cyber attacks. https://arxiv.org/abs/1806.03342v1.

[71] Guo, D., Shamai, S., and Verdú, S. (2005). Mutual information and minimum mean-square error in Gaussian channels. *IEEE Trans. Inform Theory*, *51*(4), 1261–1282.

[72] Guo, R., and Shakarian, P. (2016). A comparison of methods for cascade prediction. In *Proceedings of the 2016 IEEE/ACM International Conference on Advances in Social Networks Analysis and Mining*, ASONAM '16, (pp. 591–598). IEEE Press.

[73] Gupta, M. (2014). *Handbook of Research on Emerging Developments in Data Privacy*. Advances in Information Security, Privacy, and Ethics (1948–9730). IGI Global. https://books.google.com/books?id=5Ra5BgAAQBAJ.

[74] Hamilton, H. J., and Karimi, K. (2005). The timers II algorithm for the discovery of causality. In T. B. Ho, D. Cheung, and H. Liu (Eds.) *Advances in Knowledge Discovery and Data Mining*, (pp. 744–750). Springer.

[75] Han, J., Pei, J., and Yin, Y. (2000). Mining frequent patterns without candidate generation. In *ACM sigmod Record*, vol. 29, (pp. 1–12).

[76] Hao, S., Kantchelian, A., Miller, B., Paxson, V., and Feamster, N. (2016). Predator: Proactive recognition and elimination of domain abuse at time-of-registration. In *Proceedings of the 2016 ACM SIGSAC Conference on Computer and Communications Security*, (pp. 1568–1579). ACM.

[77] Hodge, V. J., and Austin, J. (2004). A survey of outlier detection methodologies. *Arti. Intell. Rev.*, *22*(2), 85–126. https://doi.org/10.1007/s10462-004-4304-y.

[78] Holt, T., Strumsky, D., Smirnova, O., and Kilger, M. (2012). Examining the social networks of malware writers and hackers. *Int. J. Cyber Criminol.*, *6*(1), 891–903.

[79] Holt, T. J., and Lampke, E. (2010). Exploring stolen data markets online: Products and market forces. *Criminal Justice Stud.*, *23*(1), 33–50. https://doi.org/10.1080/14786011003634415.

[80] Hornik, K., Kober, M., Feinerer, I., and Buchta, C. (2012). Spherical k-means clustering. *J. Stat. Software*, *50*, 1–22.

[81] Hubert, L., and Arabie, P. (1985). Comparing partitions. *J. Classification*, *2*(1), 193–218.

[82] IdentityForce (2019). Data breaches – the worst breaches, so far. www.identityforce.com/blog/2019-data-breaches.

[83] Khandpur, R. P., Ji, T., Jan, S., Wang, G., Lu, C.-T., and Ramakrishnan, N. (2017). Crowdsourcing cybersecurity: Cyber attack detection using social media. In *Proceedings of the 2017 ACM on Conference on Information and Knowledge Management*, CIKM '17, (pp. 1049–1057). ACM. http://doi.acm.org/10.1145/3132847.3132866.

[84] Knowles, A. (2016). How black hats and white hats collaborate to be successful. https://securityintelligence.com/how-black-hats-and-white-hats-collaborate-to-be-successful/.

[85] Kotenko, I., and Stepashkin, M. (2005). Analyzing vulnerabilities and measuring security level at design and exploitation stages of computer network life cycle. In *Proceedings of the Third International Conference on Mathematical Methods, Models, and Architectures for Computer Network Security*, MMM-ACNS'05, (pp. 311–324). Springer. https://doi.org/10.1007/11560326_24.

[86] Lab, K. (2019). Kaspersky Security Bulletin 2019. Statistics. https://securelist.com/kaspersky-security-bulletin-2019-statistics/95475/.

[87] Lakhina, A., Crovella, M., and Diot, C. (2004). Diagnosing network-wide traffic anomalies. In *Proceedings of the 2004 Conference on Applications, Technologies, Architectures, and Protocols for Computer Communications*, SIGCOMM '04, (pp. 219–230). ACM. http://doi.acm.org/10.1145/1015467.1015492.

[88] Laxman, S., and Sastry, P. S. (2006). A survey of temporal data mining. *Sadhana*, *31*(2), 173–198.

[89] LeClair, J. (2015). Small business, big threat: Protecting small businesses from cyber attacks. Tech. rep., National Cybersecurity Institute at

Excelsior College. https://docs.house.gov/meetings/SM/SM00/20150422/103276/HHRG-114-SM00-20150422-SD003-U4.pdf.

[90] Lee, H., and Yoon, Y. (2017). Engineering doc2vec for automatic classification of product descriptions on o2o applications. *Electr. Commerce Res.*, *18*, 1–24.

[91] L'Huillier, G., Alvarez, H., Ríos, S. A., and Aguilera, F. (2011). Topic-based social network analysis for virtual communities of interests in the dark web. *SIGKDD Explor. Newsl.*, *12*(2), 66–73.

[92] Liu, Y., Sarabi, A., Zhang, J., Naghizadeh, P., Karir, M., Bailey, M., and Liu, M. (2015). Cloudy with a chance of breach: Forecasting cyber security incidents. In *24th USENIX Security Symposium (USENIX Security 15)*, (pp. 1009–1024). USENIX. www.usenix.org/conference/usenixsecurity15/technical-sessions/presentation/liu.

[93] Liu, Y., Zhang, J., Sarabi, A., Liu, M., Karir, M., and Bailey, M. (2015). Predicting cyber security incidents using feature-based characterization of network-level malicious activities. In *IWSPA 2015 - Proceedings of the 2015 ACM International Workshop on Security and Privacy Analytics, Co-located with CODASPY 2015*, IWSPA 2015 – Proceedings of the 2015 ACM International Workshop on Security and Privacy Analytics, Co-located with CODASPY 2015, (pp. 3–9). ACM.

[94] Lloyd, J. W. (2012). *Foundations of Logic Programming*. Springer Science & Business Media.

[95] Macdonald, M., Frank, R., Mei, J., and Monk, B. (2015). Identifying digital threats in a hacker web forum. In *Proceedings of the 2015 IEEE/ACM International Conference on Advances in Social Networks Analysis and Mining 2015*, ASONAM '15, (pp. 926–933). ACM.

[96] Mandiant. (2013). APT1: Exposing one of China's cyber espionage units. www.fireeye.com/content/dam/fireeye-www/services/pdfs/mandiant-apt1-report.pdf.

[97] Manski, C. (2009). *Identification for Prediction and Decision*. Harvard University Press.

[98] Marin, E. (2020). *A hacker-centric perspective to empower cyber defense*. PhD dissertation, Arizona State University.

[99] Marin, E., Almukaynizi, M., Nunes, E., Shakarian, J., and Shakarian, P. (2018). Predicting hacker adoption on darkweb forums using sequential rule mining. In *2018 IEEE International Conference on Parallel Distributed Processing with Applications, Ubiquitous Computing Communications, Big Data Cloud Computing, Social Computing Networking, Sustainable Computing Communications (ISPA/IUCC/BDCloud/SocialCom/SustainCom)*, (pp. 1183–1190). https://doi.org/10.1109/BDCloud.2018.00174.

[100] Marin, E., Almukaynizi, M., Nunes, E., and Shakarian, P. (2018). Community finding of malware and exploit vendors on darkweb marketplaces. In *2018 1st International Conference on Data Intelligence and Security (ICDIS)*, (pp. 81–84). IEEE.

[101] Marin, E., Almukaynizi, M., and Shakarian, P. (2019). Reasoning about future cyber-attacks through socio-technical hacking information. In *2019 IEEE 31th International Conference on Tools with Artificial Intelligence (ICTAI)*, (pp. 157–164).

[102] Marin, E., Almukaynizi, M., and Shakarian, P. (2020). Inductive and deductive reasoning to assist in cyber-attack prediction. In *2020 IEEE Annual Computing and Communication Workshop and Conference*, (pp. 262–268).

[103] Marin, E., Diab, A., and Shakarian, P. (2016). Product offerings in malicious hacker markets. In *2016 IEEE Conference on Intelligence and Security Informatics (ISI)*, (pp. 187–189). IEEE.

[104] Marin, E., Guo, R., and Shakarian, P. (2017). Temporal analysis of influence to predict users' adoption in online social networks. In *Proceedings of the 2017 International Conference on Social Computing, Behavioral-Cultural Modeling & Prediction and Behavior Representation in Modeling and Simulation (SBP-BRiMS-2017)*, (pp. 254–261). Springer.

[105] Marin, E., Guo, R., and Shakarian, P. (2020). Measuring time-constrained influence to predict adoption in online social networks. *Trans. Soc. Comput.*, *3*(3). https://doi.org/10.1145/3372785.

[106] Marin, E., Shakarian, J., and Shakarian, P. (2018). Mining key-hackers on darkweb forums. In *2018 1st International Conference on Data Intelligence and Security (ICDIS)*, (pp. 73–80). IEEE.

[107] Marin, E. S., and d. Carvalho, C. L. (2014). Search in social networks: Designing models and algorithms that maximize human influence. In *2014 47th Hawaii International Conference on System Sciences*, (pp. 1586–1595). IEEE.

[108] Marin, E. S., and de Carvalho, C. L. (2013). Small-scale: A new model of social networks. In *2013 Winter Simulations Conference (WSC)*, (pp. 2972–2983). IEEE.

[109] Meier, L., Van De Geer, S., and Bühlmann, P. (2008). The group lasso for logistic regression. *J. R. Stat. Soc. Series B*, *70*(1), 53–71. https://rss.onlinelibrary.wiley.com/doi/abs/10.1111/j.1467-9868.2007.00627.x.

[110] Miller, C. (2007). The legitimate vulnerability market: Inside the secretive world of 0-day exploit sales. In *Sixth Workshop on the Economics of Information Security*, (p. 10). Carnegie Mellon University.

[111] Mitchell, M. (1996). *An Introduction to Genetic Algorithms*. MIT Press.

[112] Mittal, S., Das, P. K., Mulwad, V., Joshi, A., and Finin, T. (2016). Cybertwitter: Using Twitter to generate alerts for cybersecurity threats and vulnerabilities. In *2016 IEEE/ACM International Conference on Advances in Social Networks Analysis and Mining (ASONAM)*, (pp. 860–867). IEEE.

[113] Mitzenmacher, M., and Upfal, E. (2017). *Probability and Computing: Randomization and Probabilistic Techniques in Algorithms and Data Analysis*. Cambridge University Press.

[114] Montgomery, D. C. (2007). *Introduction to Statistical Quality Control*. John Wiley.

[115] Morris, R. G., and Blackburn, A. G. (2009). Cracking the code: An empirical exploration of social learning theory and computer crime. *J. Crime Justice*, *32*(1), 1–34.

[116] Motoyama, M., McCoy, D., Levchenko, K., Savage, S., and Voelker, G. M. (2011). An analysis of underground forums. In *Proceedings of the 2011 ACM SIGCOMM Conference on Internet Measurement Conference*, IMC '11, (pp. 71–80). ACM.

[117] Munkres, J. (1957). Algorithms for the assignment and transportation problems. *J. Soc. Indust. App. Math.*, *5*(1), 32–38.

[118] Nagaraja, S. (2007). Anonymity in the wild: Mixes on unstructured networks. In N. Borisov, and P. Golle (Eds.) *Privacy Enhancing Technologies*, (pp. 254–271). Springer.

[119] Nagaraja, S., Mittal, P., Hong, C.-Y., Caesar, M., and Borisov, N. (2010). Botgrep: Finding p2p bots with structured graph analysis. In *Proceedings of the 19th USENIX Conference on Security*, USENIX Security'10, (pp. 7–7). USENIX Association. http://dl.acm.org/citation.cfm?id=1929820.1929830.

[120] Nayak, K., Marino, D., Efstathopoulos, P., and Dumitraş, T. (2014). Some vulnerabilities are different than others. In *International Workshop on Recent Advances in Intrusion Detection*, (pp. 426–446). Springer.

[121] Nespoli, P., Papamartzivanos, D., MÃąrmol, F. G., and Kambourakis, G. (2018). Optimal countermeasures selection against cyber attacks: A comprehensive survey on reaction frameworks. *IEEE Commun. Surv. Tutorials*, *20*(2), 1361–1396. https://doi.org/10.1109/COMST.2017.2781126.

[122] Neuhaus, S., Zimmermann, T., Holler, C., and Zeller, A. (2007). Predicting vulnerable software components. In *Proceedings of the 14th ACM Conference on Computer and Communications Security*, (pp. 529–540). ACM.

[123] Newman, M. E. J. (2006). Finding community structure in networks using the eigenvectors of matrices. *Phys. Rev. E*, *74*, 036104.

[124] NIST (2020). National vulnerability database. https://nvd.nist.gov/.

[125] Nouh, M., and Nurse, J. (2015). Identifying key-players in online activist groups on the facebook social network. In *2015 IEEE International Conference on Data Mining Workshop (ICDMW)*, (pp. 969–978).

[126] Nunes, E., Diab, A., Gunn, A., et al. (2016). Darknet and deepnet mining for proactive cybersecurity threat intelligence. In *2016 IEEE Conference on Intelligence and Security Informatics (ISI)*, (pp. 7–12). IEEE.

[127] Nunes, E., Shakarian, P., and Simari, G. I. (2018). At-risk system identification via analysis of discussions on the darkweb. In *2018 APWG Symposium on Electronic Crime Research (eCrime)*, (pp. 1–12). APWG.

[128] Nunes, E., Shakarian, P., Simari, G. I., and Ruef, A. (2016). Argumentation models for cyber attribution. In *2016 IEEE/ACM International Conference on Advances in Social Networks Analysis and Mining (ASONAM)*, (pp. 837–844). https://doi.org/10.1109/ASONAM.2016.7752335.

[129] Okutan, A., Werner, G., Yang, S. J., and McConky, K. (2018). Forecasting cyberattacks with incomplete, imbalanced, and insignificant data. *Cybersecurity*, *1*(1), 15. https://doi.org/10.1186/s42400-018-0016-5.

[130] Oprea, A., Li, Z., Yen, T., Chin, S. H., and Alrwais, S. (2015). Detection of early-stage enterprise infection by mining large-scale log data. In *2015 45th Annual IEEE/IFIP International Conference on Dependable Systems and Networks*, (pp. 45–56). IEEE.

[131] Pastrana, S., Hutchings, A., Caines, A., and Buttery, P. (2018). Characterizing eve: Analysing cybercrime actors in a large underground forum. In M. Bailey, T. Holz, M. Stamatogiannakis, and S. Ioannidis (Eds.) *Research in Attacks, Intrusions, and Defenses*, (pp. 207–227). Springer International Publishing.

[132] Pedregosa, F., Varoquaux, G., Gramfort, et al. (2011). Scikit-learn: Machine learning in Python. *J. Machine Learn. Res.*, *12*(Oct), 2825–2830.

[133] Pei, J., Han, J., Mortazavi-Asl, B., Wang, J., Pinto, H., Chen, Q., Dayal, U., and Hsu, M.-C. (2004). Mining sequential patterns by pattern-growth: The prefixspan approach. *IEEE Trans. Know. Data Eng.*, *16*(11), 1424–1440.

[134] Pfleeger, C. P., and Pfleeger, S. L. (2002). *Security in Computing*. Prentice Hall Professional Technical Reference.

[135] Phillips, E., Nurse, J., Goldsmith, M., and Creese, S. (2015). Extracting social structure from darkweb forums. In *2015 International Conference on Social Media Technologies, Communication, and Informatics*, (pp. 97–102). IARIA.

[136] Pitman, A., and Zanker, M. (2011). An empirical study of extracting multidimensional sequential rules for personalization and recommendation in online commerce. In *Proceeding of Wirtschaftsinformatik*, (pp. 180–189).

[137] Pons, A., and Pons, E. (2015). Social learning theory and ethical hacking: Student perspectives on a hacking curriculum. In *Proceedings of the Information Systems Education Conference*, ISECON 2015, (pp. 289–299). Foundation for IT Education.

[138] Qiu, M., Sim, Y., Smith, N. A., and Jiang, J. (2015). Modeling user arguments, interactions, and attributes for stance prediction in online debate forums. In *Proceedings of the 2015 SIAM International Conference on Data Mining*, SIAM'2015, (pp. 855–863). SIAM Press.

[139] Radianti, J. (2010). A study of a social behavior inside the online black markets. In *2010 Fourth International Conference on Emerging Security Information, Systems and Technologies*, (pp. 189–194). IEEE.

[140] Rahwan, I., Simari, G. R., and van Benthem, J. (2009). *Argumentation in Artificial Intelligence*. vol. 47. Springer.

[141] Randall, D. (2006). Rapidly mixing Markov chains with applications in computer science and physics. *Comput. Sci. Eng.*, *8*(2), 30–41.

[142] Rekšna, T. (2017). *Complex network analysis of Darknet black market forum structure*. Master's thesis, Leiden University, the Netherlands.

[143] Ribeiro, M. T., Singh, S., and Guestrin, C. (2016). "Why should i trust you?": Explaining the predictions of any classifier. In *Proceedings of the 22nd ACM SIGKDD International Conference on Knowledge Discovery and Data Mining*, KDD '16, (pp. 1135–1144). ACM. http://doi.acm.org/10.1145/2939672.2939778.

[144] Robertson, J., Diab, A., Marin, E., Nunes, E., Paliath, V., Shakarian, J., and Shakarian, P. (2016). Darknet mining and game theory for enhanced cyber threat intelligence. *Cyber Defense Rev.*, *1*(2), 95–121.

[145] Robertson, J., Diab, A., Marin, E., Nunes, E., Paliath, V., Shakarian, J., and Shakarian, P. (2017). *Darkweb Cyber Threat Intelligence Mining*. Cambridge University Press.

[146] Robertson, J., Paliath, V., Shakarian, J., Thart, A., and Shakarian, P. (2016). Data driven game theoretic cyber threat mitigation. In *Proceedings of the Thirtieth AAAI Conference on Artificial Intelligence (AAAI-16)*, (pp. 4041–4046). AAAI.

[147] Roy, A., Kim, D. S., and Trivedi, K. S. (2012). Scalable optimal countermeasure selection using implicit enumeration on attack countermeasure trees.

In *IEEE/IFIP International Conference on Dependable Systems and Networks (DSN 2012)*, (pp. 1–12). IEEE.

[148] Sabottke, C., Suciu, O., and Dumitras, T. (2015). Vulnerability disclosure in the age of social media: Exploiting Twitter for predicting real-world exploits. In *USENIX Security*, vol. 15, (pp. 1041–1056). USENIX.

[149] Samtani, S., and Chen, H. (2016). Using social network analysis to identify key hackers for keylogging tools in hacker forums. In *Proceeding of ISI 2016*, (pp. 319–321). IEEE.

[150] Samtani, S., Chinn, K., Larson, C., and Chen, H. (2016). Azsecure hacker assets portal: Cyber threat intelligence and malware analysis. In *2016 IEEE Conference on Intelligence and Security Informatics (ISI)*, (pp. 19–24). IEEE.

[151] Samtani, S., Chinn, R., and Chen, H. (2015). Exploring hacker assets in underground forums. In *2015 IEEE International Conference on Intelligence and Security Informatics (ISI)*, (pp. 31–36). IEEE.

[152] Sapienza, A., Bessi, A., Damodaran, S., Shakarian, P., Lerman, K., and Ferrara, E. (2017). Early warnings of cyber threats in online discussions. In *2017 IEEE International Conference on Data Mining Workshops (ICDMW)*, (pp. 667–674). IEEE.

[153] Sapienza, A., Ernala, S. K., Bessi, A., Lerman, K., and Ferrara, E. (2018). Discover: Mining online chatter for emerging cyber threats. In *Companion Proceedings of the Web Conference 2018*, WWW '18, (pp. 983–990). International World Wide Web Conferences Steering Committee.

[154] Sarkar, S., Almukaynizi, M., Shakarian, J., and Shakarian, P. (2018). Predicting enterprise cyber incidents using social network analysis on the darkweb hacker forums. http://arxiv.org/abs/1811.06537.

[155] Sarkar, S., Almukaynizi, M., Shakarian, J., and Shakarian, P. (2019). Mining user interaction patterns in the darkweb to predict enterprise cyber incidents. *Social Network Anal. Min.*, *9*(57). https://doi.org/10.1007/s13278-019-0603-9,.

[156] Scandariato, R., Walden, J., Hovsepyan, A., and Joosen, W. (2014). Predicting vulnerable software components via text mining. *IEEE Trans. Software Eng.*, *40*(10), 993–1006.

[157] Schökopf, B., Platt, J., and Hofmann, T. (2007). *In-Network PCA and Anomaly Detection*, (pp. 617–624). MITP. https://ieeexplore.ieee.org/document/6287317.

[158] Seebruck, R. (2015). A typology of hackers: Classifying cyber malfeasance using a weighted arc circumplex model. *Digital Invest.*, *14*, 36–45.

[159] Senthilkumar, R., Deepika, R., Saranya, R., and Govind, M. D. (2016). Generating adaptive partially ordered sequential rules. In *Proceedings of the International Conference on Informatics and Analytics*, ICIA-16, (pp. 110:1–110:8). ACM.

[160] Shakarian, J., Gunn, A. T., and Shakarian, P. (2016). *Exploring Malicious Hacker Forums*. Springer International.

[161] Shakarian, J., Shakarian, P., and Ruef, A. (2015). Cyber attacks and public embarrassment: A survey of some notable hacks. *Elsevier SciTechConnect*.

[162] Shakarian, P., Parker, A., Simari, G., and Subrahmanian, V. V. S. (2011). Annotated probabilistic temporal logic. *ACM Trans. Comput. Logic*, *12*(2), 14:1–14:44.

[163] Shakarian, P., and Shakarian, J. (2016). Socio-cultural modeling for cyber threat actors. In *AAAI Workshop on Artificial Intelligence and Cyber Security (AICS)*, (pp. 193–194). AAAI.

[164] Shakarian, P., Simari, G. I., Moores, G., and Parsons, S. (2015). Cyber attribution: An argumentation-based approach. In *Cyber Warfare*, (pp. 151–171). Springer.

[165] Shakarian, P., Simari, G. I., and Subrahmanian, V. S. (2012). Annotated probabilistic temporal logic: Approximate fixpoint implementation. *ACM Trans. Comput. Logic*, *13*(2), 13:1–13:33.

[166] Shlens, J. (2014). A tutorial on principal component analysis. *Int. J. Remote Sensing*, *51*(2).

[167] Sikos, L. F., Philp, D., Howard, C., Voigt, S., Stumptner, M., and Mayer, W. (2019). *Knowledge Representation of Network Semantics for Reasoning-Powered Cyber-Situational Awareness*, (pp. 19–45). Springer International. https://doi.org/10.1007/978-3-319-98842-9_2.

[168] Skinner, W. F., and Fream, A. M. (1997). A social learning theory analysis of computer crime among college students. *J. Res. Crime Delinquency*, *34*(4), 495–518.

[169] Sood, A. K., Bansal, R., and Enbody, R. J. (2013). Cybercrime: Dissecting the state of underground enterprise. *IEEE Internet Comput.*, *17*(1), 60–68.

[170] Soska, K., and Christin, N. (2014). Automatically detecting vulnerable websites before they turn malicious. In *Usenix Security*, (pp. 625–640). Usenix.

[171] Soule, A., Salamatian, K., and Taft, N. (2005). Combining filtering and statistical methods for anomaly detection. In *Proceedings of the 5th ACM SIGCOMM Conference on Internet Measurement*, IMC '05, (pp. 31–31). USENIX Association. http://dl.acm.org/citation.cfm?id=1251086.1251117.

[172] Stanton, A., Thart, A., Jain, A., Vyas, P., Chatterjee, A., and Shakarian, P. (2015). Mining for causal relationships: A data-driven study of the islamic state. In *Proceedings of the 21th ACM SIGKDD International Conference on Knowledge Discovery and Data Mining*, (pp. 2137–2146). ACM.

[173] Stolzenburg, F., García, A. J., Chesnevar, C. I., and Simari, G. R. (2003). Computing generalized specificity. *J. App. Non-Classical Logics*, *13*(1), 87–113.

[174] Sun, N., Zhang, J., Rimba, P., Gao, S., Zhang, L. Y., and Xiang, Y. (2019). Data-driven cybersecurity incident prediction: A survey. *IEEE Commun. Surv. Tutorials*, *21*(2), 1744–1772. https://doi.org/10.1109/COMST.2018.2885561.

[175] Sun, X., Dai, J., Liu, P., Singhal, A., and Yen, J. (2018). Using Bayesian networks for probabilistic identification of zero-day attack paths. *IEEE Trans. Inform. Forensics Security*, *13*(10), 2506–2521.

[176] Swarner, J. (2017). Before WannaCry was unleashed, hackers plotted about it on the dark web. http://slate.me/2xQvscu.

[177] Swearingen, J. (2017). The creator of the Mirai botnet is probably a Rutgers student with the bad habit of bragging. http://slct.al/2wpr54l.

[178] Symantec. (2019). 2019 internet security threat report. www.symantec.com/security-center/threat-report.

[179] Tan, P., Steinbach, M., and Kumar, V. (2013). *Introduction to Data Mining*. Addison-Wesley.

[180] Tang, J., Musolesi, M., Mascolo, C., and Latora, V. (2009). Temporal distance metrics for social network analysis. In *Proceedings of the 2nd ACM Workshop on Online Social Networks*, WOSN '09, (pp. 31–36). ACM. http://doi.acm.org/10.1145/1592665.1592674.

[181] Tavabi, N., Goyal, P., Almukaynizi, M., Shakarian, P., and Lerman, K. (2018). Darkembed: Exploit prediction with neural language models. In *Proceedings of AAAI Conference on Innovative Applications of AI (IAAI2018)*, (p. 6). AAAI.

[182] Tibshirani, R., and Suo, X. (2016). An ordered lasso and sparse time-lagged regression. *Technometrics*, *58*(4), 415–423. https://doi.org/10.1080/00401706.2015.1079245.

[183] Trieu, L. Q., Tran, H. Q., and Tran, M.-T. (2017). News classification from social media using Twitter-based doc2vec model and automatic query expansion. In *Proceedings of the Eighth International Symposium on Information and Communication Technology*, (pp. 460–467). ACM.

[184] Turek, M. (2019). Explainable artificial intelligence (XAI). www.darpa.mil/program/explainable-artificial-intelligence.

[185] Veeramachaneni, K., Arnaldo, I., Korrapati, V., Bassias, C., and Li, K. (2016). Ai$^2$: Training a big data machine to defend. In *2016 IEEE 2nd International Conference on Big Data Security on Cloud (BigDataSecurity), IEEE International Conference on High Performance and Smart Computing (HPSC), and IEEE International Conference on Intelligent Data and Security (IDS)*, (pp. 49–54). IEEE.

[186] Verizon. (2015). 2015 data breach investigations report. https://cybersecurity.idaho.gov/wp-content/uploads/sites/87/2019/04/data-breach-investigation-report_2015.pdf.

[187] Verizon. (2017). 2017 data breach investigations report. www.ictsecuritymagazine.com/wp-content/uploads/2017-Data-Breach-Investigations-Report.pdf.

[188] Walden, J., Stuckman, J., and Scandariato, R. (2014). Predicting vulnerable components: Software metrics vs text mining. In *2014 IEEE 25th International Symposium on Software Reliability Engineering (ISSRE)*, (pp. 23–33). IEEE.

[189] Watts, D. (2004). *Six Degrees: The Science of a Connected Age*. W. W. Norton.

[190] Widmer, G., and Kubat, M. (1996). Learning in the presence of concept drift and hidden contexts. *Machine Learning*, *23*(1), 69–101. https://doi.org/10.1023/A:1018046501280.

[191] Xu, J., and Chen, H. (2008). The topology of dark networks. *Commun. ACM*, *51*(10), 58–65. http://doi.acm.org/10.1145/1400181.1400198.

[192] Xu, T., Sun, J., and Bi, J. (2015). Longitudinal lasso: Jointly learning features and temporal contingency for outcome prediction. In *Proceedings of the 21th ACM SIGKDD International Conference on Knowledge Discovery and Data Mining*, KDD '15, (pp. 1345–1354). ACM. http://doi.acm.org/10.1145/2783258.2783403.

[193] Yang, C. C., Tang, X., and Gong, X. (2011). Identifying dark web clusters with temporal coherence analysis. In *2011 IEEE International Conference on Intelligence and Security Informatics (ISI)*, (pp. 167–172). IEEE.

[194] Yang, T., Brinton, C., and Joe-Wong, C. (2018). Predicting learner interactions in social learning networks. In *IEEE Conference on Computer Communications (INFOCOM)*, INFOCOM '18, (pp. 1322–1330). IEEE.

[195] Yip, M., Shadbolt, N., and Webber, C. (2013). Why forums? an empirical analysis into the facilitating factors of carding forums. In *Proceedings of the 5th Annual ACM Web Science Conference*, WebSci '13, (pp. 453–462). ACM. http://doi.acm.org/10.1145/2464464.2464524.

[196] Zafarani, R., Abbasi, M., and Liu, H. (2014). *Social Media Mining: An Introduction*. Cambridge University Press.

[197] Zhang, J., Liu, B., Tang, J., Chen, T., and Li, J. (2013). Social influence locality for modeling retweeting behaviors. In *Proceedings of the 23rd International Joint Conference on Artificial Intelligence (IJCAI '13)*, (pp. 2761–2767). AAAI Press.

[198] Zhang, S., Caragea, D., and Ou, X. (2011). An empirical study on using the national vulnerability database to predict software vulnerabilities. In *International Conference on Database and Expert Systems Applications*, (pp. 217–231). Springer.

[199] Zhang, X., and Chenwei, L. (2013). Survival analysis on hacker forums. In *2013 SIGBPS Workshop on Business Processes and Service*, (pp. 106–2013). AIS.

[200] Zhang, X., Tsang, A., Yue, W., and Chau, M. (2015). The classification of hackers by knowledge exchange behaviors. *Inform. Syst. Frontiers*, *17*(6), 1239–1251.

[201] Zhao, Z., Ahn, G.-J., Hu, H., and Mahi, D. (2012). SocialImpact: Systematic analysis of underground social dynamics. In S. Foresti, M. Yung, and F. Martinelli (Eds.) *ESORICS*, vol. 7459 of *Lecture Notes in Computer Science*, (pp. 877–894). Springer.

# Index